Never One Nation

Never One Nation

Freaks, Savages, and Whiteness in U.S. Popular Culture, 1850–1877

Linda Frost

University of Minnesota Press
Minneapolis • London

Portions of chapter 1 originally appeared in "'Living Curiosities' and 'The Wonder of America': The Primitive, the Freakish, and the Construction of National Identities in Civil War America," *Journal x: A Journal in Culture and Criticism* 1, no. 1 (Autumn 1996): 85–111. Portions of chapter 3 originally appeared as "The Circassian Beauty and the Circassian Slave: Gender, Imperialism, and American Popular Entertainment," in *Freakery: Cultural Spectacles of the Extraordinary Body,* ed. Rosemarie Garland Thomson (New York: New York University Press, 1996), 248–62.

Published by the University of Minnesota Press
111 Third Avenue South, Suite 290
Minneapolis, MN 55401-2520
http://www.upress.umn.edu

Library of Congress Cataloging-in-Publication Data

Frost, Linda.
    Never one nation : freaks, savages, and whiteness in U.S. popular culture, 1850–1877 / Linda Frost.
        p.   cm.
    Includes bibliographical references and index.
    ISBN 0-8166-4489-6 (hc : alk. paper) — ISBN 0-8166-4490-X (pb : alk. paper)
    1. Popular culture—United States—History—19th century.   2. Racism in popular culture—United States—History—19th century.   3. Whites—Race identity—United States.   4. African Americans in popular culture—History—19th century.   5. Indians in popular culture—United States—History—19th century.   6. Freak shows—Social aspects—United States—History—19th century.   I. Title.
    E166.F925   2005
    306'.0973'09034 — dc22   2004022992

Printed in the United States of America on acid-free paper

The University of Minnesota is an equal-opportunity educator and employer.

12 11 10 09 08 07 06 05   10 9 8 7 6 5 4 3 2 1

To my parents —
David Frost, who taught me to love history, and
Ethel Frost, who taught me to love books.
You are both here, on every page.

Contents

Blinding Whiteness and "The Wonder of America"

Deep within the word "American" is its association with race. To identify someone as a South African is to say very little; we need the adjective "white" or "black" or "colored" to make our meaning clear. In this country it is quite the reverse. American means white.

—Toni Morrison, *Playing in the Dark: Whiteness and the Literary Imagination*

Four years before the Harper brothers were to launch their highly success-ful *Harper's Weekly*, entrepreneur P. T. Barnum recognized the financial potential of periodical publishing. Joining forces with *New York Sun* editors H. D. and Alfred E. Beach, and engaging Frank Leslie as his chief engraver, Barnum kicked off a publication of his own in 1853: the short-lived *Illustrated News*.[1] The weekly's initial editorial address stated that "there was never a better field for such an enterprise than New York. . . . More than any other city in the world, New York is the center of intel-lectual as well as industrial and commercial activity, and it is in almost every essential the metropolis of this entire continent."[2] By the time the second number of the paper appeared, the editors had revised the focus of their intended readership. Carefully explaining that while selecting New York as their "centre," the editors still wished "to be understood as speaking to every part of America where the English language is spoken. We aim at a *national* undertaking, and are happy that as far as time and steam have permitted us to judge the success of an experiment, it has been nationally responded to."[3] As if to drive the point home, this issue of the *News* includes a series of engravings detailing the ongoing construction of the Capitol building and the Washington Monument.

Barnum's attempt to create a "*national* undertaking" in the *Illustrated News* illustrates the potential power these popular texts harbored, not only as moneymakers for their ambitious owners and editors but as participants in the process of configuring their readers as Americans. Other overlapping institutions of popular culture, such as Barnum's version of the freak show, likewise participated in the implicit endeavor to identify the definitive properties of "Americanness." As Benedict Anderson has argued, nations are imagined as coherent communities by clearly establishing who *cannot* claim membership to them.[4] In the nineteenth-century United States of America, this imagining depended on a highly racialized discourse, one that assigned a savage otherness to the nation's nonmembers.

In *Playing in the Dark: Whiteness and the Literary Imagination,* Toni Morrison forefronts the role race has and does play in the creation of American national identity. Arguing that to be American means, and has always meant, to be white, Morrison contends that it is by virtue of the historical and metaphorical presence of slaves and those people of color who are metonymic of slavery's operations that whites in America have come to know themselves. As Morrison puts it, "Africanism is the vehicle by which the American self knows itself as not enslaved, but free; not repulsive, but desirable; not helpless, but licensed and powerful; not history-less, but historical; not damned, but innocent; not a blind accident of evolution, but a progressive fulfillment of destiny."[5] Homi K. Bhabha affirms the idea that this process is one of an internalized projection when he writes that "the 'other' is never outside or beyond us; it emerges forcefully, within cultural discourse, when we *think* we speak most intimately and indigenously 'between ourselves.'"[6] Americanness, as these and other scholars argue, depends on a cultural motif of human coloration that projects an image of a blackened other that is either evil or infantile and forever in the shadow, or at the throat of the white civilizer.

Morrison goes on in *Playing in the Dark* to talk about Edgar Allan Poe's *The Narrative of Arthur Gordon Pym,* claiming that "impenetrable" images of whiteness appear in that text like the ghosts of identity for which they seem to stand: "these images of blinding whiteness seem to function as both antidote for and meditation on the shadow that is companion to this whiteness—a dark and abiding presence that moves the hearts and texts of American literature with fear and longing."[7] Morrison's main interest is the exploration of this shadow, one she identifies as essentially Africanist and describes as a "reflexive" fabrication, "an extraordinary meditation on the self; a powerful exploration of the fears and desires that reside in the writerly unconscious."[8] I have used Morrison's phrase—blinding whiteness—to highlight what I see as a recurrent theme in nineteenth-century America's popular writing; that is, the rhetorical manipulation of racialized, blackened others that defines Americanness by contrast, in shadow. Whiteness blinds Barnum and the other editors, writers, and illustrators discussed in this study to the metaphoric quality of the blacknesses they love to discuss; like an Old Testament deity, whiteness robs the sight of those who look directly at it. In fact, as this study will explore, whiteness has bred centuries of shadows, hosts of imaginative projections, each darker and more dangerous, foul, rude, and stupid than the last. These projections ultimately assuage an insecure sense of national belonging for their producers and consumers, allowing them to know they are, as Morrison says, free because not enslaved, sanctified because not damned, and civilized because not savage.

But while this idea is hardly new in relation to how we scholars, bleached or blackened, have learned to reread our books, what the following chapters will bring to light is how flexible and mobile such a racialized discourse was—and had to be—if it was to pertain to more than one moment in American history or one section of the American nation. While Morrison holds that it is specifically and primarily an Africanist presence in American literary history that has defined whiteness, scholars of race generally agree that in American history overall, the blackened figures that define whiteness, as well as those figures who are defined as white themselves, have ranged widely and changed dramatically over time. According to Tomás Almaguer, as early as the colonial period, English settlers in America constructed "a collective identity based upon the categories *English, Christian, free,* and, above all, *white,*" an identity that was "specifically defined in opposition to another, non-white category of people, initially Native Americans and Africans."[9] Matthew Frye Jacobson likewise indicates an early reliance on both the African and the Indian to supply the necessarily contrasting and blackened other for American whiteness. He notes that the idea of citizenship in the early years of the American Republic was "thoroughly entwined with the idea of 'whiteness'. . . because what a citizen really was, at bottom, was someone who could help put down a slave rebellion or participate in Indian wars."[10] Since the colonial period, who has occupied this position of racialized other, whether African, Native American, Chinese, Irish, Arabic, etc., has been and is constantly changing, as has and is the whole notion of race itself.[11]

Generally agreed by sociologists, anthropologists, and historians to have little if anything to do with biology, race is now treated, in the words of Michael Omi and Howard Winant, as "a pre-eminently *sociohistorical* concept."[12] Omi and Winant coined the term "racial formation" in their work to define "the process by which social, economic and political forces determine the content and importance of racial categories, and by which they are in turn shaped by racial meanings."[13] Noting that characteristics from "temperament, sexuality, [and] intelligence" to "our very ways of talking, walking, eating and dreaming" are "presumed to be fixed and discernible from the palpable mark of race," Omi and Winant nevertheless systematically demonstrate race's essential instability.[14] Their work nicely pinpoints the central irony of the operations of race in American history and culture. While racial understandings reproduce a set of surprisingly durable social beliefs that certain traits are fixed, inherent, and natural based on the race to whom they have been assigned, the actual figures who occupy those racial categories are constantly changing. In the work of scholars like Omi and Winant, race is ultimately revealed at once as both among the most resilient and the most unstable of sociopolitical and historical categories. In Jacobson's words, the challenge for scholars of American culture and history is "not only to recognize the fluidity of race, but to find ways of narrating events, social movements, and the trajectory of individual lives in all their integrity along the convoluted path of an ever-shifting racial reality."[15]

What I want to do in *Never One Nation* is to both build on and complicate the foundation Morrison and others have provided for those of us exploring race's trace in nineteenth-century print culture. Americanness has always undeniably meant whiteness, but the others targeted by this racialized, nationalistic discourse have and continue to change. Considered together, what the following chapters will bring to a hopefully less-than-blinding light is one record of how flexible and mobile such a racialized discourse was—and had to be—if it was to apply to more than one isolated section of the nineteenth-century United States. *Never One*

Nation then argues against an assumption in the work of scholars of nationality like Anderson that national identity—at least in America— can ever be understood as a monologic or singular thing. The process of developing a sense of Americanness was indeed a preoccupation with all parts of the still statehood-granting nation in the years before, of, and following the Civil War. The period on which I've chosen to concentrate is brief—less than thirty years—yet historically dense and decisive. Changes in the United States postal system in the year 1850 augmented a rapid increase in the production, distribution, and significance of the popular periodical. It is also the year of the Compromise of 1850, per- haps the last and most significant act of Congress to spur the events that led to the Civil War. The three decades between 1850 and 1877, the date of publication of the final text I consider here and in many accounts the end of Reconstruction and one era of American history, include one of the largest riots in American history—the so-called New York City Draft Riots of 1863—as well as the largest mass execution staged in the United States, in Mankato, Minnesota, just months earlier. It is also this era that witnesses the creation and failure of a second America within the original nation's borders—the Confederate States of America—as well as the only full-scale civil war to be fought on its soil. As June Namias puts it, rather than one United States, the Civil War and Dakota wars of the early 1860s could have resulted in "three and maybe more nations: the United States of America, the Confederate States of America, and perhaps the Confederate Indian Lands of America."[16] Finally, it is also this period that sees the completion of the first transcontinental railway line in this country, an act that propels migration westward and con- cretizes the actuality of a nation-state reaching from sea to sea. What being American meant during this time to a particular group of people in a particular part of the country obviously had to vary significantly from region to region. Even though Americanness might abstractly and consistently be characterized by that list of adjectives provided by Morri- son—free, desirable, powerful, innocent, civilized—the precise shapes and faces those adjectives assumed differed greatly from New York to Richmond to San Francisco. The reason they did, of course, is that who was configured as their shadow and darkened other differed. Typically those others are racialized in ways we have been taught to recognize, coded as fundamentally and culturally nonwhite. But there are moments in which even this understanding of race is stretched when the others who define Americanness are savage national aliens rather than conventionally racialized bodies. If in the Confederate States of America to be American meant to be white, then to be non-American or *Yankee* meant occupying the space of the racialized, othered alien.[17] While no one— other than the odd Confederate writer—would necessarily argue that "Yankee" is or ever was a racial category, I believe that a racialized rhetoric was the discursive tool used by Confederate writers and editors to help consolidate an idea of Confederate Americanness in their popular press. What I believe these texts indicate is that rather than biological, sociological, or even strictly historical fact, race as a category of otherness is a discursive formation; it is in the end an argument, a linguistic effect, even a language.

While *Never One Nation* certainly engages us in the question of how racialized discourse works to preserve power for a blinded and blinding few, it likewise attempts to uncover the profound desire behind such discourse—namely, the desire to be a part of the nation overall, in and of a community that, as Anderson notes, was by necessity largely imaginary. In his list of "narratives and discourses that signify a sense of 'nationness,'" Bhabha sandwiches "the *unheimlich* terror of the space or race of the Other" between "the *heimlich* pleasures of the hearth" and "the comfort of social belonging."[18] As the final chapter of this study argues, the readers of the texts into which I here delve read them at least in part, if not primarily, in order to read themselves into communities that were increasingly lost to them, textualized and imagined versions of the stable villages of a nostalgic American past. While promoting the alienation of the racialized figures represented in them, the stories, woodcuts, and letters printed in these periodicals responded in part to a different sense of alienation experienced by those readers themselves. As Morrison says, we need to understand what makes "intellectual domination possible" in order to learn "how knowledge is transformed from invasion and conquest to revelation and choice."[19] The conclusion of this study gestures toward this kind of explanation.

While I would like to say that *Never One Nation* evolved out of a desire to improve my snowblinded vision and look whiteness in the face in the texts I read and teach, that was not exactly the case. This book came about because of the texts in which I found myself immersed. In an attempt to better understand the cultural significance of the popular magazine fiction of Louisa May Alcott with which I had worked in graduate school, I decided to recontextualize those stories within the pages of the periodicals in which they first appeared. I was in the reading room of the American Antiquarian Society in 1993 when I first opened a bound volume of issues of *Frank Leslie's Illustrated Newspaper* for the beginning of 1863. Gradually I came to realize that what was spread out in front of me constituted a cultural cross-section of that extremely important year, a montage made marvelous with detailed engravings, bits of gossip, fiction, news stories, poems, biographies of "great men," political cartoons, advertisements, and letters from readers themselves. It took me ten years to realize with what exactly I was fascinated, and one more of concentrated writing and rereading, thanks to a sabbatical, to be able to see its themes, give them names, and bring to the whole argument a shape.

Never One Nation is then as much a study of the popular nineteenth-century periodical—primarily but not exclusively the weekly, miscellany, and story paper—as it is a study of Americanness by othered proxy.[20] But it is not an exhaustive catalog of these periodicals, nor is it a study of their publication histories or range of distribution and readers. Other, better literary historians have done much of that work; Frank Luther Mott is the most enduring of these names.[21] *Never One Nation* instead looks very closely at the texts actually contained within these periodicals, some of which were undoubtedly more popular and influential than others, and many of which were not nearly as influential as the ones I never got around to addressing. Instead, I looked for those papers that seemed to best represent their region, that were concerned with a range of issues pertaining to readers both in and beyond their immediate publication home but still concerned themselves with a "home" readership.

Chapter 1 begins the study by looking at the way in which racialized otherness functioned to consolidate two regionally specific and different national identities, one in New York and another in Minnesota during the Dakota wars of 1862. Here, as in chapter 3, I consider the role played by another institution of popular entertainment—the nineteenth-century freak show—in the representation of the Native American for the varying uses of these regions. Chapter 1 also exemplifies the kinds of intersections explored elsewhere in *Never One Nation*, particularly the ways in which the political identities of class and gender support a racializing discourse used to determine American identity in different parts of the country for different political and economic ends.

Chapters 2 and 3 consider the way in which designations of class, race, and gender together configured a sense of national belonging and alienness in several New York–based publications during 1863, the year of Emancipation and the racially explosive New York City Draft Riots. Focusing on New York weeklies like *Frank Leslie's Illustrated Newspaper* and *Harper's Weekly*, these chapters argue that the Northern press was as racially responsive to the idea of Emancipation as the Confederate press was to be. I call this response "Emancipation anxiety" and trace how it manifests itself in two different ways. In chapter 2, I look at the representation of the African Americans and Irish in New York in relation to the question of "free labor" and the imagined threats to that doctrine these blackened others posed. In chapter 3, I focus on a particular freak exhibit and cultural figure—the Circassian Beauty and slave—to show how slavery became spectacle in the North, and how a gender analysis of the Beauty's performance both complicates and reveals the imperialist energies of a white Northern Americanness.

Chapters 4 and 5 consider the way in which wartime periodicals in the South helped shape an idea of Confederate Americanness, that most problematic of American identities. While the African-American slave is clearly a key racialized other to the white Confederate, the position of the slave in that nation's self-description is more complicated than might be expected. Chapter 4 looks first at the role the Confederate press played in the development of a national identity for the rebelling Southern states, then at the way in which the slave is incorporated into that definition. Chapter 5 then considers the racialized other that emerges in the Confederacy's nationalist scheme—the Yankee—and argues that, while not a strict racial category, the Yankee is in fact demonized and racialized as alien in the Confederate imagination. Even so, once the war reaches an end, the true "demon" will be the conundrum of Confederate identity overall and the slave will once again become the othered proxy for Americanness.

Chapters 6 and 7 consider the burgeoning population of California readers and consumers, particularly the ways in which the press of the American West responded to the possibilities and problems created by the newly completed transcontinental railroad. Chapter 6 argues that the image of the Chinese functions both as the key racialized other of the West, and California in particular, and as a kind of echo of another far Easterner that also endangers the idea and actuality of Western American autonomy—the Northeasterner of the United States. As chapter 7 shows, proponents of white supremacy in California were obviously troubled by the possibility that groups like the Chinese could conceivably gain citizenship by virtue of the passage of constitutional amendments thirteen through fifteen. This anxiety leads to the last I consider in the book, namely the worry over women's rights and what effect the increased public and political movement of white women might have on the racial hierarchy in California. This struggle is highlighted when a white woman from the East offers up her own critique of what she sees in the West, a critique that elicits a powerful and heated response from one segment of the Western press.

When I was doing my preliminary research for this project, I looked through these periodicals for the moments that caught my attention, then looked to see how those moments spoke to one another. *Never One Nation* is my attempt to describe and expose that conversation, a rich and textured dialogue about what it meant to be American if you were reading in New York or Mankato or Richmond or San Francisco. It is my effort to bring the category of regional affiliation into our standing vocabulary of political identity. Over the years it has taken me to make sense of this conversation, I myself have been a reader in a variety of places—Suffield, Ohio; Stony Brook and New York City, New York; Wilkes-Barre, Pennsylvania; Boston and Worcester, Massachusetts; Birmingham, Alabama. In all of these places, a powerful network of support has sustained me and helped to see this project through.

My book's fate has been in the hands of essentially six people since I first sent it off for consideration for publication: my reviewers, who offered fabulously specific and encouraging suggestions, my diligent editors Carrie Mullen and Jason Weidemann, and the impossibly patient and practically angelic Doug Armato. They all get a mighty round of applause from me. At one point or another, I worked at or received materials from all of the following libraries and collections: the American Antiquarian Society, the Bancroft Library at the University of California, Berkeley, the Boston Public Library, the Bridgeport Public Library, the California Historical Society, the Circus World Museum in Baraboo, the Elmer L. Andersen Library at the University of Minnesota, the Harvard Theatre Collection, the Hertzberg Circus Collection, the Houghton Library of the Harvard College Library, the Library of Congress, the Mervyn H. Sterne Library at the University of Alabama at Birmingham, the New

York Public Library, the Virginia Historical Society, and the W. S. Hoole Special Collections Library at the University of Alabama. The faculty and staff of these places—particularly Delores Carlito, Eddie Luster, and Heather Martin—are very fine people indeed and I thank them all for their invaluable help in getting me the documents I needed to do this book. I was very fortunate to meet Madeleine Stern and Leona Rostenberg in New York years ago when I was first working on Alcott; Stern's work on publishing and Miriam Frank Leslie has been foundational for me. Various editor-friends saw fit to put sections of this study into print as it was under construction: I am grateful to Rosemarie Garland Thomson, Ivo Kamps, and Jay Watson for their printed votes of confidence, as well as their permission to reprint sections of chapters 1 and 3. Without the generous funding I received from the Wilkes-Barre campus of Penn State University and the University of Alabama at Birmingham, I wouldn't be writing these acknowledgments now. My friends and colleagues at UAB have always been grand supporters of me, particularly my dean, Bert Brouwer, my chair, Marilyn Kurata, and the folks from the UAB Faculty Reading Group. My teaching compadre Tom McKenna and the students of our "American Others" course were there with important suggestions very early on in the process. My special cohorts in academic crime, David Basilico, Sue Kim, Danny Siegel, and Gale Temple, have always kindly and carefully listened to me babble on about various snags in my argument. In the end, I am just a lucky gal to have the like-minded buddies I do, some of whom I've known since I was an undergraduate in Ohio and others that I met just yesterday over corn fungus in Cancún. To Jana Argersinger, Noelle Baker, Jeff Bond, Kris Boudreau, Sylvia Brown, Marcia Camino, Carol Ebbecke, Libby Fay, Ellen Gardiner, Ellen Garvey, Margaret Harrill, Mark Jeffreys, Lisa Logan, Devoney Looser, Terry Martin, Chuck Meyer, Mike Morgan, Jim Nawrocki, Lee Person, Sandy Petrulionis, Ken Price, Sandy Runzo, Scott Sandage, Barbara Smith, and Ron and Mary Zboray—thanks for your reassurance, your advice, your expertise, your spare bedroom.

Finally, I would not have had the emotional energy to do this book had it not been for my family: Mom, Jenny, Jeff, Ian, Hannah, Emily, Russell, Lucy, and Cora. This book—my first—is for my parents; I know my father would have loved to see his name on the dedication page and I hope my mother will add it to the stack on her dresser. Lucy and Cora, two small someones worth doing well for, gave me something brighter to think about when the arguments wouldn't gracefully fall in line. And Russell, my husband, has given me everything else, really—time to finish this, faith that I could do it, love of a kind I never thought I'd have. It takes a village, as they say. Thank you for being mine.

ONE

Roving Savages, Regionalized Americanness, and the 1862 Dakota Wars

... in the van of a higher civilization, the native red men have, at different times, given sad and fearful evidences of their enmity to the dominant white race; ... no exhibition of Indian character had so afflicted and appalled the soul of humanity, as the fearful and deliberate massacre perpetrated by them in August, 1862.
— Charles S. Bryant, *A History of the Great Massacre by the Sioux Indians, in Minnesota, Including the Personal Narratives of Many Who Escaped*

Mr. Barnum has indeed found out that the Sioux and Winnebago Indians are the most consistent friends of the white men, for they have consented to sacrifice still another week of their home comforts, and the pleasures of their happy hunting grounds to comply with the demands of the public for their prolonged stay.
— *Frank Leslie's Illustrated Newspaper,* October 24, 1863

D—n Indians *anyhow.* They are a lazy, shiftless set of brutes— though they will *draw.*
— P. T. Barnum, letter to Moses Kimball, September 26, 1843

When P. T. Barnum brought a group of Sioux and Winnebago tribal members to his American Museum in 1863, he was participating in the performance and staging of the nation, using the persons and bodies of "real" Native Americans to flesh out the racialized assumptions of his audience members.[1] Capitalizing on a crisis of national identity spurred in part by the Civil War and recent events in Minnesota, Barnum's work in his American Museum, like that of the editors of America's popular periodicals, helped to shore up a racially determined but historically threatened and regionally specific understanding of Americanness. Although both were concerned with the definition of some kind of American identity, the New York press and the Minnesota press relied on different rhetorical and racialized others to promote their nationally defined yet regionally aligned agendas. While the Sioux of the Western plains is the primary "savage" for white settlers and government officials in Minnesota during the Dakota wars of 1862 and 1863, for the New York press and its readership, primarily concerned with what was becoming a costly, drawn out, and bloody division of the United States, the Southern Confederate took on the savage attributes of his and her Western counterparts. For the entrepreneurial P. T. Barnum, the community of greatest concern was the one defined by the marketplace. The audience's pocketbooks were what Barnum wished to control, and his presentation of the primitive served to consolidate at once the sense of Barnum's own mastery over it as well as the national membership it ascribed to his audience and disallowed his performers.

"What Is It?" or, The Freakishness of Americanness

Étienne Balibar contends that "the history of nations . . . is always already presented to us in the form of a narrative which attributes to these entities the continuity of a subject."[2] By studying the nation as a narrative, says Homi Bhabha, we can better see its fractures and mobilities:

> To encounter the nation *as it is written* displays a temporality of culture and social consciousness more in tune with the partial, overdetermined process by which textual meaning is produced through the articulation of difference in language; more in keeping with the problem of closure which plays enigmatically in the discourse of the sign. . . . If the problematic 'closure' of textuality questions the 'totalization' of national culture, then its positive value lies in displaying the wide dissemination through which we construct the field of meanings and symbols associated with national life.[3]

Benedict Anderson has suggested that the process of nation-building that took hold in the nineteenth century was in part made possible by that period's emergent print culture, and in particular, print-capitalism's emphasis on distributing its commodities to a broad-based readership.

He claims that this reading scenario made possible a kind of simultaneity that afforded readers the imaginative experience of participating in a nationalized reading community by absorbing the same texts at the same time.[4] Even so, says Kirsten Belgum in her study of the German illustrated weekly *Die Gartenlaube,* we shouldn't then assume that the nation thus portrayed and perpetuated is univocal; we need to look more carefully at the role difference plays in the narratives of nation-building.[5]

In the discourses situating the United States as a national and imperial presence, the idea of primitiveness has been and probably remains its most powerful and consistent rhetorical strain. Positioning the African, Native American, or any other(ed) American as primitive or anthropologically stunted plants these figures firmly at the beginning of narratives of evolution that, according to popular myth, were already over. Like other myths and narratives of the nation, primitiveness can act as a story that establishes, as Marianna Torgovnick points out, "definable beginnings and endings that will make what comes between them coherent narrations."[6] In fact, explorers' narratives pepper the pages of weeklies like Barnum's *Illustrated News,* and stories such as those about the "discovery" of "missing link" tribes relied on their white readers' fascination with an evolutionary model that affirmed their own racial superiority. Depicting primitives as either inhuman monsters, bestial and cannibalistic, or children, naive and ignorant, conveniently positioned them at the beginning of the story of Western civilization—one that was best exemplified in the form of the United States of America itself. This use of narrative aided in the construction of the nation by creating a hierarchically superior, white, middle-class identity that could claim national membership in a "natural" or timeless way.

The narrative of Western progress in particular was a common one in the weeklies. An 1851 image from the Boston-based *Gleason's Pictorial Drawing Room Companion* literally illustrates this familiar story of frontier expansion (see Figure 1).[7] Entitled "Progress of Civilization," the scene—which is meant to be read syntactically, from left to right—features two warriors paddling a canoe underneath a Native American village on the far left. In the center, a farm and church form the background where two well-dressed white men distribute books to tribal members and gesture to the far right of the picture where a train, factories, and steam-powered ships chug toward a future as yet hidden from the reader beyond the right edge of the image. The text reads as follows:

Figure 1. "Progress of Civilization" from *Gleason's Pictorial Drawing Room Companion* (19 April 1851): 28. Courtesy of the American Antiquarian Society.

> The white man meets the Indian in council, takes him by the hand, . . .
> and points out to him the improvements of the civilized life. . . . By de-
> grees, the log cabin rises and takes the place of the rude tent of skin. . . .
> grounds are cleared and fenced in. . . . Factories spring up, . . . cities
> founded, and those modern accessories to civilization, and improve-
> ment in all things, the steamboat and the railroad, bring us in our
> imagination to the present time.[8]

The *story* of progress highlighted by this writer was likewise employed
in the projects of other cultural agents, including P. T. Barnum. An 1873
"Advance Courier" advertisement for Barnum's "Great Traveling World's
Fair," a portable version of his American Museum, includes a picture of
the burning of the Museum in 1868 with Barnum rising god-like from
the smoky flames, one hand extended to offer "The World in Contribution" to the paying customer (see Figure 2). This world includes human
curiosities like those pictured throughout the image—Siamese twins,
dwarves, cannibals, as well as Native Americans. Like "civilization" itself,
Barnum's progress is made possible by that technological triumph, the
steam engine, which is appropriately pictured near the center of the
engraving.

The ability to assign primitiveness to other people affirmed the sense
of belonging and entitlement that American national membership promised. And enjoying the ability to do this as an audience member was a
popular form of entertainment in the nineteenth century, as the perva-
siveness and popularity of the freak show clearly demonstrates. Freak
presentation, because of its emphasis on and exploitation of racial, eth-

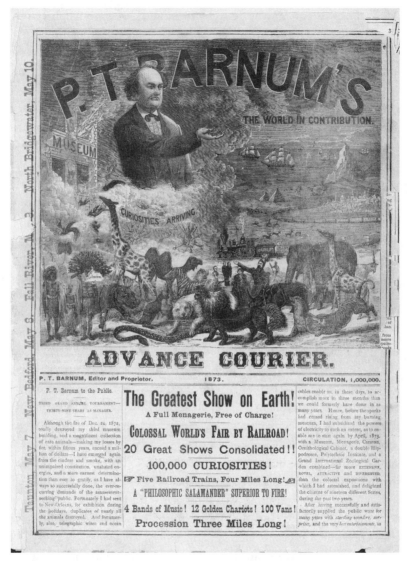

Figure 2. "Advance Courier" for P. T. Barnum's "Great Traveling World's Fair" (1873). Courtesy of the Historical Collections, Bridgeport Public Library.

nic, and cultural differences, reaffirmed white audience members' notions of who belonged to the civilized community of the United States by virtue of putting on stage those who did not. Freak shows themselves emerged from the museum tradition that gained momentum in the nineteenth century, institutions that housed displays featuring the pseudoscientific exhibition of "curiosities."[9] In fact, P. T. Barnum founded the

American Museum in New York in 1840, and Robert Bogdan credits this as the start date of the freak show as its own institutionalized form of popular entertainment, due in part to Barnum's central role in its creation.[10] Like the nation itself, the freak exhibit was a construction, a figure wrapped in cultural myth and story. And freaks were almost always shown within the context of a narrative, a showman relating the story of how they came to be in the museum and selling souvenir chapbooks that contained the freak's "history." There was, then, no such thing as a "real freak"; by virtue of their carefully plotted representation, freaks were/are always constructed.

A late nineteenth-century article pasted into the scrapbook of one fan—Nathaniel Paine of Worcester, Massachusetts—illustrates the understanding showmen and audiences shared: "A little pot-bellied negro boy, with a pointed head, and short, crooked arms and legs, would not draw more than a passing glance in the usual order of things. Call him the Turtle Boy, and he becomes a freak. People like to stare at him and trace the combination of the boy and turtle, which the genius of the showman has suggested."[11] This description brings to mind another image in Paine's text, a *carte de visite* of an African American boy labeled simply "Nondescript" — "a commonly used [nineteenth-century] phrase for animals not yet classified or described by science" (see Figure 3).[12] Draped in what appears to be a bear hide, the little boy rests his congenitally shortened arms on a rock, the setting for the portrait simulating a meadow complete with grass, rocks, and painted tree background. Despite the child's obvious physical deformity, his status as a "freak" results less from this than it does from the way he is represented overall, couched in trappings of the primitive (e.g., the piece of fur he wears, the outdoor setting of the studio, and the "on-all-fours" position his abnormally shortened limbs appear to necessitate).

In fact, not only the primitivization, but the bestialization of human exhibits was a mainstay in freak representation. "Krao, the Missing Link," "Susie, the Elephant Girl" and "Jo-Jo, the Dog-Faced Boy" are all examples of this practice that "posited that certain malformations were the result of crossbreeding man with beast."[13] Evidence of the fascination with, yet culturally sanctioned revulsion for miscegenation, this literalization of the animal nature of the primitive and savage in freak exhibits affirmed and expanded associations already existing in the culture regarding native, non-Western peoples and their shaky, or simply non-

Figure 3. "Nondescript" from the *Freaks of Nature* scrapbook of Nathaniel Paine. Courtesy of the American Antiquarian Society.

human status. A well-known 1860 Currier and Ives political lithograph features the freak, "What Is It?" or "Zip the Pinhead," a microcephalic African-American man, William Henry Johnson, whom Barnum began exhibiting in 1860 (see Figure 4).[14] In an illustrated catalogue to Barnum's American Museum, "What Is It?" is described as a blend of ape and man: "While his face, hands, and arms are distinctly human, his head, feet and legs are more like the Orang Outang [orangutan], indicating his mixed

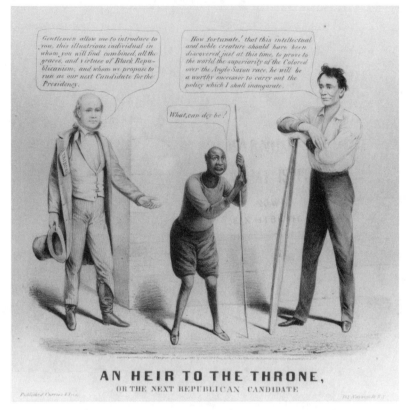

Figure 4. "An Heir to the Throne, or the Next Republican Candidate," Currier and Ives print (1860). Courtesy of the American Antiquarian Society.

ancestry" (108).[15] The Currier and Ives cartoon uses this "nondescript" missing-link representation to satirize Republican support of African-American rights in the 1860 presidential campaign; entitled "An Heir to the Throne," the print features *New York Tribune* editor and well-known abolitionist Horace Greeley, and presidential candidate Abraham Lincoln standing behind the "What Is It?" figure, extolling *his* virtues as a presidential candidate. Barnum's narrative for the "What Is It?" freak exhibit not only relies on the color of Johnson's skin, but on specific racialist ideologies circulating in the culture—namely, the less-than-human status of the African-descended slave in America. "An Heir to the Throne" also shows how such an exhibit, and all its attendant meanings, is put to overt political use, here by Northern opponents of Greeley/Lincoln "radicalism." Freaks were often popular—and profitable—

because their representation reinforced racialist attitudes and ethnocentric distinctions upheld in the dominant culture. Their exhibition further underscored the narrative of civilization and progress that maintained the audience member's position of privileged membership in that community. Represented as potentially dangerous and often sexualized, the freak exhibit simultaneously served to titillate and reassure the white viewer.

Journals of Civilization

About ten years after Barnum started the American Museum, a mid-century publishing boom in the United States catapulted the production and circulation of periodicals like the *Illustrated News*. Frank Luther Mott attributes both the Compromise of 1850, as well as the 1852 Post Office Act, with this "beginning of a new era in the history of American magazines."[16] The Compromise of 1850 included a series of measures passed to appease both proslavery and antislavery proponents that significantly heated up the debate over slavery overall and actually impelled the onset of the Civil War eleven years later; that debate in part took place in the pages of periodicals. In addition, the 1852 Post Office Act reduced postal rates and revised the relationship between subscriber and publisher, making the distribution of print materials more feasible and affordable. As a result, throughout the midcentury, periodical types and titles proliferated as they never had before. Women's magazines like *Godey's Lady's Book,* journals of fine literature like the prestigious *Atlantic Monthly,* abolitionist papers like William Lloyd Garrison's *Liberator,* story papers like Robert Bonner's enormously successful *New York Ledger,* family-oriented weeklies and miscellanies like *Harper's Weekly* and *Frank Leslie's Illustrated Newspaper,* true-crime papers like the *National Police Gazette,* and even pornographic periodicals, such as the scandalous *Venus Miscellany,* provided Americans with a wide range of reading material. While varying markedly in content and quality, all of these publications shared one major aim: to reach the widest group of readers possible. And, although they accomplished it in different ways, these texts likewise served an important ideological function: to create a community of readers described by ambitious editors like Barnum as national.

Ronald Zboray uses the term "fictive people" to refer to this kind of constructed community, indicating the trend toward "cultural coherence" reflected in the print culture of nineteenth-century America, which was both a force in and product of the period's rapid increase in industrialization.[17] Technological improvements in the printing process and supporting industries like the railroad, which were responsible for dramatically propelling the distribution of print matter, increased both the mass of printed materials as well as the possibility that they might find readers. These readers, inundated with reading material and socially scattered as a result of the increased movement of Americans away from their home communities, attempted to find their experiences reflected in the variety of texts that lay before them in a somewhat hit-or-miss fashion. Zboray argues that while "these somewhat experimental practices of the reading public mitigated against the creation of a national literature, . . . readers *had* to find their commonalities in literature that would sell the most copies."[18] And while this search for self in the popular press may in part explain the rise in formulaic fiction that dominated the periodicals at this time, it does not explain the differing slants on the same news events reported in papers coming from different parts of the country. Both the availability of information regarding the event and its relevance to that region's audience determined its reportage.

Likewise, how the papers were read and distributed would have affected their success as producers of totalizing national ideologies. Anderson has argued that the newspaper was the primary vehicle of this nation-building in the nineteenth century, given that newspapers contribute to an imagining of community via an imaginary and doubled sense of simultaneity. According to Anderson, nineteenth-century readers of newspapers were informed about the same set of events and circumstances, each at the same time—"each communicant is well aware that the ceremony he performs [of reading the paper] is being replicated simultaneously by thousands (or millions) of others of whose existence he is confident, yet of whose identity he has not the slightest notion"—and these events themselves share a simultaneity of existence because of their juxtaposed presentation on the page; Anderson calls this phenomenon "calendrical coincidence."[19] But what Anderson describes as a joint and comprehensive attempt to create an imagined nationalized body of readers is a process complicated by the historical context of midcentury America, in which different regions were being conceived of as different kinds of Americas. Readers at this time were *not* necessarily reading the same materials at the same time but were often reading regionalized versions of events that placed emphasis on those accounts that had partic-

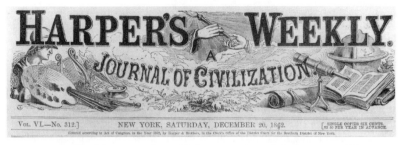

Figure 5. Masthead for *Harper's Weekly* (20 December 1862). Courtesy of the American Antiquarian Society.

ular relevance for their area. Moreover, while a reader in, say, Ohio may in fact have been reading the New York-produced periodical *Frank Leslie's Illustrated Newspaper*, s/he may not have been doing so at the same time his/her New York counterpart may have been; often periodicals were circulated through the mail among family and friends, a practice that widely extended a periodical's network of readers, as well as the time frame in which it might be consumed.

The nation-building narrative of "progress" represented as the evolutionary path humanity takes from primitivity to civilization, also varied between regions. These different narratives are highlighted in the mastheads of the periodicals catering to different readership areas. The New York-based *Harper's Weekly* masthead establishes a theme of intellect and social class to which the reader was assumed to belong, or—as was probably more likely to be the case—aspire (see Figure 5).[20] A painting palette, an inkwell, and a lyre illustrate the refined, artistic nature of the paper while a telescope, globe, compass, and open book indicate its scholarly and scientific dimensions. Between the words, *Harper's Weekly*, one hand passes the light of knowledge to another while the words, *Journal of Civilization*, form a gently curving arc bridging the two collections of images. As *Harper's Weekly*'s masthead professes the journal to be an organ of civilization, so too its lead article in 1857 argues that the Union itself—which should, according to the article, be maintained at almost any cost and certainly the cost of compromise over slavery—is a manifestation of the same. According to *Harper's Weekly*'s writers, the Union is, "only another name for freedom, progress, and civilization."[21] Anything outside of the boundaries and margins of that Union consequently belongs to that which is not civilized—to the primitive and savage. What *Harper's Weekly* concludes in its opening number is the most common

Figure 6. Masthead for the *St. Paul Pioneer and Democrat* (5 September 1862).
Courtesy of the American Antiquarian Society.

form of othering during this midcentury period; that those who belong to the Union are civilized, "active, intelligent, free citizens" who have voted for a continued compromise in the organization of the American states. Those who do not belong to it, or who do not support it, are primitive, savage. In quite a different vein, but still relying on this same narrative of civilization's progress, the masthead of the flagship *St. Paul Pioneer and Democrat* shows an industrious, smoke-pumping town in the middle of the wilderness as framed by a hole in the forest foliage through which a voyeuristic—and clearly covetous—Indian peers (see Figure 6).[22] While both texts rely on the positive implications of conferring civilization on its reader, the shape that civilization assumes is determined by the site of its published imagining.

The Wrongful Possession of a Continent

In the middle of the Civil War in August of 1862, war broke out on another front—in the newly admitted Western state of Minnesota. Having been systematically cheated out of their tribal annuities and subsequently starved by Indian agents and traders, the Dakota in the area rose up against the white settlers, whom they recognized as generally responsible for their misery. The tribe was led by Little Crow, a generally conciliatory leader who favored peace and compliance with white ways and laws, until he was approached by the younger warriors of the Dakota and agreed to lead his people into battle. The conflict began when one brave seeking food dared another to steal eggs from a white farmer; his companion claimed he would show his courage by shooting the whites of the farm. Fighting began in August and continued throughout the summer, leading to the deaths of hundreds of whites and Dakota, the imprisonment of some three hundred warriors, and the largest formal execution in U.S. history, when 38 Dakota men were hung the day after Christmas in 1862.[23]

The sensational nature of the uprising caught the attention of many Northeastern papers, but this new war also provided another opportunity for affirming the white identification of the periodical's readership. *Frank Leslie's Illustrated Newspaper* ran a half-page engraving on the cover of their October 25 edition depicting a murdered family; two women and one man lie on the ground, victims of what the caption calls the "Indian Outrages in the North-West," with the most gruesome detail being a naked infant skewered to a tree (see Figure 7).[24] The caption reads "An American Family Murdered by the Sioux Indians, in a Grove Near New Ulm, Minnesota," highlighting the need for readers to identify with the victims and perceive the attack as an act of war against the entire American community, not only those settlers living in the area itself. In this instance, then, the presentation of the primitive serves to strengthen ties between Northeastern and Western readers into one national community, and to eclipse the national otherness of the citizens of New Ulm, a German settlement, by highlighting the racial difference of the Sioux.

Despite such "sympathetic" reports, though, the Western press generally believed that its Eastern counterpart was much more forgiving of the Sioux than they should have been, given the Eastern press's attempts to open up the question of possible white wrongdoing as an origin for the trouble. In fact in 1864, Charles S. Bryant and Abel B. Murch co-authored their *History of the Great Massacre by the Sioux Indians, in Minnesota, Including the Personal Narratives of Many Who Escaped* in part as an attempt to refute the calls for sympathy the Dakota had supposedly received in the Eastern press. Bryant and Murch discount that any of the Dakota sympathetic causes proposed for the conflict are correct; the "antecedent exciting causes of this massacre" are listed but, according to Bryant and Murch, each theorist is "satisfied that the great massacre of August 1862 had its origin in some way intimately connected with his favorite theory, and were the question raised, What was the cause of the great Southern rebellion? the answers would be perhaps quite as various."[25] By begging the question, Bryant and Murch draw attention to the different wars being fought in America at the time and

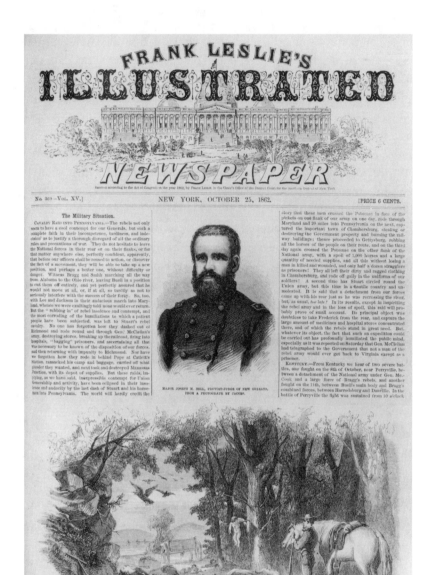

Figure 7. Front page of *Frank Leslie's Illustrated Newspaper* (25 October 1862). Courtesy of the American Antiquarian Society.

the different nations fighting to win them. Nevertheless for these authors, *this* war, unlike that going on between the North and South, does contain a primary cause:

> Let us, for a moment, look at the facts in relation to the two races who
> have come into close contact with each other, and, in the light of these
> facts, judge of the probable cause of this fearful collision. . . . The white
> race stood upon this undeveloped continent ready and willing to execute
> the Divine injunction, to replenish the earth and SUBDUE it. The savage
> races in possession, either refused or imperfectly obeyed this first law of
> the Creator. On the one side stood the white race in the command of
> God, armed with his law; on the other, the savage, resisting the execution
> of that law. The result could not be evaded by any human device. God's
> laws will ever triumph, even through the imperfect instrumentality of
> human agency. In the case before us, the Indian races were in the wrong-
> ful possession of a continent required by the superior right of the white
> man. This right, founded in the wisdom of God, eliminated by the ever-
> operative law of progress, will continue to assert its dominion, with vary-
> ing success, contingent on the use of means employed, until all opposition
> is hushed in the perfect reign of the superior aggressive principle.[26]

The quote on the text's cover page is thus fitting for its authors' purpose: "'For that which is unclean by nature thou canst entertain no hope; no washing will turn the Gipsy white.'"[27] What Bryant and Murch rehearse is the prevailing racialized belief that, given the dictates of Manifest Destiny, only God can or should alter the movement of U.S. settlers into the Western territories and homelands of the native tribes. In the end, then, for these writers, the war for white dominance in the West is propelled by an act of God, a divinely sanctioned progress reliant upon skin color: "on the one side stood the white race in the command of God, armed with his law [to replenish the earth and SUBDUE it]; on the other, the savage, resisting the execution of that law."

The weekly *St. Paul Pioneer and Democrat* covered the events with clear intent: to highlight the Sioux threat to future white settlement of Minnesota in order to replenish the state's dwindling reserve of white soldiers.[28] In order to affirm that there was as great, if not greater need for an American military presence in the West as there was in the South, the press needed to underscore the danger posed by the Dakota not only to the settlers of the region, but to the idea of America overall. This was effected largely by feminizing America "herself," a common move in nationalist rhetoric. The Western press drew a portrait of Dakota savagery that linked the vulnerability of the region with the vulnerability of its white women, figures who themselves represented American morality and purity.[29] More than 300 warriors were taken captive after the August battles, and the Minnesota press registered the local settlers' desire to hang them all. In the rhetorical exchange between Minnesota legislators and the White House regarding the fate of the Dakota prisoners reprinted in the *St. Paul Pioneer and Democrat,* the rape of white women consistently emerged as the most common evidence of the Sioux's savagery. Governor Alexander Ramsey in a September speech to the Minnesota House and Senate details the destruction in terms of "infants hewn into bloody chips of flesh, or nailed alive to door posts" as well as "rape joined to murder in one awful tragedy, young girls, even children of tender years, outraged by their brutal ravishers till death ended their shame."[30] *Harper's Weekly* printed a woodcut in the December 20, 1862, edition with the caption, "Identification of Indian Murderers in Minnesota by a Boy Survivor of the Massacre." In the image, a small white boy points his finger at a hulking darkened warrior whom the boy accuses of "the murder and outrage" of his mother and sisters.[31] Despite the heightened emotional quality of this rape rhetoric, President Lincoln notes in his pardon of all but 39 of the warriors that, after "careful examination of the records of the trials," he could find only two seemingly valid accounts of rape.[32]

Nevertheless, the settlers and representatives of the United States government in Minnesota wanted brutal retribution. Lieutenant Governor Ignatius Donnelly wrote that "with prompt action [the Sioux] can be exterminated or driven beyond the State line, and the State once more placed on such a footing that she can, with some prospect of success, invite immigration. There should be no restoring of the Sioux to their old status ... *they must disappear or be exterminated.*"[33] In his speech to a joint Minnesota House and Senate meeting, Governor Alexander Ramsey describes the "outrages" of the war, highlighting the need to establish definitive boundaries for the nation being carved out of this region—social, as well as geographic boundaries—and reinforcing the *lack* of boundary on the part of the Dakota. This lack signals a missing morality on which the idea of a "civilized" America depends:

> Our course then is plain. The Sioux Indians of Minnesota must be exterminated or driven forever beyond the borders of the state. . . . They have themselves made their annihilation an imperative social necessity.

> Faithless to solemn treaty obligations, to old friendships, to the ties of blood, regardless even of self interest when it conflicts with their savage passions, incapable of honor or of truth or gratitude; amenable to no law; bound by no moral or social restraints—they have already destroyed in one monstrous act of perfidy every pledge on which it was possible to found a hope of mutual reconciliation.[34]

No mention is made, of course, of the agents' theft of the Dakota's promised annuities, pay for the land they "sold" to the United States government, just as no mention is made of the government's attempts to destroy tribal unity by economically and ideologically undermining their religious and cultural beliefs and practices. The political rhetoric of Minnesota's white government relies on nineteenth-century conceptions of the primitive and savage to outline the limits of national membership, a line difficult to draw so sharply without the racial difference always already attributed to the Dakota. While it is, according to Governor Ramsey, the Dakota's "savage passions" that make it impossible "to found a hope of mutual reconciliation," it is in fact the representation of those same "passions" that make possible the definition of a group to whom the Dakota would finally be forced to submit.

White Western officials needed to keep the fires of the Indian wars burning in order to insure continued financial and material support from the federal government; one October *Democrat* editorial reads: "We are surprised, pained, even alarmed, to find the idea gaining ground in many circles that this war is over. . . . This war is not alone with the Sioux of the Mississippi; it is a war of the white race against the brutal, inhuman savages that infest the country between the Mississippi and the Pacific."[35] But the fact that writers and legislators had to assert, in such powerful terms, the ongoing threat posed by this "infestation" of native peoples may indicate to some degree the perceived fragility of and ambivalence toward that threat in the minds of the American public at large. Reports of the execution invariably included this emotionally charged and even sympathetic description:

> The most touching scene on the drop was their attempts to grasp each other's hands, fettered as they were. . . . We were informed by those who understand the language, that their singing and shouting was only to sustain each other—that there was nothing defiant in their last moments, and that no "death-song," strictly speaking, was chanted on the gallows. Each one shouted his own name, and called on the name of his friend, saying, in substance, "I'm here! I'm here!"[36]

Figure 8. Engraving of "The Execution of 38 Sioux Indians..." from *Frank Leslie's Illustrated Newspaper* (24 January 1863): 285. Courtesy of the American Antiquarian Society.

The execution was itself "staged" in the press via a pictorial depiction in both *Harper's Weekly* and *Frank Leslie's Illustrated Newspaper* that literalizes the containment of the Dakota favored by the whites of Minnesota (see Figure 8).[37] Squares composed of militia soldiers and townspeople surround the central structure, indicating not only the vastly more numerous representatives of the white race in this space of supposedly endangered whiteness, but their ability to effectively surround and strike down those who threaten them. The city buildings of Mankato, Minnesota, site of the execution, form the scene's background and it is a significantly more "civilized" scene than one might expect, given the sensational descriptions of the West that have preceded its appearance.

Savagery, Southern-style

In the periodicals of the Northeast covering the conflict in Minnesota, the discourse of savagery extends beyond the notion of the warring Dakota to include the Confederate, even while it draws on popular ideas regarding the Indians themselves. When it gets coverage in *Harper's Weekly,* the Dakota uprising is presented in such a way as to link the Western drama with that of the war being played out in the South. The first mention of the uprising occurs on September 6, 1862, and on September 13, 1862, a cartoon showing Indians fighting alongside Confederates appears with a caption described as extracted from "JEFF DAVIS's last message" that will supposedly "serve to explain the News from Minnesota": "'I am happy to inform you that, in spite ... of ... threats, used in profusion by the agents of the government of the United States, the Indian nations within the confederacy have remained firm in their loyalty and steadfast in the observance of their treaty engagements with this government.'"[38] The connection between Confederate savage and Indian savage is here brought powerfully to the fore as the Confederacy's president himself supposedly affirms the tribes' allegiance to the Southern nation-in-waiting, an allegiance punctuated by an illustration of the most recent acts of "barbarism" committed by the most savage of American savages, the Sioux themselves. In these instances, *Harper's Weekly* reiterates the theme that those who oppose the Union, already described in the paper as simply another name for the idea of civilization, must be savages, opposed to the construction of a higher order of society such as the members of the Union represent.

During the years 1862 and 1863, Confederate savagery is a minor theme in *Harper's Weekly* and *Frank Leslie's Illustrated Newspaper*. John Morgan's Raiders merit two large woodcuts in *Harper's Weekly*'s in the same months that the U.S. settlers of Minnesota fight the Dakota in the West. This simultaneity allows for a kind of rhetorical exchange or borrowing of imagery; the depictions of Morgan's "Highwaymen" in *Harper's Weekly* utilize a range of images most commonly found in Indian captivity narratives. In these engravings, the men riding with Morgan swing Yankee infants by their feet to crush their skulls against trees and buildings; Mary Rowlandson describes a similar practice in her prototypical captivity narrative when the Algonquin braves who take her captive kill Anglo infants by "knocking" them on the head. Confederate guerrillas torture and brutalize children and animals by shooting at or around them, and lascivious Raiders lead women with faces down-turned suggestively away. One description accompanying an engraving appearing in the August 30, 1862, issue of *Harper's Weekly* entitled "John Morgan's Highwaymen Sacking a Peaceful Village in the West," states the following:

> The bond which unites members of a guerrilla band together is love of plunder, lust, and violence. War, as carried on by civilized armies, has no attractions for them. ... Such God forsaken wretches can not be found anywhere in the world out of the Feejee Islands and the Southern Slave States.[39]

This writer calls upon his/her reader's popular conception of the inhabitant of the "Feejee Islands" to complete this image of the savage Confederate; in the popular imagination, the Fiji Islands constitute the primary global site of cannibal activity—cannibals being, as Torgovnick points out, a mainstay of primitive and savage representation.[40] In 1872, thirty years after Barnum had exhibited his first "Cannibal Chief" at the American Museum and more than forty years after the first South Pacific cannibal had appeared anywhere on display in the American museum circuit, four "Fiji Cannibals" appeared in Barnum's Great Traveling Exhibition, "savages" supposedly captured during a raid by a Christianized Fiji king.[41]

The savagery associated with cannibalism appears in other forms in Northern depictions of the Confederate. A few months earlier, *Harper's* had published a report in their "Domestic Intelligence" column entitled, "Our Wounded and Dead Scalped and Mangled," in which a report of a reprinted letter written by S. R. Curtis, Brigadier-General, states that "the General regrets that we find on the battle-field, contrary to civilized warfare, many of the Federal dead who were tomahawked, scalped, and their bodies shamefully mangled, and expressed a hope that this important struggle may not degenerate to a savage warfare."[42] While such a letter points to Confederate-Native American alliances and conflates the "savagery" of the Indians with the "savagery" of Rebel soldiers, reports of more shocking Confederate behavior are depicted in cartoons like one that appeared in *Harper's Weekly* (see Figure 9). Products of "Secesh Industry" cover the page like artifacts in museum cases, items that include a goblet made from a "Yankee's skull," paperweights made out of Northern soldiers' jawbones, furs stitched from scalps and beards, hair-pieces and necklaces made out of Union teeth, and a doorbell handle constructed from the skeleton of a Union soldier's hand.[43] *Frank Leslie's Illustrated Newspaper* ran a similar cartoon a month earlier called "The Rebel Lady's Boudoir." The featured room is a study in Yankee skulls, one resting under a bell jar on a table built out of the leg bones of a dead Union soldier, another fashioning a teakettle and matching cup, and yet another lending authenticity to a skull and crossbones wall-hanging. The ironically demure "Rebel Lady" placidly reads a letter as her baby plays with his very own Yankee skull. The caption, taken from the "Report of the Congressional Committee on the Conduct of the War," is telling:

Figure 9. "Some Specimens of 'Secesh' Industry," engraving from *Harper's Weekly* (7 June 1862): 368. Courtesy of the American Antiquarian Society.

> The outrages upon the dead will revive the recollections of the cruelties to which savage tribes subject their prisoners. They were buried in many cases naked, with their faces downward. They were left to decay in the open air, *their bones being carried off as trophies,* sometimes, as the testimony proves, to be used as personal adornments, *and one witness deliberately avers that the head of one of our most gallant officers was cut off by a Secessionist, to be turned into a drinking-cup on the occasion of his marriage.*[44]

Here, the Northern press writer racializes as alien the Confederate soldier by grafting onto him a popular image of Indian savagery; just as the "savage tribes" use their enemies' body parts for trophies or leave them "to decay in the open air," so the Southern male—*white* male—has similarly used those of his Yankee opponent. In his letter to "my dearest wife," the Confederate soldier responsible for this particular example of Rebel savagery says that he is "about to add something to your collection ... a baby-rattle for our little pet, made out of the ribs of a Yankee drummer-boy."[45]

Northeastern popular periodicals did not neglect to capitalize on the popularly understood primitive nature of racialized groups like the Dakota in their reportage of these Confederate atrocities. Rather, they extended this classification, including in the fold that figure who most immediately—and dangerously—threatened the definition of nationality most relevant to its region. Even without the visible markers of race, the Northeastern press managed to "other" the Confederate by way of racialized discourse. A physical threat to those living in and fighting for the North, the Confederate here threatens the very concept of civilized humanity, something for which, as *Harper's Weekly* has already proclaimed, the Union undeniably and singly stands. Not the infantile primitive the African-American slave was so often represented as being, the Confederate soldier endangers the civilized boundaries of American citizenry as only the "headhunting" tribesman of the Fiji Islands or the "savage" Sioux of the Western plains can. What is most ironic about these representations, however, is how *little* they rely on the barbarism of the Southern slavery system to prove the barbarism of the Southern slaveholder him or herself. Confederates in these instances are typically savage *not* because they perpetuate the enslavement and debasement of other human beings, but because they threaten the life and dignity of the Union soldier, a figure obviously metonymic for the Union itself.

Packaging America: A Nation Commodified

The figure of the "savage" of the Dakota wars became a rhetorical strategy used by different communities to benefit their individual causes and strengthen the sense of each community's borders overall. The Western press highlighted the savage nature of the Sioux in order to regain military, financial, and public support for their ongoing and increasingly hostile movement into native lands. The Northern press used the savage in part to echo these conclusions—conclusions that had a more regional and immediate effect and relevance in the West than they did the East— but to also extend the domain of the racialized other to include the Confederate. But savagery for the likes of P. T. Barnum was valuable in an even more local and individualized way. Barnum used this rhetoric to show not only how barbaric the Indian was, but how effectively that savagery could be contained by the skillful and courageous showman— and it made Barnum a nice profit. Barnum relied upon this discourse to build a sense of intrigue and danger that, in turn, created a spectacle worth paying for. As did the writers, illustrators, and editors responsible for the depiction of the "savage" Indian in the popular press, Barnum commodified Native Americans to effect his own purpose. Using the racialized rhetoric available to him, Barnum appropriated primitive and savage discourses to construct a community over which he represented himself as having singular control. Obviously not a national or regionalized community in and of himself, Barnum nevertheless constructed a paternalistic and economic relationship between himself and the Native Americans he exhibited that positioned him as dominant via the primitive and savage discourses already in place as markers of national identity.

In 1843, almost twenty years before the Dakota uprising, Barnum brought what he called simply "a band of Indians from Iowa" to perform war dances in the American Museum's Lecture Room. In his autobiography, he notes that the dances seem to be considered by the Native Americans as "realities" rather than performances and claims that "when they gave a real War Dance, it was dangerous for any parties, except their manager and interpreter, to be on the stage."[46] Lydia Maria Child, who attended one such performance at the museum, described it as "terrific to both eye and ear," saying that she "looked at the door, to see if escape were easy."[47] She claims that she "was never before so much struck with the animalism of Indian character" and she backs up her observations with an appropriately bestial string of metaphors: "Their gestures were as furious as wildcats, they howled like wolves, screamed like prairie dogs, and tramped like buffaloes."[48]

Beyond emphasizing the reality of the performance itself, Barnum's strategy for showing the Indians was to simultaneously heighten and contain the danger he claimed they posed. He used a rope to draw a physical barrier between the dancing warriors and audience members, and interpreters and managers to "handle" the natives, much as a circus tamer handles big cats. In all cases, Barnum represents himself, the white showman, as completely in control of the Indians' movements. Twenty years after Child visited the Museum, Barnum again exhibited a group of ten or so chiefs there. In one of his autobiographies, he details his handling and rhetorical framing of the Kiowa chief Yellow Bear. Barnum notes that he called the chief "probably the meanest, black-hearted rascal that lives in the far West. . . . He has tortured to death poor, unprotected women, murdered their husbands, brained their helpless little ones; and he would gladly do the same to you or to me, if he thought he could escape punishment."[49] During this introduction, however, Barnum would pat Yellow Bear "familiarly upon the shoulder, which always caused him to look up to me with a pleasant smile, while he softly stroked down my arm with his right hand in the most loving manner."[50] Barnum here shapes the audience's experience of Yellow Bear by positioning him within a specific narrative and by maintaining control of that narrative, speaking a language to which Yellow Bear does not apparently have access. Barnum therefore emphasizes his control of this "black-hearted rascal" by exploiting both halves of the monster/child primitive binary, telling the story of Yellow Bear's barbarism while making him look like a docile, not-very-bright child. But it isn't just the Indians who are rhetorically contained in Barnum's exhibition; his audience, as well, sits within his theatre, consuming the commodified oddities Barnum feeds them.

Barnum featured Sioux chiefs and their songs and dances again at the museum during the winter of 1863, following the execution of the thirty-eight warriors in Mankato. During this several-month period, *Frank Leslie's Illustrated Newspaper* simultaneously ran news accounts of ongoing Indian attacks in Minnesota, along with informal advertisements of Barnum's shows in an entertainment/gossip column called "The Idler About Town." On one hand highlighting the danger these "real" Indians continue to pose to white Western settlers—"Towns are still building stockades and block houses for refuge, and prowling bands of Indians steal and murder constantly"—*Leslie's* "Idler" column almost simultaneously depicts the Indian chiefs in Barnum's employ as "wild children of Nature" whose "songs and dances are among the most curious exhibitions we ever witnessed."[51] Later, the "Idler" pronounces them "the most consistent friends of the white men" because they decide to extend their museum stay.[52] In an explanation of a November 14, 1863, woodcut, "Sioux Dancing the Scalp Dance," a *Leslie* reporter remarks that having "a scene like this sent to an illustrated newspaper in the middle of the nineteenth century seems strange and more strange when it comes from within the borders of one of the States, and not from the yet unbroken wilderness. But the Sioux war is still raging."[53] Such coverage served not only to further identify the nation emerging from the "yet unbroken wilderness," but also to amplify the fascinated fear Barnum counted on to fill the seats of his lecture hall in the American Museum. This fear, of course, was not Barnum's own. In fact, what Barnum may have thought and felt about the "savages" he displayed was motivated by quite different forces than those brought out by *Leslie's*.

In a letter to Moses Kimball, proprietor of Boston's version of the American Museum and a close friend, Barnum complains about the Indians who perform at the American Museum in 1843—"5 Indians,

2 squaws, and a little [?papoose] five or six years old."[54] Given that Kimball will be the next to show this group ("You may as [well] get your
puffs preliminary in the papers," Barnum tells him, "I [?think] that I
can let them leave here Saturday after[noon]"), Barnum shares his own
experiences with these supposedly savage "curiosities":

> The lazy devils want to be *lying down* nearly all the time, and as it looks
> so bad for them to be lying about the Museum, I have them stretched
> out in the workshop all day, some of them occasionally strolling about
> the Museum.
> D—n Indians *anyhow*. They are a lazy, shiftless set of brutes—
> though they will *draw*.[55]

Despite his "insider" position, Barnum clearly agrees with the general
popular consensus that the Indians are, as he puts it, "brutes." But for
Barnum, this is not a distinction that helps to separate Northerner from
Southerner or even settler from Sioux; it is, rather, a distinction between
a cooperative employee who works in tandem with his/her employer to
attain market-driven goals, and the less complicitous worker who does
not accept the market's—and, therefore, his capitalist employer's—goals
as his/her own. Barnum's staging of the Indian as racialized other links
the Indian to the market Barnum has created in the American Museum.
Although he uses a primitivizing discourse to justify this performance
and as a means to appeal to his audience by shoring up their basically
illusory, abstract state of Americanness via the physical bodies of the
nonwhite, non-American Dakota, the driving force behind this instance
of "blinding whiteness" is economic. It is ironic, to say the least, that
for Barnum, conqueror and controller of these dangerous warriors,
the biggest problem he has with them is that they always "want to be *lying down*."

He Bad Injin—He Gone

Whether, as *Frank Leslie's Illustrated Newspaper* put it, the "Sioux war"
was still raging or not, clearly it was in the best interest of a number of
different groups to believe that it was. For the Western press, continuation of the war meant maintaining continued public support for an
organized move into Dakota lands that necessitated removal of the
Dakota themselves, a move that insured continued white domination of
the area. Perpetuating the idea of an Indian threat to white settlers was
the best argument Western officials could make for increasing their share

of military resources at a time when such resources were scarce indeed. In the Northeast, however, where concentrated populations of potential soldiers were greater and the decisions regarding the war in the South were daily being made, the Dakota conflict likewise supplied the press with a fresh batch of imagery to further delineate who and what Northerners were killing and dying for in the South. If the Union was itself an actualization of civilization, then those who had taken a stand against it could only be uncivilized. To emphasize the threat of secession—in this scheme, literally a move away from civilization—the Confederate was rhetorically aligned with the image of the raping-and-killing savage currently being recirculated as a result of the fresh conflict in Minnesota. For P. T. Barnum, savagery sold, as did the racially self-congratulatory sense of superiority his largely white urban audience members saw reaffirmed on the stages of the American Museum. Behind the scenes, Barnum's creation of a community was less driven by nation-building— itself, an economic issue driven by the rush to claim resources—than it was propelled by personal gain, but Barnum's appropriation of that rhetoric tells us one thing very clearly: in order to construct America, America had to be sold. As America's capitalist economy was beginning to take shape and sellers competed for buyers, the nation at large was routinely commodified by competing groups. Whether it was the editors of the weekly *St. Paul Pioneer and Democrat,* Barnum with his American Museum, or writers of sensational serialized fiction, the producers of these cultural texts attempted to present a version of the United States that would bring to those with the greatest claim on its membership the most resources and the most power.

In 1869, the Dakota wars were revived by the prolific and ubiquitous author of the best-selling dime novel, *Seth Jones,* for even more varied purposes. Appearing originally in Philadelphia's popular weekly story paper *Saturday Night,* Edward Sylvester Ellis's serialized *Red Plume: A Tale of the Minnesota Massacres* ran from August 21, 1869, through December 18, 1869.[56] Seven years after the fact, the initial run of *Red Plume* ironically covers the same span of months as did the original conflict and consequent execution in Minnesota. Later republished as an adolescent boys' story, *Red Plume* is an excellent example of the popular Western adventure tale.[57] The cast of characters includes all key frontier figures— Captain Swarthausen, an upstanding ex-soldier turned Western settler; the captain's housekeeper, Mrs. Muggins, and her somewhat befuddled, humorous husband, Snoopy; John Fielding, a Quaker and one of the tale's suitors; Hugh Prescott, his wife, and their love-struck daughters, Lillian and Edith; a foppish cousin from the East, Adolphus Pipkins; and the Prescott's black "servants," Dinah, Cato, and Elijah or "Lige." Once the Swarthausen-Prescott community is attacked by local marauding bands of Sioux, two more characters arrive on the scene: Jubal Judkins or "Old Jud," the Natty Bumppo of the tale, and Red Plume, a friendly Sioux warrior who has devoted his life to saving white people from his own angry tribesmen. The story follows the group as they are separated from one another and barely escape a barrage of attacks by the Sioux. They lose Mrs. Muggins to a well-aimed Indian bullet, work through a range of romantic traumas, and finally reach the safety of Fort Grandson where they are saved by a U.S. Army battalion.

The representation of the Sioux in *Red Plume* is not, of course, particularly positive. Depicted by even one of their own—Red Plume—as bloodthirsty and murderous beyond redemption, the Sioux attackers in the story meld into one common enemy, one opposing force to the various kinds of civilization these settlers bring to the wilderness. In one instance, John Fielding argues that they should treat with kindness a warrior that part of the party has managed to take captive. Fielding offers the brave food (which he refuses), then convinces everyone, including the dubious Red Plume, that they should release him. Later, when a shot comes out of the forest and narrowly misses "the brain of Lillian by scarcely a hair's breath," Red Plume informs the party that the shooter is in fact the same warrior Fielding convinced his cohorts to forgive and to free.[58] Edith can't tell if it is the same man—" 'There isn't enough difference between your people's looks for me to distinguish them apart at that great distance,'" she explains to Red Plume—but the two other white women agree that Red Plume must be right: " 'Red Plume never makes a mistake,' added Lillian, placing her white, delicate hand upon the swarthy, muscular shoulder of the Sioux with all the confiding faith of a child."[59] Without another thought, Red Plume raises his rifle and shoots the offending brave dead: " 'Neber do dat more,' said Red Plume, as he coolly reloaded his piece; 'he bad Injin—he gone.'"[60] And so he is, as Red Plume himself is made to go at the end of the story when Ellis concludes that Red Plume and the Otter, another white-friendly Sioux, disappear "somewhere in the Great West, serving as scouts, hunters or runners for the advanced military posts."[61]

While it would be difficult to argue that Ellis depicts the Native American in the person of Red Plume as something other than the primitive savage we've already seen the rebelling Minnesota Sioux of the popular press to be, in many ways, it's not the Sioux who emerges as the most dangerous racialized other in this tale. Although Ellis indeed describes the various warriors as leaping here and there "like panthers" (he even names the chief whom Red Plume confronts in the final segment of the story "Leaping Panther"), the unquestionably white John Fielding leaps like a panther too.[62] Ellis even refers to Red Plume midway through the novel's run as an "aboriginal American."[63] Red Plume himself is both undeniably good and undeniably alien and he follows the necessary destiny of all such good aliens by conveniently disappearing himself into the disappearing West by the end of the text. In *Red Plume,* we never really see enough of any of the "bad Injins" to see them as anything other than the shadowy but worthy adversaries such adventure tales demand they be.

In fact, the only character depicted as consciously and systematically evil in *Red Plume* is an African American. Lige apparently steals whiskey from his upstanding master, aligns himself with the Sioux, and attempts to betray the community of white settlers he serves by delivering them into the hands of the killing braves. Once they see how vulnerable Lige's actions have made them to the Sioux, various characters—including the all-forgiving John Fielding—claim that they never really trusted him to begin with. Although the other black characters that serve the Prescott family are not depicted as intentionally duplicitous in the way Lige is, they nevertheless endanger the whites' survival and are therefore represented as deeply problematic as well. Cato is forever getting into potentially disastrous scrapes for which only his complete ignorance and lack of awareness can account, and his mother, Dinah, is described as being so fat at one point in the story as to be potentially fatal to the rest of the group. She can't outrun the warriors that are in hot pursuit of the settlers and Old Jud refuses to let the other members of the fleeing Prescott party slow down in order to help her. "'Ef we've got to lose any one, it may as well be her,'" he tells them; "'Like as not she'll sink the boat anyway when she gets into it.'"[64]

It seems clear that for Ellis, while Indians make good copy and even at times valuable allies, the same is clearly not true of African Americans. Hardly virtuous, at the least troublesome, and at the worst definitively villainous, Ellis characterizes the African American as a clear threat to white survival. In *Red Plume,* this also means survival of the nation, as one of the calling cards of American national identity was white settlement of the Western frontier. In casting his African American characters as threats to this settlement, Ellis in *Red Plume* demonstrates a kind of cultural fear I call Emancipation anxiety. As the definition of Americanness officially shifted in 1863 to include freed slaves and already free blacks living in the United States, the response in the white-marketed popular press in the Northeast was swift and clear. It is this response—a racialized response itself heavily overdetermined by class-complicated notions of endangered Americanness—to which I now turn.

TWO

Emancipation Anxiety and the New York City Draft Riots

EMANCIPATION IS ENTIRELY SAFE.
—Advertisement for Augustin Cochin's *The Results of Emancipation* in *Frank Leslie's Illustrated Newspaper,* January 24, 1863

If I taught you more cunning, you would destroy everybody.
—Woman to Spider in Nigerian trickster tale

There is no question that Abraham Lincoln's "Proclamation" of Emancipation and the passage of Constitutional Amendments Thirteen, Fourteen, and Fifteen were at least among, if not the, most outstanding legislative achievements of the nineteenth century.[1] According to the editors of *Freedom: A Documentary History of Emancipation, 1861–1867,* "no event in American history matches the drama of emancipation."[2] Encompassing as it does the breadth of the public debate regarding slavery, the clash of economic and social orders within the United States, the war that ensued in part as a result of that clash, and the painful period of rebuilding and reconstruction following that war (a period many would argue has not yet reached its end), the "drama of emancipation" surely does stand alone. Lincoln's proclamation came too late for some and didn't go far enough for others, but it remains nevertheless the first institutionally sanctioned step toward the national abolition of slavery. It was inarguably a defining moment in the history of American citizenship.

Even more than abolition, Emancipation became a racialist and nationalist force for American citizens in the nineteenth century. As Kathleen Diffley has noted, the freeing of the slaves and the consequent gain of American citizenship by African Americans fundamentally altered the way in which those already classified as American citizens—those understood to be "white"—viewed themselves as members of a national community.[3] Despite the fact that civil equality was not the actual result of Emancipation, the idea that African Americans, a people historically and theoretically classified as less than human, would no longer be denied basic civil liberties by slavery ripped through the popular American imagination, reconfiguring all kinds of racialized categories. To call what resulted from the conversation surrounding and the events leading up to and including Emancipation "anxiety" is clearly an understatement. Nevertheless, it remains a functionally useful term for the alarmist response in the popular white-dominant imagination to the shift in social relations Emancipation promised. Over and over again in the pages of the popular press, writers relied on a pervasive fear of the insurrections in Haiti and what was then Santo Domingo, using them as examples of what was undoubtedly to come as a result of Emancipation. But at the same time that New York-based periodicals like *Frank Leslie's Illustrated Newspaper* were predicting explosive upheaval in the South as a result of Emancipation, when civil unrest occurred, it did so in the Northern city itself. The violence and brutality of what have come to be known as the New York City Draft Riots were not ultimately provoked by, but aimed at, the city's African-American population.[4] The actuality of the New York riots and the way in which a popular newspaper like *Leslie's* responded to them illustrate how intertwined yet shifting conceptions of class and race are, particularly when they act as markers of American belonging and entitlement.

Who Freed the Slaves?

In his essay, "Who Freed the Slaves? Emancipation and Its Meaning," Ira Berlin sums up the scholarly debate regarding the historical event of Emancipation overall.[5] According to Berlin,

> The debate over the origins of Civil War emancipation in the American South can be parsed in such a way as to divide historians into two camps: those who understand emancipation primarily as the product of the slaves' struggle to free themselves, and those who see the Great Emancipator's hand at work.[6]

According to Berlin, historians who promote "self-emancipation," or the idea that the slaves were solely responsible for their hard-won freedom, are responding in part to ethnocentric, white-centered histories of Emancipation that wrongly neglect the work and actions of the slaves in their own freedom. For some historians, Frederick Douglass's address given at the dedication of the Emancipation Monument in Washington, D.C., in 1876 reflects this hallowing of the Great Emancipator; in the speech, Douglass claims that it was under Lincoln's "wise and beneficent rule" that enslaved blacks "saw ourselves gradually lifted from the depths of slavery to the heights of liberty and manhood."[7] But this swing of the historical pendulum in favor of social history's reprivileging of nonelitist, noncentralized mass populations does not, according to Berlin, complete the picture either. Again, according to Berlin:

> Slaves were the prime movers in the emancipation drama, not the sole movers. Slaves set others in motion, including many who would never have moved if left to their own devices. How they did so is nothing less than the story of emancipation.[8]

Berlin's mediating ideas are mirrored by many other historians of Emancipation. John Cimprich in his study of the end of slavery in Tennessee argues that the self-emancipatory actions of contrabands—runaway slaves—spurred legislative action, but that both were necessary for the end of the "peculiar institution": "Although contrabands had gained virtual freedom, only white politicians could make it legal."[9] In the introduction to their study of the gradual emancipation process in Pennsylvania, Gary B. Nash and Jean R. Soderlund indicate that they intend to balance what they claim has been a distorted discussion of the "triumph...of Christian moralism and the philosophy of natural rights" in the institution's demise there:[10]

> Of the states south of New England, slavery died first in Pennsylvania and it died there the fastest. But its death was a complicated matter in which slaves themselves were far more involved than has been understood and in which masters were more notable for shrewd calculations of how to extricate themselves at little cost from an involvement in owning fellow human beings than for a rise in their moral sensibilities caused by participation in commercial enterprise or anything else. Nor was the transition to a free labor system smooth, because while masters might give up their slaves, they did not easily relinquish ideas about the people whose labor they formerly commanded absolutely.[11]

Leslie A. Schwalm writing about Emancipation in the sea islands and low country of South Carolina reemphasizes the assertive role slaves took in the appropriation of their own freedom while simultaneously underlining an official, military presence in their accomplishing of that goal: "On the mainland, the wartime dissolution of slavery had accelerated with the arrival of Union troops; slaves eventually took matters into their own hands to secure slavery's final destruction. Still, even their self-emancipation relied, in part, on the perceptions of former slaves and planters as to the strength and duration of Union presence."[12] Victor B. Howard reiterates in various moments of his study of Emancipation in Kentucky the conjoining of institutional and noninstitutional forces to effect slavery's abolition. While stating definitively that "the initiative taken by large numbers of blacks thus lay at the heart of slavery's decline in Kentucky," Howard also makes clear that Lincoln's move to change border-state policy on slavery—a move he was forced to make due to the "disruptions" runaway slaves caused by linking themselves with the Union forces in the state—was key to its ending.[13] T. Stephen Whitman's remarks in his study of slavery and manumission in Baltimore and early national Maryland further support the idea of the black-initiated, but two-toned liberation process outlined by Berlin. "What emerges from this study of early nineteenth-century Baltimore and Maryland," Whitman concludes, "is the criticality of black efforts to obtain freedom; those efforts in combination with rural planters' decisions drove events in the city."[14] William H. Williams in his study on the end of slavery in Delaware—a state that did not officially ratify the Thirteenth Amendment abolishing slavery until *1901*—describes a kind of equality of agency in the struggle when he notes that "Lincoln's Emancipation Proclamation and the subsequent flight of enslaved African-Americans from their owners ended slavery throughout most of the Confederacy by April 1865"; Patience Essah writing about slavery's *official* end there in 1901 notes that even then, it was the appeal of a tenuously and newly empowered, largely white, Republican majority in the Delaware legislature to black voters that finally pushed the legislation through.[15]

In other words, most historians writing on the subject seem to agree with Berlin that Emancipation was a process that worked because of the combined efforts and energies of both blacks *and* whites, both resisting slaves and empowered government officials. Berlin explains that this is the philosophy of the editors of the *Freedom* series, the most in-depth study of Emancipation to be undertaken to date; he argues that it is as crucial to maintain Lincoln and the Emancipation Proclamation's positioning in whatever history of Emancipation is written as it is to maintain the original and central efforts of enslaved and freed African Americans of that time:

> The Emancipation Proclamation's place in the drama of emancipation is thus secure—as is Lincoln's. To deny it is to ignore the intense struggle by which freedom arrived. It is to ignore the Union soldiers who sheltered slaves, the abolitionists who stumped for emancipation, and the thousands of men and women who, like Lincoln, changed their minds as slaves made the case for universal liberty. Reducing the Emancipation Proclamation to a nullity and Lincoln to a cipher denies human agency just as personifying emancipation in a larger-than-life Great Emancipator denies the agency of the slaves and many others, and trivializes the process by which the slaves were freed.[16]

As all these comments show, Emancipation was indeed a process, a path taken by both whites and blacks during these years of and surrounding the Civil War. What Berlin and other critics make apparent, however, is that the Proclamation itself occupies a special position, installing itself as a defining moment in the history of the liberation of America's slaves and the redefinition of American citizenship and nationhood overall.

Emancipation Anxiety and American Whiteness

On January 1, 1863, slaves living in those states yet at war with the Federal government of the United States of America were legally emancipated by President Abraham Lincoln; on January 17, *Frank Leslie's Illustrated Newspaper* speculated on reactions likely to follow this event. Abolitionists, it said, "will find it difficult to understand that the President has no power over slavery, except in his military capacity" while Europeans hostile to the United States may try to represent "the President as . . . supporting slavery when he has the power, while claiming the cheap credit of abolishing it when he has no power."[17] Turning to the potentially negative consequences of the Proclamation, the writer explains that those hostile to American interests "will seek to represent [the Proclamation] as a firebrand thrown into the heart of the South for the sole and fell purpose of exciting servile insurrection and reviving the horrors of Santo Domingo."[18]

Santo Domingo (now the Dominican Republic), "Hayti," and the slave uprisings that occurred in both countries between 1791 and 1802 become highly charged tropes for expressing a white Northern anxiety about Emancipation. According to Eric Foner, the overthrow of slavery on Saint-Domingue, the French colony located on the western third of the island of Hispaniola (the island on which both Haiti and the Dominican Republic are located), "resulted from a black revolution in which most of the white population was massacred or fled into exile, the armies of England and France were defeated by the former slaves, and much of the countryside was laid waste."[19] It was the first national emancipatory victory in the Western Hemisphere and one that created the second "independent nation in the New World."[20] The fact that Haiti's revolution did not spur financial prosperity there or improve what was described as the overall standard of living for its finally freed citizens, became key points of discussion for opponents of abolition in America.[21] More so than this fear of economic loss to the South, the fear of the destruction of white property and the loss of control over resources hitherto dominated by white consumers were key for citizens of the northeast United States. These were the "horrors of Santo Domingo" most horrible to white Northern readers.

But while white Northern writers warned their readers that Emancipation was sure to lead to black insurrection in the South, the *real* terrorism that would occur as a result of Emancipation would be prompted and perpetuated not *by*, but *against* blacks. As Robyn Wiegman writes,

> the emancipation of five million slaves was neither a widespread cultural recognition of black humanity nor the proud achievement of the democratic ethos. As the late nineteenth century's turn toward the Ku Klux Klan and mob violence makes clear, the transformation from slavery to "freedom" was characterized by a rearticulation of cultural hierarchies in which terrorism provided the means for defining and securing the continuity of white supremacy.[22]

In fact, one insurrection did occur at about this time, and it was the largest and most devastating of its kind yet in American history. It did not, however, occur in the South and it was not a direct result of Emancipation. In July of 1863, a body of New Yorkers rioted against the recently announced draft in the city and more than a hundred people—among them a bulk of African Americans—were killed. *This* insurrection certainly predicted what *would* follow Emancipation—the terrorizing, lynching, and murder of African Americans in the South after the Civil War. It also illustrates how Americanness and whiteness were defined oppositionally and opportunely, in relation to politically vulnerable nationalities and ethnicities. These two narratives of insurrection—a fantasized black uprising and a very real white one—emerge during the Emancipation period in New York City and work relationally to further define who should have possession of American identity. The contradictions and complexities of these narratives verify that the notion of Americanness circulating in them is no fixed entity. Stuart Hall argues that we must learn "to reconceptualize identity as a *process of identification,* [as] . . . something that happens over time, that is never absolutely stable, that is subject to the play of history and the play of difference."[23] This is certainly the case in the incidents of 1863 in New York City. Whiteness for a white is not, as Ruth Frankenberg notes, typically easy to see; while it does seem to constitute "a set of normative cultural practices," it is "visible most clearly to those it definitively excludes and those to whom it does violence. Those who are securely housed within its borders usually do not examine it."[24] Frankenberg argues that whiteness does have "content inasmuch as it generates norms, ways of understanding history, ways of thinking about self and other, and even ways of thinking about the notion of culture itself," but she also stresses its relational qualities: "'Whiteness' is indeed a space defined only by reference to those named cultures it has flung out to its perimeters."[25] Stuart Hall complicates this idea, though, when he argues that this "dialogic relationship to the other" means that the other has also necessarily been internalized— "the Other is not outside; but also inside the Self, the identity."[26] Whiteness then defines itself via conceptions of blackness, but the seeds of these conceptions lie within the realm of whiteness itself.

What "blackness" meant in 1863 to one white Northern population can be seen in several images culled from *Frank Leslie's Illustrated Newspaper.* Once the question of racial purity in an increasingly mixed America was no longer "skintight," race shifted from an essentially exteriorized concept to a philosophically considered, scientifically poised interiority.[27] Notions of the African and the African American as animalistic and savage or, conversely, infantile and slow-witted circulated in varying discourses in the culture.[28] In a political cartoon appearing in *Leslie's* in 1862, the enslaved black man is represented as a black bird in a cage, a bird for which Uncle Sam is offering "Bub" Maryland a quarter—"now go and let that black bird loose," he coaxes (see Figure 10).[29] While the cartoon seems to comment on the absurdity of the exchange, the bird nevertheless depicts the slave as one of the anomalies of the animal

Figure 10. Political cartoon of a slave bird in a cage talking with Uncle Sam and Maryland, from *Frank Leslie's Illustrated Newspaper* (5 April 1862): 336. Courtesy of the American Antiquarian Society.

kingdom that can, quite imperfectly, simulate human speech: "Jis de eberlasting nigger I is," sings the caged animal. Highlighting the always primarily embodied presence of the slave as both commodity and animal, another *Frank Leslie's Illustrated Newspaper* woodcut depicts "The Great Government Sale of Confiscated Blood Stock" in New Orleans.[30] The center illustration shows a black stallion held by a black man and, while horses dominate the frame in sheer numbers, the slave holding the horse occupies the image's central space. The question is implicit: to what "blood stock" does the title refer?

While the image of the New Orleans sale of horses (and men) appeared after Emancipation, descriptions and images directly commenting on Emancipation itself likewise reiterate these racist concepts. One *Leslie's* reporter covering the Emancipation Day celebration near Charleston, South Carolina comments on the presence of "Sambo" there and highlights the power the minstrel show had in perpetuating a particular kind of African-American figure for Northern female readers: "Two thirds of our boarding-school misses believe that a contraband is a dark gentleman with a triangular collar of some two feet high in new pumps and broadcloth, a set of white ivory, a fine tenor voice, a rather handsome banjo and a remarkably bad hat."[31] The reporter goes on to replace this stereotype with one of his own, relying on a familiar bestial rhetoric to do so:

> We had for passengers, on this occasion, what a rebel would esteem his fortune—being no less than scores of colored individuals of all stripes, sizes, modes of dress and hue. . . . the steamer Flora from Beaufort . . . was literally jammed with niggers, who grinned and chatted like so many monkeys.[32]

The accompanying image emphasizes the simian characteristics often, if not typically found in pictorial representations of African Americans at the time.[33]

The prospect of the African American achieving what Wiegman calls "Emancipation's theoretical effect—the black male's social sameness," contributes to what I see as the larger over-reaching anxiety regarding American identity in the mid-nineteenth century.[34] When the black slave theoretically achieved political and legal equality, the threat of this "social sameness" potentially made racialized, white Americanness much more difficult to define. The idea of former slaves competing for work with white "free laborers" threatened both an increase in competition for economic resources as well as the ideological premises of work defined as "free," defined in opposition to slavery.[35] In general, the event of Emancipation sparked an anxiety always already present in American culture as to what truly constituted American identity—as well as highlighting the potential for loss of white privilege. Santo Domingo became metaphoric for what was seen by many Northerners as an apocalyptic end to white American privilege and exclusivity.[36]

William Neal Cleveland, father of future American president Grover Cleveland, argued two years before Emancipation that the "mysterious matter" of "servitude" should be left "in the hands of God" and not "girdled" by "the iron hand of prohibition":

> Ah! my brethren, think not that in such circumstances the southern section of our dear land shall thrive. For a time there might be no apparent decay, be ere two generations shall have come and gone, depend upon it, the history of Louisiana will be as the history of Santo Domingo.[37]

In a speech given in the House of Representatives in June of 1862, Samuel Sullivan Cox of Ohio returns time and again to the image of Santo Domingo, suggesting that the rewriting of slave laws in the South by the

Union government will force Southern legislators into "rash acts," acts that will in turn become an "excuse for converting the war into a Santo Domingo insurrection, turning the South into one utter desolation."[38] "There would be re-enacted the scenes of Hayti," says Cox, "a war of extermination between black and white, until after scenes of carnage and horror, the black man would be swept away."[39]

Cox's unlikely fear of black genocide rhetorically shifts attention from what truly disturbs him—the loss of American white "purity" and exclusive white power. Relying on conventional proslavery arguments to win his readers' appeal, Cox reprints a piece from the *London Times* describing "the freed negro of Hayti" as "a lazy animal, without any foresight, and therefore requiring to be led and compelled. He is decidedly inferior, very little raised above a mere animal. . . . In Jamaica, emancipation has thrown enormous tracts of land out of cultivation, and on these the negro squats, getting all he wants with very little trouble, and sinking, in the most absolute fashion, back to the savage state."[40] With an apocalyptic flair, Cox lists statistics for black crime in Ohio, black prostitution, and the possible decline of Ohio property value if "the numberless itinerant blacks from the South are to be admitted to the State."[41] He concludes by lamenting the "fate" of the "Anglo-Saxon-Celtic population of the United States" if political equality is legislated—namely, the browning of America's European-descended white population.[42] Despite "reassuring" comments like those published in *Leslie's* "Idler About Town" column—an 1863 note on the Baby Show at Barnum's American Museum comments that "it has brought out some of the finest infants in the world, and has proved beyond all peradventure that the race is by no means degenerating"—the anxiety fueled by such anti-Emancipatory rhetoric is almost always forcibly linked to popular notions of racial mixing and racial "degradation."[43] Racial distinction is equated with national membership; Emancipation necessarily blurred the lines of both.

The fear of racial mixing—"amalgamation" and "miscegenation"— is the central theme of a satiric cartoon published as a broadside in 1864 by Bromtey and Company in New York.[44] "Political Caricature No. 2: Miscegenation, or The Millennium of Abolitionism" features pairs of white and black men and women participating in a range of leisure activities together. The representations of the whites and blacks are strikingly, and intentionally, divisive. A tidy, white Horace Greeley eats ice cream with "Miss Snowball," a large round-headed, big-grinned mammy.

Charles Sumner holds hands with another such character, introducing "my very dear friend, Miss Dinah, Arabella, Aramintha Squash" to Abraham Lincoln, who notes that he "shall be proud to number among my intimate friends any member of the Squash family, *especially the little Squashes*." Miss Squash, who curtsies slightly to the bowing Abe, notes that she knew Mrs. Lincoln when she "washed for her 'fore de hebenly Miscegenation times was cum. Don't do nuffin now but gallevnat 'round wid de white gem'men!" Two more oversized and simian-featured black men seduce white abolitionist Anna Dickinson and a sister lecturer. When her beau asks Dickinson when "Brodder Beecher shall make us one!" she answers, "Oh! You dear creature, I am so agitated! Go and ask Pa." The other white lecturer lounges on her black beau's lap.

This broadside is intriguing in part for the bold images of implied sexuality it uses to shock and disturb its white readers. These are pictures, after all: visually realized scenes rather than narrative or editorial remarks on the hypersexualized nature of the Jezebel image or the brutal and sexually rapacious Reconstruction-era black man. In fact, the African Americans portrayed in this broadside are frightening without the sexual overtones; cartoonish and overly large, the black men's heads are twice the size of their white female companions' and the black women similarly tower over their thin white male paramours. Miss Squash is almost as tall as the notoriously long-limbed President Lincoln and when she laughs, she actually brays: "he—ah! he—ah! he ah!" While other black and white couples cavort around the park and viaduct where the scene takes place, an all-black couple rides in a carriage in the middle of the scene, noting that they must watch not to "cut" the walking Sumner with their carriage. The white driver of the carriage remarks— presumably to himself—that he must have been desperate to take this position—"my heys! I wanted a sitiwation when I took this one." An Englishman, a German man, and an Irish woman all make similar asides. Both the German and the Brit are simply astounded by what they witness: "Mine Got," says the German, "vat a guntry, vat a beebles!" The Irish woman who, like the grumbling white disenfranchised driver, faces away from the center of the action, says with disgust, "and is it to drag nagur babies that I left old Ireland? Bad luck to me." What this scene adds to the more stereotypical images of the bestialized African American is another kind of blinding whiteness, one that enlists a range of immigrant attitudes in its racialization of the national conflict depicted in the broadside. The racialist comments made by the German man and the Irish woman are here obviously inflected with overtones of class disparity. Likewise, the white driver of the black couple that occupies the center of the text mutters to himself the words, "white driver, white footmen, niggers inside," indicating what he understands to be the obvious and absurd inversions of race and class happening around him. In America, being on the inside of power—whether that meant inside a circle of economic gain, political and social visibility, or national belonging that invariably promises, if not actually provides, the rest of these benefits—becomes a complicated and conflated racialized class issue. As this cartoon indicates, the central concern of the disgruntled figures here revolves around the loss of one's social and economic positioning or opportunity; even the not-very-white category of the Irish woman—a figure to which I will momentarily turn—is included in this group of despairing potential Americans. Those least concerned with the loss of this status remain those most firmly ensconced at the top of the social and economic ladder, politicians like the President and Sumner, leading businessmen like Horace Greeley, and public figures like Anna Dickinson. But where everyone *else* seems to fall in terms of this socioeconomic spectrum remains the key question and one visibly answered here in terms of race.

Caught in the Web:
Emancipation Anxiety in "The Crab Spider"

While some writers indeed tried to smooth over the worries of writers like Cox and Cleveland—Augustin Cochin's *The Results of Emancipation,* for instance, came to the conclusion that "EMANCIPATION IS ENTIRELY SAFE" according to one *Leslie's* advertisement—the fear of Emancipation's incendiary effects on white America appeared in genres other than that of the congressional speech or the political cartoon.[45] In "The Crab Spider," a story by John B. Williams, M.D., appearing in the Prize Story series of March 1863 published in *Frank Leslie's Illustrated Newspaper,* the fear of Emancipation is encoded in a science fiction tale about an overgrown spider. Indigenous to Santo Domingo, the crab spider of the title terrorizes and ultimately destroys an elite German health spa. "The Crab Spider" resonates in complex ways with white fear of the liberated movements of the African American, with West African and African-American folktales featuring the anansi spider trickster figure, and with events that occurred in New York later that year—namely, the New York Draft Riots when the anarchy so many had predicted indeed seemed to have come to Northern streets at last.

"The Crab Spider" appeared on March 28, 1863; it was the second "Prize Story" Williams published in *Frank Leslie's Illustrated Newspaper*. Williams himself was a popular fiction writer, publishing what appear to be primarily thrillers, often with fantastical plots, in a range of Northern-based story papers like Philadelphia's *Saturday Night* and various dime novel series, including the Eliott, Thomes, and Talbot's "Brilliant Novel-lettes" series. Aside from scattered facts like these, it is difficult to uncover much else about him. (He may have taken his medical degree from Yale in 1860—if he indeed actually *had* a medical degree.) Like many, if not most, of the popular writers from the nineteenth century, little but odd titles remain to testify to his presence.[46]

"The Crab Spider" takes place in Hundsruck, Germany, where the thermal springs of Spinbronn once served as a natural spa for that region's afflicted citizens. The tale focuses on the downfall of the spa: as Williams initially describes it, the waters of Spinbronn had created a place of hope for its patients—and a bustling practice for its doctor. However,

> in the present day the waters of Spinbronn are no longer mentioned in the *Codex*; in this poor village only a few miserable woodcutters are to be found, and, sad thing to state, Dr. Haselnoss has departed.[47]

"The Crab Spider" is the story of how this came to pass, of how a once-thriving, economically secure community was gutted and destroyed.

The body of the story is narrated by Counsellor Bremer, younger cousin to Christian Weber, the man who moves into the role of the spa's physician. Bremer explains that the spring from which the spa's lucrative waters come is located in a cavern made inaccessible by the spring's thermal fumes. Visitors to the spa typically bathe in the cascade falling from this cavern, and the trouble begins when several bathers see "a human skeleton fall from the cascade, as white as snow" (5). The local physician provides scientific evidence as to how this could have occurred, but, almost to spite him, "all that the cavern contained of remains, slime and detritus were disgorged during the following days. A veritable ossuary descended from the mountain; skeletons of all kinds of animals, quadrupeds, birds and reptiles, in a word, all that could be conceived the most horrible" (5). The cavern empties itself out and soon after, the spa itself follows suit as its clients disperse in fear. Dr. Christian Weber, a young physician ending a ten-year stint in Santo Domingo that he left once "the revolt among the negroes broke out," comes to take over (5). "I need not recall to your mind," says Bremer, "the barbarous treatment our compatriots suffered at Hayti. Dr. Weber had the good fortune to escape the massacre and to save a portion of his fortune" (5).

Weber brings with him evidence of his travels: from "Hayti a quantity of paper-boxes, full of the strangest insects," all kinds of exotic fowl including one white peacock, and "an old negress, named Agatha, a frightful creature, with a flat nose and lips as thick as the thumb" who becomes a local spectacle (5). Bremer explains his initial disgust and fear of "Black Agatha" as he calls her, especially of her "extraordinary physiognomy," but soon recalls his warming affections for her—"she was such a good woman, and knew so well how to make spiced pies"—explaining that she becomes the primary source of information about his mysterious cousin. Agatha confides in Bremer that Weber is actually a sorcerer; she remains in a state of constant fear of him. When, predictably, Weber's sole patient and friend, Sir Thomas Hawerburch, disappears in the cavern, Weber forces Agatha into a death-like trance, using her as his conduit to the source of the trouble in the springs:

> At the approach of her master, Agatha began to tremble. The doctor entered abruptly with his lips pressed together, and with despair painted on his face.... He had scarcely entered the room before the sparkling eyes of my tutor seemed to seek something; he perceived the negress, and without a word being exchanged between them, the poor woman began to cry out:
> "No! No! I will not!"
> "And I will not!" replied the doctor, in a harsh commanding voice.
> One would have said that the negress was seized with some invincible power. She trembled from head to foot; and Dr. Weber pointing to a chair, she sat down on it with the rigidity of a corpse....
> The doctor approached the negress, and passing his hand over her forehead with a rapid gesture, said:
> "Are you there?"
> "Yes, master." (6)

In her trance, Agatha reveals that a crab spider is living in the cavern at Spinbronn and that it has indeed killed Sir Thomas. When Weber asks if the spider is large, Agatha is emphatic: "oh master, never, never have I seen one as large. . . . It is as large as my head!" (6). The villagers, led by Weber, smoke the beast out and kill it.

The story ends with the narrator's speculations on the feasibility of the spider's abnormally bloated bulk; "it does not seem to me absurd to admit that insects living in the high temperature of certain thermal springs—which surrounds them with the same conditions of existence and development as the burning climate of Africa and South America— may attain a fabulous size" (6). The doctor returns to America with "his negress and his collections" and the storyteller concludes: "The great political events of the period absorbed the whole attention of Germany and France to such a degree that the facts I have related to you passed completely unnoticed" (6).

Williams's text clearly warns his reader of the potential destruction of white property and financial prosperity as a result of the free movement of a murderous beast indigenous to a country torn by uprising. Weber almost loses his entire fortune in the Santo Domingo rebellion and indeed the physician living at the spa prior to Weber's arrival does lose his position there as a result of the displaced black spider. The story suggests that creatures like the crab spider are harmless as long as they stay pinned in specimen cases, confined to their natural habitat, or anthropomorphized into servants like Black Agatha. But once they are freed and permitted to roam wild in a place "with the same conditions of existence and development as the burning climates of Africa and South America," these beings could certainly "attain a fabulous size." Black Agatha, for instance, frightens the narrator, who is a child at the time of the story's occurrence, but he comes to understand that, despite her grotesque form, she is an innocuous, if conspicuous presence in the community. Noted by Bremer to be a spectacle to the townspeople not unlike Weber's insect and bird collections, and certainly as much of a possession of his as these—Agatha consistently refers to Weber as "master"—Agatha is the domesticated version of the murderous spider. The analogous figure freed lives only to feed on the whites that cross its path while Black Agatha alone displays the ability to "see" into the depths of the spider's cavern. Of course, Weber's authority over Agatha and his ability to control and manipulate even the things she sees, heightens his own power and authority in general.

Williams's use of the spider is interesting here in part because of its resonance with the spider trickster figure of African and African-American folklore—the anansi of West Africa and Aunt Nancy of the Americas. Like other tricksters, anansi is clever, deceitful and manipulative; as Lawrence Levine and Roger Abrahams have both noted, all such trickster stories seem to also say something about the operations of power in general—"to remind us to be on guard constantly for others' tricks, and at the same time to admire those who are able to win the contest by their wits."[48] But "The Crab Spider" reduces what in African folklore is a powerful trickster to a hidden monster. It splits the trickster into two connected, yet distinctly polarized figures—the spider and Black Agatha—thereby illustrating the bifurcated nature of the stereotype that depicts the African as both murderous, savage beast and slow-witted, weak servant.

In one version of the anansi story included in Joel Chandler Harris's *Seven Tales of Uncle Remus,* Brer Rabbit and the other creatures experience what is described as an annual "call" to see Aunt Nancy. According to Uncle Remus, Aunt Nancy was "de granny er Mammy-Bammy-Big-Money. . . . Her rule went furder dan whar she live at, an' when she went ter call de creeturs, all she hatter do wuz ter fling her head back an' kinder suck in her bref an' all de creeturs would have a little chill an' know dat she wuz a-calling' un um."[49] In a Nigerian version of the "Hausa" Spider tale, a woman tells Spider she will teach him more cunning if he brings her the tears of a lion, an elephant tusk, and the skin of a dingo. Spider somehow manages to bring all the required items to the woman, who then attempts to kill Spider with her calabash. When he asks her what she's doing, the woman replies, "If I taught you more cunning, you would destroy everybody."[50] In Williams's story, this power is in the hands of the great white doctor; he even controls the voodoo-esque trance into which Black Agatha slips in order to reveal the mystery of the cave. But the one whose cunning seems to be most feared is not Weber, but the African-Americanized spider. It is the spider who will destroy this place of healing and hope. And even though Weber is clearly the white master in this scene of slavery, his time in the non-European state of Santo Domingo has to some degree gotten under his white skin. He exhibits what the reader is led to believe is an unhealthy interest in exotic animals as well as a dangerous knowledge of the art of "black" magic: he is, according to Black Agatha, a "sorcerer."[51] The danger the crab spider poses then is not simply the loss of life, limb, and property, but the loss of a morality and civilization marked European. The illustration of the spider's burning cave that accompanies the story harkens back to images of burning plantations in Haiti and Santo Domingo during the revolts there, as it also does the now-burning plantations of the Confederacy in the United States. The other image accompanying the piece depicts a very white man being attacked by a very black spider (see Figure 11). Whiteness here indicates education, prosperity, and mastery— all the attributes Dr. Weber exhibits. But whiteness in "The Crab Spider" also indicates physical and social vulnerability as the image of the spider attacking the man graphically represents, and as Dr. Weber's cultural blackening, via his interests in aberrant faiths and beasts, shows.

As well as race and color, gender plays a key role in determining who has the most claim to prosperity in "The Crab Spider." Only two females figure in the tale, but the body of each provides a direct link to the heart of horror in the cavern. The "white as snow" skeleton that first falls from the cascade is assumed to be the victim of a murder; it is only later that local townspeople remember that fifty years before, a young girl, Louise Muller, who had been living with her grandmother, disappeared while gathering herbs. With the benefit of hindsight, Bremer tells the reader that "the poor young girl had, no doubt, been attracted in the gulf by the mysterious influence which acted daily on more feeble creatures. . . . what was this influence? No one knew; but the inhabitants of Spinbronn, superstitious as are all mountaineers, pretended that Satan inhabited the cavern, and terror spread through the neighborhood."[52] When Bremer [a young boy at the time of the events relayed in the story] goes with the doomed Sir Thomas to the cavern, he experiences an episode of almost supernatural fear and power, mostly inspired by the memory of Louise Muller's body:

> Night was slowly approaching. An indefinable agony oppressed me. Suddenly this history of the young girl who had disappeared came back to my mind, and I descended the rock with a run, but when I arrived before the cavern I stopped, seized with inexpressible terror. While casting a glance through the black shadow of the spring, I had discovered two red immovable points; then I saw something agitated in a strange manner in the midst of the darkness. Fear had given to my sight and all my organs an extraordinary acuteness of perception. (6)

The Baron in the Spider's Clutches.

Figure 11. Illustration accompanying "The Crab Spider," from *Frank Leslie's Illustrated Newspaper* (28 March 1863): 5. Courtesy of the American Antiquarian Society.

Despite the fact that Bremer returns to the cavern at this point in the story in order to explore what has happened to his friend Sir Thomas, the fear the place and situation engenders is one linked first to the body of the "white as snow" girl. She becomes the spider's first victim as well as the symbol of what's to follow for the spa at large. Louise Muller's white skeleton functions in the text as a racialized caveat. As the black spider attacks the white man at the bottom of the first page on which "The Crab Spider" appears, the poem "Lines on the American Struggle" written by Mary Alice Sewell appears in the page's far-left column, illustrated by a picture of a weeping white Columbia, her face in her hands.[53] Despite the fact that the poem lauds the Union cause to drive out slavery—"no more the slaves shall cry,/For white-winged Liberty, serene, stands smiling by"—the woman who visually represents the piece as a personification of the United States at large isn't smiling about anything. Columbia's teary significance bleeds across the page, suggesting not just a feminized nation in mourning, but the mourning of all such white women whose lives have been irrevocably changed by a war fought over the fate of black people.[54] In fact, the poem begins not with images of war, but of lightness and darkness, of a nationalized bridal virginity "sullied":

> Weep, weep, Columbia, from thy banner fair
> The stars are falling through the darkening air.
> Sullied thy greatness, quenched thy pomp and pride,
> In which thou deck'st thee like a noble bride.[55]

Even as these female bodies—white, violated, mutilated, and sacrificed—serve as physicalized realizations of the threat engendered by freed black bodies, be they spiders or slaves, so too Agatha's black body serves another function. Her presence reminds the reader of the white man's "natural" power over the black. Agatha's female form provides the doctor with all kinds of things necessary for the retention of his position of economic and personal power: personal service, intimate labor, knowledge, and even sight into the world of the black unknown. Agatha is a translator, a body that sees what the blinded white cannot. Even as the white Louise Muller is necessary for this plot, propelling fear into and through the village via the very bones of her picked-clean skeleton, the equally necessary blackened Agatha provides insight, service, and herself as an object to be possessed and controlled by the white man.

Anxiety Made Manifest: The New York City Draft Riots

While the narrator informs us that the events of "The Crab Spider" were ignored because they were eclipsed by the Revolution in France and other continental happenings, Williams's text inevitably exhorts his reader to pay heed to the danger believed to hide in the cavern of American history. Bremer notes that "it does not seem to me absurd to admit that insects living in the high temperature of certain thermal springs—

which surrounds them with the same conditions of existence and development as the burning climate of Africa and South America—may attain a fabulous size," adding that "the great political events of the period absorbed the whole attention of Germany and France to such a degree that the facts I have related to you passed completely unnoticed."[56] Williams certainly seems to be suggesting that the slave, transported from his/her originary Africa, or South America, or West India, may indeed "attain a fabulous [political] size" if climactic conditions agree—perhaps even the size of the revolutionaries in Santo Domingo. This makes the story a caveat regarding the dangers of slave insurrection and Emancipation overall. The trope of Emancipation representing a return to the insurrections of Haiti and Santo Domingo also serves as a projection. When Williams says that the events of his story went "completely unnoticed," he alludes to the French Revolution as the primary political focal point that stole this story's thunder, an event of plentiful barbarity and carnage itself in one of the world's most self-proclaimed "civilized" countries. To prophesy the horrors of Santo Domingo may have allowed white Northerners to imagine a bloodletting worse than the one in which they were already embroiled. It also may have served to imagine or create in the American imagination a racially propelled situation that itself would be more catastrophic, somehow, than the events of slavery had already been.

Nevertheless, the ironic fact for *Leslie's* New York-based readers was that while insurrection *was* right around the corner, it wasn't coming from around the corner they were watching. In its July 25th edition, *Leslie's* reported that on July 11, 1863, it had been announced that 30,000 New Yorkers between the ages of 18 and 45 were to be drafted for military service. The paper explained that "the number of poor men drawn far exceeded, as a matter of course, that of the rich, their number to draw being so much the greater, but this was viewed as a proof of the dishonesty in the whole proceeding."[57] On July 13, 1863, after the first round of controversial draft calls were announced that pulled heavily from the immigrant and working classes of the city (a $300 fee could exempt anyone from military service who could pay it), a group of New Yorkers rioted. The three-day insurrection resulted in a devastating wave of murder and looting. More than a hundred people were killed, including a number of African Americans who were publicly mutilated, beaten, burned, and lynched.

It is clear in *Leslie's* and other newspapers' reports that African Americans were the key target in this cruel event. Rioters burned to the ground buildings that either housed blacks or those sympathetic with them. The Colored Orphans Asylum stood out as one such casualty. Ernest A. McKay in his history of the riots writes that

> a wild horde, made up mainly of Irish, rushed to the Colored Orphans Asylum on Fifth Avenue between Forty-third and Forty-fourth streets. Hundreds of rioters ran through the four-story building stealing anything in sight. Women and children stood beneath the windows and caught bundles of bedding and clothing that men tossed to them. Trunks of crockery, carpeting, and furniture were moved out in the mad fury. The mob was not satisfied with simple robbery. Some, bent on destruction, carried axes, and others cried, "burn the niggers' nest." Soon a fire started. Volunteer firemen, in contrast to the behavior of the hoodlum firemen, bravely tried to put out the fire but were foiled when the mob chopped the hoses. Luckily, the orphans had time to escape out the back of the building and were taken to the Twentieth Precinct.[58]

"Never, perhaps," noted one writer for *Leslie's*, "has a mob destroyed a home raised by charity to shelter the poor orphan."[59] Blacks were doomed whenever they were caught by the mob; again, according to *Leslie's*, "During the excitement, wherever negroes were seen they were pursued and horribly beaten. One negro, in Spring Street, in a melee, shot a white man, when he was pursued, caught, stripped and hung in Charlton St., his shirt being set on fire as he swung in his last agonies."[60] Another writer noted that "feeling against negroes is so great that the *Francis Skiddy*, which has black waiters on board, was warned against landing at the wharf, and was therefore obliged to return to Albany."[61] Iver Bernstein notes that racial tension had been high in New York City that spring before the draft was initiated, due in part to a decision made by local shipping companies to use black workers as scabs to break a longshoremen's strike. As a result, groups of Irish longshoremen initiated many of the attacks, beginning on Monday, July 13.[62] According to Bernstein, some of the more gruesome aspects of these assaults bear the mark of acts demonstrating sexual domination, dehumanizing and objectifying the victims in order to emphasize the power of their attackers.[63] And these were surely gruesome attacks; according to Bernstein,

> laborer George Glass yanked crippled black coachman Abraham Franklin and his sister Henrietta from their rooms a few blocks away, roughed up

the girl and dragged Franklin through the streets. A lamppost was found and Franklin was hanged. The military arrived, scattered the crowd and cut down Franklin's body, but when the soldiers departed, the corpse was hoisted up again with cheers for Jefferson Davis. Then the crowd pulled down Franklin's body for the final time. In a grisly denouement, sixteen-year-old Irishman Patrick Butler dragged the body through the streets by the genitals as the crowd applauded. After yet another hanging in this neighborhood, rioters cut off their black victim's fingers and toes.[64]

Attacks like these differed significantly from others that targeted government officials and wealthy New Yorkers. While warning that "we must be careful here not to ascribe too much structure and rationality to such emotional behavior," Bernstein nevertheless comments that

> it is certainly worth wondering whether bonfire lynch murders and drownings of black victims were the final acts in much improvised dramas of conquest and purification. Fire and water would symbolically render harmless what these rioters perceived as the post-emancipation social power of their black neighbors.... Through sexual conquest and purification, many white workingmen may have hoped to erase the threat of a new black dignity at a time when the social and political status of black people was especially unsettled.[65]

In spite of the horrific nature of this brutality and the coverage *Leslie's* does provide of the riots' focus on New York blacks, the newspaper's reports of the riots do not forefront the murder and maiming of black New Yorkers as the event's central tragedy.[66] The cover images for *Leslie's* August 1 edition show no attacks on black individuals, and only one of the many images contained in the double-page spread of the riots inside the issue shows a scene of a "negro hanged by the mob."[67] When *Leslie's* publishes the results of inquests conducted regarding those killed in the riots, no African Americans are even listed. The highest number recorded, in fact, are the Irish—44—a statistic that serves to concretize their culpability for the riots more than anything else.[68] Even as it promotes its own distortion of the events, *Leslie's* coverage of the riots ultimately reveals the complicated nexus of identities at work in this moment of American crisis.

For those historians particularly concerned with the intersections between race and class in the United States in the nineteenth century, the New York riots have largely been recognized as the two-pronged race/class explosion they were. For Eric Lott, minstrel performers' mention of the riots illustrates W. E. B. Du Bois's perception that "the racial violence of the draft riots was inseparable from a class context that was manipulated to serve the ruling elites."[69] For David Roediger, the riots took working-class racism "to new depths."[70] For Noel Ignatiev, they become the ultimate and disturbing expression of Irish resentment about fighting a war to free a people against whom the Irish felt pitted for American citizenship.[71] Complicated by the economically polarized targets of the rioters themselves, the racially ambiguous position of the Irish rioters, and the larger moment and context of national conflict in which they occurred, the riots are nothing if not historically and ideologically confusing. But brutal, confusing, and contradictory as they might have been, the riots do emphatically indicate at least one thing: the complex and inseparable strains of political identities that both ensured and denied American national membership at this time.

While the broadside "Miscegenation, or The Millennium of Abolitionism" attempts to enlist a range of nondomestic, non-American identities, including the Irish, into the nationalizing racialism it promotes, *Leslie's* depiction of the Irish in its coverage of the riots relies on a class-marked definition of Americanness to further alienate them. As the Confederate was represented as savagely un-American not because of his/her savagery in relation to the slave, but because of his/her savagery in relation to the Union soldier, so *Leslie's* portrays the Irish's participation in the riots as shocking not because of their role in the racially motivated destruction of African-American life and property, but because of the ill-gotten goods they obtain in the process.[72] *Leslie's* August 15 issue contained this note: "The recent riots in this city were made the opportunity of furnishing many of the poor Irish shanties in the 2d avenue; but alas! the police paid the possessors of the newly furnished apartments a visit, and carried their ungodly spoils away, in many instances taking the dishonest appropriators with them."[73] A cartoon published in *Leslie's* in the fall following the riots shows a "Proprietor of Crib" boasting that his shanty looks "ilegant since I fetched the piano in—and the pig and the poultry take to it so nat'ral like!" (see Figure 12).[74] Both indicate the evident *lack* of claim the Irish have to these commodities and markers of middle-class American identity—home furnishings, a piano—and the cartoon equates the Irish with the animals who share his "crib," relying on a familiar motif of racialized discourse.

FRANK LESLIE'S ILLUSTRATED NEWSPAPER.

A RESULT OF THE NEW YORK RIOTS.

Proprietor of Crib—" *Begorra, the shanty looks ilegant since I fetched the piano in—and the pig and the poultry take to it so nat'ral like!*"

Figure 12. "A Result of the New York Riots," political cartoon from *Frank Leslie's Illustrated Newspaper* (31 October 1863): 96. Courtesy of the American Antiquarian Society.

The racially ambiguous Irish rioters' actions against a more affluent group of undeniably white New Yorkers clearly indicates a class-based antagonism. But while certainly among the most exploited and disenfranchised residents of the United States, Irish rioters simultaneously attempted to consolidate their own precarious racial identity by lashing out against New York's black community. According to McKay, the Draft Riots stand out in United States history not only because they were the most costly riots to occur to that date in terms of life and property loss (a reliable figure for the sum of deaths is 119, more than 300 more wounded, and a total of 1.5 million dollars in property damage), but because unlike other American riots, they were "directed against the government as well as the rich and blacks."[75] The confusing range of the rioters' targets—blacks, wealthy New Yorkers, government officials—seems to indicate more than anything else the equally confusing nexus of powers and identities that confer and deny American national belonging; the representatives of the government are perhaps the most obvious of these.

Leslie's later reporting of the riots indicates another set of boundaries between which American membership was bordered, harkening back to notions of Jacksonian honorable work. While warning readers of the lazy, criminalized, not-quite-white immigrant who attempts to lay claim to American resources to which he is not entitled, *Leslie's* also disparages a connection with the upper class who disdain dirtying their hands—and endangering their lives—with the work of war. Another *Leslie* cartoon, "Dodging the Draft," depicts a "Mr. Nob de Snob" trying to fake his way into a draft exemption by arguing that he supports "me mothaw and me Orphaun infawnt, aw" by "aw—manual labah" (see Figure 13).[76] Who has the most rightful claim to American membership lies somewhere in the middle of these images.

In the pages of *Leslie's Illustrated Newspaper,* the New York riots are not an example of explosive and damaging racial tensions and violence; they are, rather, a lesson in class management. The attempt of the Irish to reach beyond the limits of their class is forefronted, thereby granting race a less visible role in the events of the riots themselves. But what *Leslie's* reporting of the riots does not reveal, the riots themselves do: namely, the kind of violence that will be enacted in the attempt to curtail national belonging in the South after the war. Evidence of the "fabulous size" to which Emancipation anxiety grew in the antislavery North, the New York riots stand as a singular example of the conflation of political identities that together constituted Americanness at this moment. While the Northern press nervously predicted the fantasized and murderous black revolt that was sure to accompany the freeing of the slaves, it carefully blinded itself to the racial aggression that *did* follow hard on Emancipation's heels.

FRANK LESLIE'S ILLUSTRATED NEWSPAPER.

DODGING THE DRAFT—A SWELL'S STRATAGEM.

MR. NOB DE SNOB (a Broadway Swell, as he appeared before the "Committee on Exemptions.")—"*Aw—these persons are me mothaw and me Orphaun infawnt, aw. I suppaut them by aw—manual labah.*"

Figure 13. "Dodging the Draft—A Swell's Stratagem," political cartoon from *Frank Leslie's Illustrated Newspaper* (19 September 1863): 420. Courtesy of the American Antiquarian Society.

THREE

The White Gaze, the Spectacle of Slavery, and the Circassian Beauty

> I still have faith in a beautiful Circassian girl if you can get one very beautiful. . . . have one or two of the most beautiful girls you can find, even if they cost $4000 or $5000 in gold. . . . But after looking the thing over, if you don't find one that is beautiful & possesses a striking kind of beauty, why of course she won't draw and you must give it up as a bad job & not get them, for there is nothing in her to attract & fascinate, and the papers would cry her down & it would prove a loss. But if she is beautiful, then she may take in Paris or in London or probably both. But look out that in Paris they don't try the law and set her free. It must be understood that she is free. . . .
> —P. T. Barnum, May 1864

As the Northern popular press predicted the calamitous effects of Emancipation, consumers of American popular culture experienced an attendant longing for the institutions of slavery. This desire often manifested itself as simply a fascination with slavery and was reflected in the way in which the popular press and institutions of wide-appeal entertainment— nineteenth-century fixtures like the minstrel show and freak exhibit— recreated slavery as spectacle. Long before the actual moment of Emancipation, concerned and often simply curious Northerners scrambled to see former slaves speak from the lecterns and podiums of the abolitionist lecture circuit. Less overtly politicized audiences thronged to see minstrel performances that reminisced about the days on the old plantation, and at the very moment of Emancipation itself, as well as beyond, visitors paid their dimes to see the Circassian Beauty in Barnum's American Museum. Probably less anxious than desirous, these spectators of Barnum's were presented with images of a conflated and contradictory bondage, a spectacularized slavery that incorporated elements of racial purity, physical desirability, and sexual availability. By midcentury, white Americans had become accustomed to the idea of the African American as a kind of spectacle, albeit with variant shades of meaning given the context in which s/he was displayed. But in the figure of the Circassian Beauty—a performer pointedly *not* represented as black—these meanings double back on themselves. While the Irish rioter in *Frank Leslie's Illustrated Newspaper* becomes a kind of trope for American national identity's multiple and confusing manifestations of class and race, the figure of the Circassian Beauty reveals the intersections of popularly held conceptions of slavery, whiteness, imperialism, and American womanhood. The Circassian Beauty's various appearances in the century show us too how race can be layered on race and what a blinding white gaze can do.

The White Gaze and the Spectacularized Slave

In John B. Williams's Emancipation-anxious "The Crab Spider," the central path to power is determined by who controls who sees what—and by extension, who controls who *knows* what. For Williams, sight largely determines who will have the most significant forms of control. Despite her startling abilities to discern the secret of the cavern, Agatha's otherworldly sight is controlled by Weber and she herself is a prime spectacle for the German villagers who come, as Williams puts it, "from a distance of six leagues to see her."[1] The way that Weber controls Agatha's sight is visual as well: "the sparkling eyes of [Weber] seemed to seek something; he perceived the negress, and without a word being exchanged between them, the poor woman began to cry out."[2] Just as Agatha has only to be "perceived" by her white master to be known—and consequently, feel pain at the knowledge to which Williams refers—similarly, the spider has only to be seen to be destroyed. As soon as Agatha communicates her own vision of the spider, forced from her by the penetrating gaze of the doctor, Weber rounds up the posse that will then go to the cavern and smoke the spider out. The controlling imperialist gaze at work here controls via representation; that Agatha supplies the image that will lead to the spider's demise—against her will, we should add—may even suggest the complicity many nineteenth-century Americans felt African Americans had in their own enslavement.[3]

As *Leslie's* Emancipation-celebration reporter indicated, perhaps the most pervasive and powerful vehicle for representation of the African American and slave in the North before the Civil War was the minstrel show. "Two thirds of our boarding-school misses believe that a contraband is a dark gentleman with a triangular collar of some two feet high in new pumps and broadcloth, a set of white ivory, a fine tenor voice, a rather handsome banjo and a remarkably bad hat," the reporter notes, recalling the image of the Northern black dandy that often kicked off the song cycles of the typical blackface minstrel performance.[4] A recent wave of historical inquiry has concretized the significance of this institution of popular entertainment, indicating its value not only as an indicator of pro- and antislavery sentiment, but also as a gauge of class tension.[5] Above and beyond anything else though, the minstrel show created a situation in which Northern audiences became accustomed to the spectacle of the African American as a comical and entertaining slave figure, whether a black man in whiteface or a white man in blackface. What these slave figures and their performances indicated, however, varied.

According to Alexander Saxton, the Civil War-era minstrel show served at once to critique Republican party politics, lament the instigation of any war that "unnecessarily" upset the happy-home feeling of the Southern plantation, and laud the efforts of working-class soldiers actually engaged in the work of war.[6] According to Saxton, minstrels

> readapted the plantation myth to wartime purposes, their message being that a struggle against slavery was neither necessary to save the Union, nor desirable. The "plantation nigger" now lamented the inexplicable "white folks" war that was causing everyone so much trouble.[7]

Eric Lott elaborates on the nostalgia encoded in the minstrel show, a nostalgia, which, while clearly linked to the political events of slavery's institutionalization and downfall, is also linked to the anxieties and disruptions of white Northern life. "Minstrel nostalgia," Lott argues, "intimated by emotional antidote all the forces in American life that seemed to be pulling the country apart.... as social allegory it was a superbly concise mediator, pinpointing if not insisting on the home sicknesses just then contributing to the slavery controversy, or at least making it harder to bear."[8] Lott also refers to Saxton's discussion of the plantation nostalgia inherent in the minstrel show, noting how it turned "the South into a kind of timeless lost home, a safe, imaginary childhood," providing a deeply satisfying emotional entertainment experience for "a wide variety of white audiences."[9] And so it seems it easily could have, particularly given the loss Americans felt as a result of the increased geographic mobility in the nation, manifested as family members struck out on their own in search of better economic opportunities or found themselves separated by the events of the war. For Lott, "minstrel-show nostalgia, usually for home and family life on the plantation" acts as "a condensed, fortuitous mapping of white desire in dark skin."[10]

The popularity and ubiquity of the minstrel show in the North undoubtedly naturalized a sense of the slave-as-spectacle as well as the "rightness" or naturalness of the white gaze that shaped these shows' depictions of black people. But the minstrel show wasn't the only place where largely white audiences could direct their white gazes at spectacularized black slaves. In a highly different venue, white antebellum Northerners gazed upon the former and runaway slave in his or her capacity as a speaker on the abolitionist platform. Leon Litwack notes that this was no easy position for the former slave to occupy, given their white audiences' preconceptions of and expectations for this figure.[11] But such speakers were by far the most popular and best draws for an abolitionist event:

> "The public have itching ears to hear a colored man speak," one abolitionist wrote to Garrison, "and particularly *a slave*. Multitudes will flock to hear one of this class speak." Such was the response to Frederick Douglass, for example, that he soon became a leading abolitionist orator. The Negro who committed himself to the abolitionist cause incurred obvious risks. If the average white man expected anything of the Negro, it was that he acquiesce in the racial status quo and act the clownish, childish, carefree, irresponsible Uncle Tom that whites had long presumed him to be. But the Negro abolitionist betrayed the white man's trust and confidence; more than that, he confounded by his very example the white man's rationale for a benevolent guardianship over an inferior and helpless race. Rare, indeed, was the Negro abolitionist who did not have to face a hostile mob at some point in his antislavery career; it was the price he paid for having committed the most unpardonable sin of all—impudence.[12]

In fact, as other historians have noted, part of the difficulties that led Douglass to split with the Massachusetts Anti-Slavery Society was the fact that his speaking was starting to appear "too learned"; society members warned him that "'people won't believe you were ever a slave, Frederick, if you keep on this way. . . . Better have a *little* of the plantation manner of speech than not.'"[13] Clearly, these white Northern audiences—despite their political predilection for abolition and its supposed attendant concern for the personal and political growth and development of African Americans in general—expected a stylized African-American speech and performance that did *not* extend beyond the plantation.

These speakers were extremely powerful, nevertheless, as well as popular with their audiences, and it is worthwhile to reconsider white audiences' fascination with them. One can't help but notice the hint of sensationalized appeal ex-slaves must have brought with them to the podium in this scholarly description:

> Audiences flocked to hear these speakers describe the whippings administered by overseers, the separation from loved ones sold down the river, and the often hectic efforts to get beyond the reach of slave catchers and bloodhounds. . . . Henry Bibb moved audiences to tears with a recital of how his wife, naked and bound, had been brutally whipped by an intoxicated slaveholder.[14]

Although it focuses on the hardships and dramatically compelling scenarios these speakers imparted in their presentations, such a description also raises questions about the underlying sexualized appeal these appearances may have promised white Northern audiences, particularly in those accounts involving the fate of female slaves. Indeed, the role gender plays in the popularity of the African American performer is one to which I want to turn now as it functions in the case of the first performative freak P. T. Barnum displayed.

The Mammy of the Father of the Nation

The first living, human curiosity P. T. Barnum ever exhibited was a slave. It was through the display of Joice Heth, billed as the 161-year-old nurse of George Washington, that Barnum was to perfect the art of human presentation and performance, including in these presentations the sale of pictures and written histories of the freaks he displayed.[15] Like Black Agatha of Williams's "The Crab Spider," people came from miles around to see the figure of this old, (mis)represented woman. Barnum bought the rights to exhibit Heth in August of 1835. A slave (although one Barnum never outright owned himself), Heth had already been performing in Philadelphia as the hymn-singing nurse of George Washington.[16] Barnum and his assistant, Levi Lyman, displayed Heth from the time they acquired the rights to do so until her death on February 19, 1836. As well as a figure of considerable cultural significance, given her supposed relationship to the national icon of George Washington himself, Heth became the first symbol of Barnum's own performative deceptions—his "humbug" writ large in the form of an elderly black woman. According to Bluford Adams,

> The exhibitors stoked public interest during the tour by spreading rumors that Heth was actually an automaton or the great-grandmother of living Kentucky slaves. They ignited another journalistic explosion after Heth's death by staging the dissection of her body—an event that exposed their ruse when it revealed her true age to have been no more than eighty.[17]

Adams goes on to argue that, given the write-up Barnum himself provides of the Heth exhibitions in the satiric pseudo-autobiography *The Adventures of an Adventurer,* Barnum attempts to "rewrite the Yankee as an antiabolitionist slaveholder," using Heth in the argument over the place of slavery in the ideology of the Founding Fathers. Not only representing her as a positive influence on someone considered to be one of the most influential figures in the history of the American nation, Barnum also depicts Heth as "a willing partner to his swindle," and therefore party to the "ex-slave confidence men" that appeared in later proslavery novels.[18] Barnum therefore founded his career on the exhibition of a woman whose performance-value lay in her enslavement to a white man—or rather, white men, including Washington, her "real" owner, and Barnum himself. Part of the public appeal of this display undoubtedly resided in the apparently acceptable political position of the Northern businessman who was not only willing to tolerate, but actually exploit, the economic practices of the Southern slaveholder. As Heth's history with Barnum demonstrates, slavery itself sold and, as is the case in "The Crab Spider," the site where this marketing often takes place is the body of a black woman. Because Heth is represented as the mammy of the Father of the Country, the appeal of Barnum's exhibit seems to be the reassurance it offers his audience that slavery, at least as an oddity, is acceptable because it is out of slavery that the nation itself, here figured in the person of George Washington, emerged.[19] Not only coloredcoded, the slavery commemorated here is also a slavery of women.[20]

The question of the slave woman functioning as a freak performer becomes even more complicated and perplexing the deeper into Barnum's career and the realm of American popular entertainment we dig. David Roediger has discussed the complicated intersecting notions of slavery circulating in the nineteenth century, focusing on terms like "white slavery" that were used to highlight horrendous conditions for factory operatives and wage laborers while sidestepping, if not actually reinforcing, the primary definition of slavery in the South.[21] The term "wage slavery" was indeed frequently used and typically its use implicitly

> called all slavery into question. But the far more common term *white slavery* immediately undercut any such implications by leaving open the possibility that it was the "slavery" *of whites* that deserved censure. Much of the labor discourse on *white slavery* took just that stance and at times strongly supported the slavery of Blacks.[22]

Roediger goes on to note that the workers for whom the term "white slaves" was used often themselves rejected it:

> To be a slave, even a white slave, was to be associated with degradation. . . . To be a slave also implied connection with blackness. . . . Comparisons of white workers with slaves, which are too often considered as simply *class* expressions, were shot through with resonances regarding America's racial realities. To ask workers to *sustain* comparisons of themselves and Black slaves violated at once their republican pride and their sense of whiteness.[23]

"White slavery" then as a hopelessly problematic term brings to the fore the inextricable interconnectedness of the forces of race and class in the United States. But it signifies even more; the term "white slave" eventually came to mean a prostitute. Roediger notes that "genteel factory women who rejected the term . . . knew that slavery implied sexual exploitation as well," clearly indicating a popular understanding of the underlying sexual politics of slavery itself.[24] In fact, it is in the figure of Barnum's Circassian Beauty, literally depicted as a slave who was white, that we can most clearly detect these interlocking, yet battling strains of sexuality, enslavement, race, class, and nationality, all somehow inexorably turning to the pornographic.

Barnum's Circassian Beauties

By early 1856, P. T. Barnum had gone bankrupt; the year before, he had sold his collections at the American Museum to John Greenwood Jr., his former manager, who also traveled for Barnum to procure the "oddities and amusements" for which Barnum was by this time famous.[25] In a letter written during this time to the Massachusetts legislator and dentist Dr. David K. Hitchcock, Barnum first alludes to his financial frustrations then proceeds to talk about one of the Museum's latest endeavors:[26]

> Greenwood in getting up the "Congress of Nations" wants two beautiful Circassian slaves. I have written Mr. Brown, our consul in Constantinople, about it, but it struck me that you could perhaps manage it through your young dental Turk [Hitchcock's student]. . . . He wants to *hire* 2 beautiful Circassian girls & their mother or father or some other protector for 1 to 2 years. I suppose they would have to be bought, then give them their freedom and hire them, making contract through U.S. consul. Will you tell me whether it is feasible to get them & do what you can to aid Greenwood in the matter?
>
> For my own part, I have renounced business & care forever.[27]

Nothing apparently came of this request, just as nothing came of Barnum's claim to have "renounced business" forever, but the transaction Barnum suggests—the purchase of two enslaved women, their emancipation, and the subsequent conversion of them into wage laborers as "freed" employees of Barnum—is an extremely interesting one for 1856. In effect, given the path by which they would hypothetically attain their freedom—guaranteed labor for Barnum as exhibits in his museum— these women would convert not into wage laborers, but into wage slaves, metaphorically "bound" to the man who brought them into America in the first place.

While this initial attempt to procure a Circassian woman for the museum apparently failed, in May of 1864, Barnum wrote of the matter again to Greenwood who was then in Cyprus. This time, Barnum clarified the value of the figure he sought:

> I still have faith in a beautiful Circassian girl if you can get one very beautiful. But if they ask $4000 each, probably one would be better than two, for $8000 in gold is worth about $14,500 in U.S. currency. . . . you can also buy a beautiful Circassian woman for $200 [?$2000], do so if you think best; or if you can hire one or two at reasonable prices, do so if you think they are pretty and will pass for Circassian slaves. But in any event have one or two of the most beautiful girls you can find, even if they cost $4000 or $5000 in gold. . . . But after looking the thing over, if you don't find one that is beautiful & possesses a striking kind of beauty, why of course she won't draw and you must give it up as a bad

job & not get them, for there is nothing in her to attract & fascinate, and the papers would cry her down & it would prove a loss. But if she is beautiful, then she may take in Paris or in London or probably both. But look out that in Paris they don't try the law and set her free. It must be understood that she is free.[28]

Barnum's instructions tell us several things. The legendary beauty of the Circassian woman or girl bought in the slave markets of Constantinople supposedly constituted the primary appeal for American audiences of the freak Barnum would term the "Circassian Beauty." Barnum notes this when he advises Greenwood to be sure to obtain a girl or woman who will "draw." But Barnum also seems quite prepared to engage in slave trafficking in order to win such an entertaining prize; this was a practice he supposedly opposed in his own country at this time. "Look out that in Paris they don't try the law and set her free," Barnum warns Greenwood after clarifying the amount Greenwood should spend on the "Beauty"—as much as four or five thousand dollars in gold.[29] The fact of the Circassian Beauty's slave status was represented somewhat differently once she appeared on the American Museum's stage, but it remained a constitutive part of her performative identity as a freak exhibit. And it is precisely this performativity that Barnum's message further reveals; he tells Greenwood to go ahead and hire one or two women if he can't actually buy any, but only if he thinks "they are pretty and will pass for Circassian slaves." The Circassian Beauty was in fact a complex and contradictory figure in nineteenth-century American popular culture, a woman who represented far more to the consumers of that culture than just the "striking kind of beauty" with which Barnum seems most concerned here.[30] In the middle of a war finally understood as an attempt to abolish slavery, Barnum introduces a new slave into the American popular imagination, one who embodies a range of racially complicated traits attributed to her by Barnum and the popular press. It is of course, something other than just ironic that Northern white American audiences were willing to pay to see another embodiment of that very institution their sons, fathers, brothers, and husbands were dying in order to destroy. As we'll see, the figures of the Circassian Beauty and the Circassian slave become gathering points for assumptions regarding abolition, racial mixing and miscegenation, the sexuality and gender of American women (both white *and* black), and notions of American imperialism. The figure of the Circassian Beauty highlights not only popularly circulating fears on the part of white Northerners regarding the effects of Emancipation, but how race interacts with and co-defines understandings of gender and sexuality as well. Who actually played the part of and physically realized the Circassian Beauty likewise complicates this issue of representation even more. The Circassian Beauty becomes an overdetermined signifier of the dominant cultural concerns of Victorian America, embodying notions of imperialism and Orientalism, Manifest Destiny and Victorian domesticity, the purity of the white race, and the sexualization of the African-American woman.

In response to Barnum's requests as indicated in his letter above, a Circassian Beauty was finally procured for the museum and put on exhibit sometime in 1864, but the woman's regional origin and the circumstances in which she was obtained remain a matter of some historical dispute. Zalumma Agra, alleged daughter of a Circassian prince and fugitive from a country caught in the land struggles of the Crimean War, had, as the story goes, never actually been sold into the slavery of the Turkish harems, but was rather *about* to be sold when Greenwood arrived on the scene to "rescue" her. He then went on to "rescue" Zalumma from savagery by assuming the role of both guardian and tutor and overseeing her education. So goes the Barnum tale; according to Robert Bogdan, there is an alternative story:

> According to an unpublished version by John Dingess, a contemporary of Barnum, Greenwood returned from his trip empty handed. A few weeks after his return a young woman came to the museum looking for work. She had bushy hair but nothing remarkable enough to make her a museum attraction. Disappointed by Greenwood's lack of success, but still bent on getting a Circassian, Barnum saw in her the possibility of creating his own Circassian, and he hired her. A Turk, residing in New York, was consulted as to appropriate dress and name, and in a short time the girl appeared at the museum in her silks as a full-fledged Circassian.[31]

Bogdan claims that Barnum's presentation of the Circassian Beauty "launched the prototype of a self-made freak," what he calls "a creation that wove the history of science together with tales of erotic intrigue from Asia Minor, current events, and a good portion of showman hype."[32] Circassian Beauties sprang up at dime museums and sideshows following Barnum's presentation of Zalumma, and they were to continue as a freak mainstay up until the beginning of the twentieth century. But the point of greatest interest to me is what Bogdan here notes as Barnum's "seeing" of a possibility in creating his own Circassian in the person of this woman whose only unique characteristic is her "bushy hair." In fact, the Circassian Beauty's signature hairstyle most closely resembles a huge Afro, and this defining characteristic—one affiliated with the African American woman—resonates oddly yet resoundingly with the rest of her identifying significations: her racial purity, her sexual enslavement, her position as colonial subject, her beauty. The Circassian Beauty blended elements of white Victorian True Womanhood with traits of the enslaved African American woman in one curiosity, the market potential of which perhaps only a Barnum would have been savvy enough to recognize.

Bogdan places the Circassian Beauty within the "exotic mode" of freak performance, highlighting the way in which the Circassian, like such freak exhibits as the "Wild Men of Borneo," were touted as examples of the primitive, inaccessible and preferably dangerous lives lived either geographically or chronologically far away from white middle-class America. Particular aspects of the popularly circulated story of the Circassian were likewise emphasized in the Circassian Beauty's performance; she was not only beautiful, but a kind of cultural ambassador for a humble, mountain-farming people at the mercy of the tyrannical Russians with whom the Circassians were at war and the 'primitive' Turks who dealt in the trade of their women. The Caucasus area in which Circassia was located likewise had a special significance to pseudoscientific, anthropologically minded Americans as well. The German anatomist, Johann Friedrich Blumenbach, introduced the term *Caucasian* when he argued that, based on his measurements of skulls obtained from Caucasus, Caucasus was the "origin not only of Europeans, the Caucasian type, but of all humans":

> According to monogenist thought, God formed humans in their pure
> form. As they spread out over the globe, they degenerated in appearance.
> Blumenbach's and other monogenists' ideas led to the widely led conclu
> sion that the purest and most beautiful whites were the Circassians, one
> tribe of the Caucasian region of Russia, a mountainous area on the Black
> Sea close to Turkey, then the Ottoman Empire.[33]

Racial superiority, then, to some degree concretized the Circassian Beauty's beauty, making her the whitest, most racially pure specimen of a human woman to be found on earth.[34] Perhaps this accounted for the marketability of the Circassian Beauty: the whitest of the white, yet a slave, the Beauty combined the purity of the white woman with the sexual availability of the slave. She could at once be both worshipped and raped.

Circassian Beauty or Circassian Slave?

Part of the contradiction and complexity of the Circassian Beauty resides in her not-quite-but-almost slave status. The celebrated fact of the Circassian slave's racial purity is sustained in spite of the evil and dark Turk who desires her and who attempts and sometimes succeeds in making her a member of his harem. On one hand, the image of the Turk echoes a primitivity that the Northern popular press popularly attributed to an array of opposing forces at home: the Confederate who not only maintained the slavery of a colonized and oppressed people, but who "barbarically" killed and maimed Union soldiers in the Civil War then being fought, and the African American whose free movement in U.S. society not only threatened white dominance of resources and their use, but the hegemonic definition of what it actually meant to be an American. The unsullied purity of the Circassian Beauty therefore seems in part to represent a Northern anxiety about racial mixing, particularly in regard to the anticipated effects of Emancipation. In her role as a symbol of endangered-yet-rescued whiteness, the Circassian slave mirrored white Northern representations of the white American woman herself, potentially endangered by the "dark" and savage forces suddenly "unleashed" in the South.

The story Barnum tells in the autobiographical *Struggles and Triumphs; or, Forty Years' Recollections of P. T. Barnum* about Greenwood's attempt to obtain a Circassian woman for show at the museum highlights the otherness of Eastern and specifically Turkish culture that undergirded the Circassian Beauty as an exotic and compelling figure. The steamer on which Greenwood sailed to Constantinople also carried the harem of a Turkish Pasha. One day while sitting on deck, Greenwood made the mistake of offering his hand to help one of the women step over a fence erected to separate the harem's members from the rest of the travelers. Greenwood is "immediately seized by two of the Pasha's attendants, violently shaken, and taken to task in Turkish for daring to offer to touch the hand of one of his Excellency's women."[35] Saved by an English- and Arabic-speaking Greek acquaintance, Greenwood is, according to Barnum, lucky not to have been "bastinadoed, or even bow-strung."[36] This incident even merits an engraving in Barnum's text, an image that seems to resonate with the next and final episode of Greenwood's search for the Circassian Beauty. In the illustration, a veiled woman in flowing robes stands on a partition above the other travelers as if put on display like a slave in the market place, or an exhibit in a freak show. Greenwood is held by two of the Pasha's thugs while the harem's lord stands in the background, his mouth an elongated "o." The helpful Greek stands in the left-hand side, hands open in a supplicating manner.[37]

Having narrowly escaped this difficulty, Greenwood puts himself in further danger by "posing" as a slave-buyer and touring the slave markets of Constantinople. As Barnum puts it,

> To carry out his purpose of getting access to the very interior of the slave-marts, he dressed himself in full Turkish costume, learned a few words and phrases which would be necessary in his assumed character as a slave-buyer, and, as the Turks are a notably reticent people, he succeeded very well in passing himself off for what he appeared, though he ran a risk of detection many times every day. In this manner, he saw a large number of Circassian girls and women, some of them the most beautiful beings he had ever seen.[38]

Unfortunately for Barnum, Greenwood doesn't seem to do much more than view these women, for Barnum simply notes how Greenwood left Constantinople and traveled back to New York, having obtained many wonderful curiosities. Barnum here clearly plays up the exoticism of the environment from which his Circassian Beauties originated by highlighting the danger posed to Greenwood by his own naturalized cultural practices, behaviors as simple and mundane to the American reader as helping a woman step over a fence. Moreover, the danger that surrounds Greenwood masquerading as a Turk—something that is evidently terribly difficult for him to do despite the fact that he is there to engage in the same slave-buying practice as the other Turks—further heightens the sense of intrigue surrounding the Circassian women themselves as they move, mysteriously veiled, through a society largely invisible to the Western male eye. Throughout his description of this incident, Barnum plays up the qualities of Orientalism that Edward Said argues were in fact distilled in Western thought during the nineteenth century: the Orient's "sensuality, its tendency to despotism, its aberrant mentality, its habits of inaccuracy, its backwardness."[39] It is significant that even while Greenwood does not here necessarily win the prize he practically risks his life to obtain, he is able to *see* "a large number of Circassian girls and women," an experience of victorious cultural penetration, given the protected and isolated nature of the harem. Greenwood's gaze is passed on to the audience via the freak exhibit itself and it is this transaction that the freak performance depends upon.

Zoe Meleke: Biographical Sketch of the Circassian Girl

Of course, it was the controlled viewing of this figure that made money for Barnum and other showmen during this time. And that viewing was not merely controlled by the money it cost to see the Beauty herself, it was further controlled by the showman/manager, who cast the audience's viewing of the freak within a particular context. Barnum published a freak history of one of his Circassian Beauties in 1880 called *Zoe Meleke: Biographical Sketch of the Circassian Girl.* The freak history was a chapbook—in this case, just 16 pages long—in which the freak's identity, place of origin, capabilities and manner of procurement were all discussed in relative detail. The pamphlet probably reflects, however imperfectly, much of what the showman actually said during "Zoe Meleke's" time on stage. Designed to complement the showman's presentation and introduction of the freak to audiences, freak histories and freak portraits were sold at exhibitions, and proceeds from their sale in part went to the freak performer him or herself. Barnum's description provides personal biographical information on Zoe Meleke, a historical context of sorts detailing Circassia's political difficulties to which Zoe falls victim, an explanation of her loss of Arabic and gain of English (something perhaps better explained by Zoe's probable American, not Circassian, background) as well as the writer's personal beliefs on women's education and social status.[40] It is an intriguing and confusing document. Clearly intended to arouse the patriotic spirit of the reader, *Zoe Meleke* indicates more of the politicized tensions that undergird the signification of the Circassian Beauty.

Zoe is presented to the American people as an entity—spiritual perhaps, but certainly delectable—to be consumed: "Among the most charming attractions offered to the American people of the present day, as a most chaste and delicate curiosity, is a young and beautiful native of Circassia" (1). Almost all freaks were performative, not simply in their construction as, say, "missing links" when they were actually micro-cephalic, or as "half-boys" when they had been born without legs, but because they also performed various acts of skill or amusement. "Arm-less wonders" would cut paper dolls out in front of their audience with their toes and Tom Thumb and the "giants" in Barnum's employ would stage David and Goliath battles. Zoe's particular talents are not so clearly defined in her history, but it is stressed that she is proficient in those "charms" which amplify "female beauty and intellect"; she writes arti-cles for publication, is "affable and pleasing in conversation" and is not only "naturally of a high order of intellect," but "thoroughly refined by education and classical culture" (2, 4). What begins to make Zoe stand out seems not so much to be her affiliation to the life she has supposedly just left of exotic, enticing if immoral sensuality and power, but rather her rapid assimilation into American culture and Western civilization, particularly her assimilation into the American domestic sphere—what historians and scholars have dubbed the "Cult of True Womanhood."[41] "She expresses her preference for America over Europe," Barnum's anony-mous writer informs us, "and thinks the people of the United States are the most prosperous and free in the world" (3). Freedom here is defined in terms of American prosperity and how "far in advance of all the other nations of the world in modern improvements" America is, particularly "in the application of steam to ships—to railroad cars, and to all kinds of machinery; in the invention of works of art, of the telegraph, and the great progress in agriculture" (3).

Not only is America "free" because of its technological advance-ments, but because of its attitude toward women. While "it was long be-fore the intellectual rights of women were acknowledged" and "frivolity and other feminine faults were favorite themes for satire with the writ-ers of the age of Charles the Second," Barnum's author assures us that this is no longer the case: "The flippant invectives on the sex, of which the writers of a former age indulge, would no longer be tolerated in soci-ety. . . . To no class is mental culture of more importance than to woman" (5). The writing becomes more and more rhetorical and dogmatic as it progresses in this vein, the author carefully qualifying that while women should be educated to protect them from the "horrors of melancholy," the author does not "mean that women should be eminent linguists and mathematicians. The education I wish them to receive would be confined to the bestowing upon them powers of thought, and treasures for thought" (6). By the end of this passage, the author understands that not only has he (?) made a case for the selective education women should receive and why, he has also illustrated the benefits Zoe has undoubtedly gained by leaving her uncivilized Circassia behind and accepting America into her heart—and head: "'The face that is the index to no mental excellence will lose its power, and the eyes brightened by no ray of genius, its luster.' What more can be said in the behalf of this lovely Circassian girl?" (6).

The history continues to expound on not only Zoe, but Circassia and how "its women are as beautiful as houris, and that the slave markets of Turkey have long been an emporium for the sale of these lovely but unfortunate creatures, to supply the seraglios and harems of the Sultans and his subjects"(8). Practically invisible to the people of the West, Circassia is, as the author assures us, merely a diamond in the rough: "The steady onward march of civilization will probably reveal, perhaps within the generation of the majority of our readers, amid the spurs and slopes and glades of the mountains of Circassia, another Golconda, another Potosi, another California, or all combined; and argosies, bearing untold wealth, the product of her womb, may, even within the present century, be plowing the waters of every clime" (9). Much of the Circassian Beauty's attraction seems to lie in the potential for gain locked within Circassia's as yet uncolonized (at least by Western forces) territories. But the Circassian Beauty herself is described as the most promising of the as yet largely unrealized natural resources Circassia has to offer: "the Circassian Girl, who is now a refined, intelligent and Christian woman, might have been enrolled upon the scroll of humanity, in company with the great mass of her countrywomen, as the beautiful but ignorant *habitat* of a Pagan's harem" (11–12). When Mr. Long, Zoe's Western rescuer and guardian and Barnum's Circassian connection, is exalted for his redeeming work with her and the author notes that "visitors have come by the scores to see this Circassian beauty," one wonders to what *this* beauty actually refers (14). Is it the beauty of the Circassian woman or is it the beauty of the barbarian "civilized" into Christianity and Western culture that fascinates her numerous fans and onlookers? What, if anything, is the difference?[42]

While the United States had not yet joined the globally colonizing efforts of Britain, Spain, France, Holland, and other European countries (it would take until the end of the nineteenth and beginning of the

twentieth until America actually became fully involved in these movements), it was certainly very much involved in such battles within what
was self-described as the nation's boundaries, i.e., obliterating Native
American tribes, driving out Mexicans from its Western territories, struggling to maintain economic power over African Americans and a massive immigrant population, etc. All of these struggles invariably invoked
the rhetoric of colonization, of Manifest Destiny and the racial superiority of a "civilized" white American populace. But this rhetoric was
(and is) gendered, which complicates our understanding of it.[43] While
the Circassian Beauty superficially appears to highlight some kind of
celebration of emancipation, of release from a bondage both sexual and
spiritual in nature, her immediate alignment with a powerfully colonialist, paternalistic force—a Greenwood who would buy such a girl if
possible, a Long who would civilize and cultivate her to an agreeably
American taste, or a Barnum who would exhibit her as a consumable
entertainment commodity—effectively reinscribes the colonial force
from which she has supposedly been rescued. The Circassian Beauty as
a freak is rescued from both Russian and Turkish oppressors only to be
realigned with an American colonizer; she, in fact, chooses this colonizer, welcoming her own "refinement" and reshaping herself into an
acceptable mate for him. Not only does Zoe's story as Barnum's author
tells it discount the possibility of the Circassian Beauty as an exemplar
of liberation, it, in fact, recasts her cage in the form of Victorian womanhood. Rather than an exotic, sensuous harem dweller, Zoe is now—
thankfully, we are assumed to understand—"a most chaste and delicate
curiosity."

The slavery that Zoe Meleke escapes is treated somewhat differently
in the pages of the 1866 story paper, *Frank Leslie's Chimney Corner.*[44]
"The Sale of Circassian Women" focuses the reader's attention toward
the injustices done to these women in general, describing the inequities
in Circassian society that could lead a woman to happily anticipate her
sale at the Constantinople markets. The brief article begins with a description of "the smugglers" who carry these women to Turkey, and notes
that, despite the dangers of the journey they must endure, these young
women and girls—12 to 14 years old generally, when they are, as the
author puts it, "disposed of by their fathers and brothers"—"look forward to their sale at Stamboul as their grand settlement in life."[45] According to the writer, their lives are so miserable at home, this change is

much welcomed: "For among the Circassians, as among every other un-civilized people—the hardest work falls to the lot of the women, who, in consequence, become soon wrinkled and aged, assuming the appearance of veritable hags at a very early period."[46] The article's description of the girls' sale leaves the reader with a very clear picture of who is ultimately at fault for this pathetic situation:

> in most cases, one of the male members of the family accompanies the precious merchandise to the place of sale, and receives the money himself from his future brother or son-in-law, generally investing on his return a part of the proceeds of the sale in the purchase of some contraband article, such as gunpowder or salt, or whatever may happen at the moment to be most in request among his countrymen.[47]

However much the girls may desire this situation, what the author finally stresses is the complete objectification they undergo by the male members of their families who hope to profit by them. As the article indicates, when the girl prepares to leave her home, she does so "amidst the tears of her mother and sisters, while her father and brothers . . . launch her upon the market, with anxious speculations as to the amount which a commodity so valuable, though to them useless, may bring."[48] In many respects, this brief sketch mirrors the transactions of Southern slaveholders engaged in the sale of their own mixed-race children, born to raped female slaves on their plantations. Rather than stressing the ultimate improvement these girls' lives will experience—the idea that their lives might be improved is mentioned as a kind of self-deception on the part of the girls—this writer makes it very clear that profit drives the men who buy and sell them, a motivation quite different from the desire to "civilize" described as the force behind Barnum's procurement of Zoe.

The Circassian Slave, or The Sultan's Favorite

Slavery and colonial activity are at the heart of a story written by Maturin Murray Ballou, "Lieutenant Murray," called *The Circassian Slave; or, The Sultan's Favorite: A Story of Constantinople and the Caucasus,* which was first published serially in *Gleason's Pictorial Drawing Room Companion* in 1851. *The Circassian Slave* was republished as a dime novel by Gleason's firm, for which Murray wrote, and of which he later assumed leadership.[49] Widely traveled himself, Murray specialized in exotic tales of faraway lands and stories of the sea. *The Circassian Slave* is in part such a tale, but it is also a document that promotes an American ethic of naturalized individualism set within an exotic context. Prefaced by a statement of authenticity of the character of the lands and people described, Murray's story opens on a "hot, sultry summer" afternoon at the slave markets in Constantinople: "here are Egyptians, Bulgarians, Persians and even Africans; but we will pass them by and cross to the main stand, where are exposed for sale some score of Georgians and Circassians."[50] After describing the "motley crowd" that throngs the market place, Murray notes how bursts of laughter would periodically break "from an enclosed division of the place where were confined a whole bevy of Nubian damsels, flat-nostriled and curly-headed, but as slight and fine-limbed as blocks of polished ebony" (10). These African women lie "negligently about, in postures that would have taken a painter's eye" but, as Murray assures us, "we have naught to do with them at this time" (10). Indeed we don't, for Murray proceeds to the sale of the Circassians, who are described as "fair and rosy-cheeked" and exposed "only so far as delicacy would sanction, yet leaving enough visible to develope [sic] charms that fired the spirits of the Turkish crowd" (10). Murray's story will not be about slavery as Americans know and practice it, although his characterization of the "Nubian damsels" in the slave market is grounded in the American stereotype of African women's promiscuity. That the Circassians are exposed "only so far as delicacy would sanction" likewise supports the notion of white women's modesty and sexual propriety. In fact, the story focuses on one Circassian woman in particular—Komel Gymroc or "Lalla" as she is known in the Sultan's harem to which she is eventually sold—who is simply not slave material. *The Circassian Slave* promotes an ideology of slavery that suggests that those who remain in it, who survive in it, are probably best suited for that life. This was a common theme of many proslavery arguments; that slavery suited those who were enslaved within it.[51] The Circassian society Murray describes raises its daughters to anticipate—happily, for the most part— a life of luxury and wealth in the Turkish harems. But Komel, whom the Sultan realizes to be of "the better class of her own nation," does not deserve the life of a harem slave (14). Slavery then is not depicted negatively, necessarily, but rather as a realistic choice for a certain group of people. And while Murray indeed leaves the "Nubian damsels" behind, the brief but telling image of them as sexualized and "negligently lying about" remains as another indication of whom slavery may in fact suit.

Komel, we learn, is a sixteen year-old Circassian who has been taken into bondage against her will by a jealous lover. She is bound by her affections to a childhood companion, Aphiz Adegah, and they are depicted as blissfully united prior to Komel's abduction: "They had grown up together from very childhood, played together, worked together, sharing each other's burthens, and mutually aiding each other; now quietly watching the sheep and goats upon the hillsides, and now working side by side in the fields, content and happy, so they were always together" (22). Circassia is a land in tumult, described in much the same way as Barnum's author described it:

> Circassia, the land of beauty and oppression, whose noble valleys produce such miracles of female loveliness, and whose level plains are the vivid scenes of such terrible struggles; where a brave, unconquerable peasantry have, for a very long period, defied the combined powers of the whole of Russia, and whose daughters, though the children of such brave sires, are yet taught and reared from childhood to look forward to a life of slavery in a Turkish harem as the height of their ambition. (21)

Over and over, Murray stresses that this tale will actually address the question of slavery and its appropriateness. A reader could see Murray suggesting that without other, more intellectually stimulating options, there is little reason for Circassian girls to long for something different than this sexual possession and slavery to luxury. In fact, he seems to suggest that slavery in this case might even be a kind of mercy. The beauty of Circassia's women is an act of compensation on the part of Providence because, according to Murray, they are "unendowed with mental culture" and in "want of intellectual brilliancy" (21). "No wonder, then," he explains, "educated, or rather uneducated as they are, that the visions of their childhood, the dreams of their girlish days, and even the aspirations of their riper years, should be in the anticipations of a life of independence, luxury and love, in those fairy-like homes that skirt the Bosphorus at Constantinople" (21). In this capacity, these women have attained positions if not of power, at least of prestige: Circassia's "daughters have been the mothers of the highest dignitaries of the courts, and Sultan Mahomet himself was born of a Circassian mother" (21). Murray does not clearly condemn or condone the slavery he depicts; rather, he describes it as possibly the best thing for which many of these less-than-bright women can hope. And this slavery has not prevented their attainment of esteem; they are, after all, mothers to many powerful men. One is tempted to draw an analogy here between depictions of mammy figures like Barnum's Joice Heth who indeed "mothered" George Washington, arguably the most popular "great man" in the American nineteenth-century imagination. But there is a tremendous difference between these situations, one for which the Circassian's impossibly pure whiteness may account. No biological child of Joice Heth could have hoped to attain a position of equivalent power in nineteenth-century America. In a sense, then, Murray here seems to use the plight of the Circassians to reflect a problematic notion of white American womanhood: that a woman may, by virtue of her role as a mother, attain a more elevated status than the society in which she is enslaved allows. If not openly disconcerted, Murray at least sounds wistful that such a situation exists. The slavery of the harem itself is described as a luxurious and mindless one. Komel walks into a "gilded cage" when she enters the harem of the Sultan to which she has been sold: "the costly and grateful lounges, the heavy and downy carpets, the rich velvet and silken hangings about the walls, the picturesque and lovely groups of female slaves that laughed and toyed with each other, mingling in pleasant games, the rich though scanty dress of these favorites of the Sultan, all were confusing and dazzling to her untutored eye" (13). And while "days and weeks passed on in the same routine of fairy-like scenes, and the Sultan's slaves counted not the time that brought to them but a never varying dull monotony of indolent luxuriance," Komel's "natural" intellect suffers in such a sweet but stifling atmosphere (40).

The quality of laziness that Said emphasizes is constitutive of the Orient in Western discourses of Orientalism is sharply juxtaposed with Komel and her loved ones. And of course, it is just this quality of intellect and restlessness that further heightens Komel's attractiveness for the Sultan. Described as "a noble specimen of his race, tall, commanding, and with a spirit of firmness breathing from his expressive face," the Sultan is himself the son of a Circassian (11). While he does not seem to be intellectually deficient in any way, he does exhibit "a doomed darkness of expression" that causes Komel to tremble before him; one wonders if in fact the Sultan does not here exhibit a trace of the mulatto in his "doomed" and "dark" expression (11). He is, after all, the son of a slave. The Sultan seems at once a potential symbol of the mixed-race male in America as well as a representation of Eastern tyranny, cruelty, and oppression: "Stern and imperious by nature, it was not usual for him to evince such feeling as had exercised him towards [Lalla/Komel], and it was plain that his heart was moved by feelings that were novel there" (12). Komel on the other hand, is the essence of American Victorian womanhood, "trapped" in an Eastern body:

> She possessed all that soft delicacy of appearance that reminds the sterner sex how frail and dependent is woman, while she bore in her face that sweet and winning expression of intellect, that, *in other climes more favored by civilization,* and where cultivation adds so much to the charms of her sex, would alone have marked her as beautiful. . . . The monarch and all Constantinople knew that her people generally looked forward with joy to the time when they should be old enough to be taken to the Turkish capital, and seek their fortunes there, and the fact of this being so different apparently with Lalla, created the more curiosity to ferret out her story. (15–16; emphasis mine)

Troubled by the emotional intensity that accompanies his new acquisition, the Sultan calls a slave to bring him his pipe and he is "soon lost in the dreamy narcotic of the tobacco" (12). The Sultan does not know precisely how to handle his new feelings, given that he has been taught to "look upon the gentler sex as toys, merely, of his own" and, when it comes to the question of possession of Komel, he remains the savage (29). When Komel's lover, Aphiz, comes to the palace in search of her, having earned a favor from the Sultan by coincidentally saving his life from Bedouin thieves, the Sultan immediately imprisons and attempts to execute him (he does not, of course, succeed). When Komel begs the Sultan to free Aphiz, her pleas are received by him "in that cold, irascible spirit that seems to form so large a share of the Turkish character" (34). The Sultan's memory is unfortunately short, and because he doesn't remember "how unlike her people she had already proved herself" and doesn't realize "that his high station, his wealth, his pomp and elegance" are thought of by Komel "only as the flowers that adorn the victim of a sacrifice," he does not anticipate what we readers do—her escape (46). Komel returns to her homeland with Aphiz who has also escaped from the Sultan's clutches and, despite the years that pass, the "Brother of the Sun . . . does not forget [the woman] who had so entranced his heart, so enslaved his affections, and then so mysteriously escaped from his gilded cage" (67).

Joanna De Groot argues that the nineteenth-century discourse of Orientalism was a means by which men explored "*their own* identity and place in the world as sexual beings, as artists and intellectuals, as imperial rulers, and as wielders of knowledge, skill, and power."[52] For De Groot, "the concepts of 'sex' and 'race' which came into use in European culture, elite and popular, did not just make the control of women or natives easier, but also expressed the conflicts, desires and anxieties which were part of the lived relationships between sexes and races, the *realities* of sexuality and imperial power."[53] The Circassian slave of both Barnum and Murray is a woman of controlled possibility. She has been pulled from the debauchery and tyranny that characterizes the harem in these documents, a debased state that has less to do with slavery than Western descriptions of a weak and evil Orient.[54] The Circassian slave then becomes the idealized colonial subject, she who is primed for "civilization" and who exhibits the naturalized individualism and intellect of Western and particularly American culture, traits that allow her to attract without effort. Komel, Murray's Circassian slave, is particularly evocative to the Sultan, who purchases her not only because she is beautiful and intellectually and emotionally sensitive, but also because she is deaf and mute. (She has been struck so by the murder of a defender and friend on the night of her capture into slavery; she regains her hearing and speech after seeing Aphiz in the Sultan's palace). For Murray, the worth of Komel as a subject with the potential to be civilized is apparent on *sight*. The same is true of Barnum's Zoe Meleke, whose primary achievement seems to be her ability to see America as the bastion of civilization and progress that it claims to be. But of course what is of greatest interest to Barnum is the value of the Beauty for his business purposes; she is a sight to be seen, an object to be held in the gaze of white Northerners, concerned about the rampant changes brought on by Emancipation and perhaps momentarily reassured by this brief experience of (re)possessing slavery. The Beauty also permits the visitor to the American Museum to feel reassured regarding the place and aspirations of the 'true' American woman. In one fell swoop, the Circassian Beauty soothes anxieties caused by Emancipation, by questions of slavery's relevance, the future economic, political, and social positioning of African Americans in the United States, and the attendant changes in the status of women in the country. Intelligent and beautiful, the Circassian Beauty of these texts represents the appropriate positioning of the white American woman in nineteenth-century culture—an object to be looked at, desired, and educated. Released from a sexual captivity in the harem, these Beauties are recaptured by a white Northern gaze.

The only thing that is *not* made clear in these texts is the significance of the trait Barnum apparently highlighted above all others and that ultimately bound all Circassian Beauties together—their bushy hair. In the end, the ultimate subduing of the anxiety caused by Emancipation in this instance is in the reinstallation of the Circassian Beauty as a white slave in its final meanings. The ultimate use of the Circassian Beauty and the way in which she reflects the blackness that was also constitutive of her performance is pornographic.

Sex, Pornography, and the Circassian Beauty

Cartes de visite, or postcards, of the Circassian Beauties sold and circulated in the latter part of the nineteenth century represent these women in a variety of settings and poses.[55] One Beauty is fully clothed in a long white gown with a high neck and looks more like a Western bride than a harem slave, encircled in the photograph by a large wreath made of branches. This interpretation of the Circassian Beauty seems to visually realize much of what the texts discussed above say about her: that she is charming, delicate, intellectual, and chaste—the perfect realization of Victorian American womanhood. But this image practically stands alone when considered within the context of the majority of the surviving visual images of these performers. Rather than highlighting the Beauty's modesty and chastity, her propriety and intellectual capability, these photographs emphasize her exoticism and eroticism. Some of the Beauties display their stockinged legs in reclining postures; one woman, photographed by the Obermuller and Son studio on Cooper Square in New York, reclines on a bench, her silky tunic provocatively sheering at her waist and her legs stretched to her side. The setting for the photograph is primitive, palms framing the Beauty as she leans on an animal skin draped over the bench. Another Obermuller portrait features a Beauty reclining on a roughly carved rock in a parlor of a house, stairs rising off to the left. She too boasts long legs, silk stockings, and a loose leotard, her ankles crossed demurely at the bottom of the rock. Another, photographed by the Henshel studio in Chicago—"Instantaneous Art Portraits" promises the print—wears a white camisole with short pantaloons, long white gloves, and a long velvet ribbon tied in a large bow around her neck (see Figure 14). Her shoulders bare, she leans against a column while cupids dance on the building's border below her in *bas relief.* She draws one leg up to allow her knee to rest on the building's

Figure 14. *Carte de visite* of a Circassian beauty. "Miss Fatima, age 20" is written on the back. Courtesy of Harvard Theatre Collection, The Houghton Library, Harvard University.

edge and the other extends before her; elbow bent, she rests her head in the cup of her palm. She is almost smiling.

Other images emphasize the exotic dress of the Orient—a woman with ropes of huge pearls around her neck, over and under her bosom and down the length of her arms, another with a tightly fitted silk gown, "stars of the East" embroidered along its hem, an ornately bordered cape over her shoulders. Often the studios incorporated tropical plants and animal skins into the background of the photograph. All of these women exude the slight sense of mystery necessary for the exotic flavor of the performance. Most are tantalizingly attired. All share one thing in common: their huge, bushy hair.

According to Bogdan, the women performing as Circassians soaked their hair in beer and teased it to make it frizz and stand up.[56] In fact, the hairstyle of the American-made Circassian Beauty has seemingly nothing to do with popular images of the time of women living in harems in Turkey; in the engraving that accompanies Murray's story in *Gleason's Pictorial Drawing Room Companion,* Komel/Lalla is veiled, her long straight black hair shimmering beneath it. She is carefully covered, dressed in traditionally puffy pants and layers of shifts, shawls, and scarves. But the American Circassian Beauty always sported large, Afro-like hair and, as these images show, usually less rather than more clothing. These women look more like nineteenth-century pin-ups than they do harem dwellers and this brings yet another facet of the Circassian Beauty's signification in American culture to light. Textually, Barnum's writer describes Zoe Meleke as the very model of Victorian womanhood— modest, intelligent and pure, racially as well as sexually—but as these images show, visually, the Beauty is something quite different, a sexual-ized figure intended to entice. She may well represent the reason why Victorian patriarchal culture constructed such a controlling domestic ideology; the Circassian Beauty embodies a sensual pleasure and sexual power that, in the harem of Western myth, would have marked her value.

But while somewhat confusing, the signature hairstyle of these women is clearly vital to our understanding of the Circassian Beauty's signification in American culture. If we go by John Dingess's story of the procurement of Zalumma Agra for the American Museum in 1864, the fact that the first woman hired to perform the role of the first American Circassian Beauty had bushy hair may be the reason why it became the freak's trademark. The freak original quickly became that figure's prototype

for all similar performances; as Dingess comments, thirty years after
Zalumma's first appearance, freak lecturers other than Barnum would
still announce that their Zalumma (who was not even old enough for
the story to be true) "'was brought to this country by John Greenwood
for Barnum's American Museum.'"[57] But the Circassian's bushy hairstyle certainly echoes other of Barnum's exhibits, most especially his
display of Fiji Cannibals and other so-called primitive groups.[58] One
image captured by the "freak photographer," Charles Eisenmann of
New York City, shows a woman in a tightly-fitted fringed bodice and
shorts, her bosom and hips amply displayed (see Figure 15). She wears
stockings and is photographed against the typical leafy set. Unlike the
other Circassians who look very Anglo/European, this woman looks
Middle-Eastern, even African. She is identified on the back of the photo
as "Egyptian, age 20, born in Cairo." Her hair stands a triumphant two
feet from her head. The primary resonance of the Circassian Beauty's
hair for contemporary audiences must have been images of African and
tribal women circulating in the culture. Perhaps it is no accident that
the two primary characteristics of these Circassian Beauties are their
bushy hair and their evocative postures; just like the "Nubian damsels,
flat-nostriled and curly-headed," lying "negligently about" in Murray's
story, the images of the African-American woman's hair and promiscu-
ous sexuality were mythic cultural stereotypes that nineteenth-century
audiences would have swiftly put together.[59] In fact, as Patricia Hill
Collins argues,

> the treatment of Black women's bodies in nineteenth-century Europe
> and the United States may be the foundation upon which contemporary
> pornography as the representation of women's objectification, domina-
> tion, and control is based. Icons about the sexuality of Black women's
> bodies emerged in these contexts. Moreover, as race/gender-specific
> representations, these icons have implications for the treatment of both
> African-American and white women in contemporary pornography.
> I suggest that African-American women were not included in pornog-
> raphy as an afterthought but instead form a key pillar on which contem-
> porary pornography itself rests.[60]

The Circassian Beauty as an image in American popular culture began
in a story of her slavery, but to qualify as a true freak commodity, Barnum and his cohorts had to reinvent her. The Circassian Beauty becomes a kind of minstrel figure, a bushy-haired slave with heightened

Figure 15. *Carte de visite* of a Circassian beauty. "Zumigo the Egyptian, age 20, born in Cairo" is written on the back. Courtesy of the Harvard Theatre Collection, The Houghton Library, Harvard University.

sexuality in white face (and body). In fact, the white slave of the Circassian Beauty may well have helped to usher in the sexualized connotations of that phrase; racially pure, she is marked by sexual violation and commodification. Given these connotations, the two performative variations into which the Circassian Beauty eventually evolved make sense. As the century wore on, some Beauties became subsumed into albino family groupings, highlighting their overly whitened skin, while others became snake charmers, beautiful women seducing phallic animal totems. De Groot in her reading of Orientalist art in the nineteenth century argues that the women portrayed by European painters and artists were "socially marginal, sexually powerless, and vulnerable, and regarded by westerners and Middle Eastern societies as inferior, morally suspect, even virtual prostitutes."[61] Further, she claims that these women "'become' whoever artists want them to be, yet they were actually flesh-and-blood women whose lives were no less real for being hidden from history."[62] Just as the "real" Circassians are lost in the artistic Orientalism of male European art, the "real" performers of the American Circassian Beauty are likewise lost, nameless or renamed women hidden behind the photographed performance of the freak show. While these women were almost certainly never native Circassians, they were commodified within the market of American popular entertainment, as were their Eastern sisters within the slave markets of Constantinople. Who they actually might have been has been suggested by circus press agent Dexter Fellows, and this suggestion illustrates how the disempowering and enslaving representation of women in American culture continues, one culture's slavery merely revamped and grafted onto another, with one racial identity layered on another. Given that the lighter the skin of the Circassian Beauty, the more likely she was to impress upon her audience her racial purity, Fellows explains that "whenever a showman encountered an unpigmented Irish or Norwegian female, he forthwith engaged her, at a salary far in advance of what she was capable of earning at the washtub, as 'Zuleika, the Circassian Sultana, Favorite of the Harem.' Such, at least, was the history of the Circassian lady from Jersey City."[63] Just like the "lucky" Circassian girl who got out of the workhorse world of her countrywomen by entering the slavery of the Turkish harems, the immigrant girl in New York could leave the drudgery of the "washtub" behind to join the market of commodified bodies in the American freak show. What the image of the Circassian Beauty may finally show us is how the signification of women in nineteenth-century American culture, the representations of her sexuality, her intellectual capability and freedom, her body and its control, as well as her position as a commodity in capitalism, not only depended upon the popular representations of women from other cultures, but in fact duplicated those meanings. The Circassian Beauty then depicts a slave from the harem in a culture that understood slavery in relation to its reality in the South. She is then recast within the net of Victorian American domesticity and finally packaged as a sexualized commodity of public entertainment, a force that likes its women and cultural others beautifully caged.

FOUR

A Peculiar Identity in the Confederate
Southern Illustrated News

As the proprietors frankly tell us, the journal is yet in its incipiency, but promise much future improvement, and this is all we ought reasonably to expect, under the circumstances. An infant must be nurtured, trained, and properly cared for, before it grows to the fair and stalwart proportions that delight the eye and senses of the beholder. It is the duty of Southerners to afford the means for this proper training; they will not be true to their obligations as patriots in every sense of the word, if they do not, by their encouragement and liberal patronage, support this journal . . .
— *Southern Illustrated News,* October 18, 1862

. . . if there is a human being on earth whom I respect more than another, it is a well-bred, intelligent old negro house-servant. I can hardly tell you how such a servant impresses me. I love him, I honor him. He makes me feel that there is something innately right, something really beautiful, in our "peculiar" Southern "institution," for which we are so reviled by all the world.
— "Getting Married," *Southern Illustrated News,* October 25, 1862

In the "Salutatory" address of the inaugural issue of Confederate Richmond's *Southern Illustrated News,* published in September of 1862, the editors make this announcement:

We propose to issue an Illustrated Family newspaper of which the present number is a specimen, devoted to literature, to public instruction, and amusement, to general news, and to the cause of our country in this trying hour when she is engaged in a terrible, but resolute and hopeful struggle for her liberty and independence.[1]

Throughout its run—which lasted almost the entire duration of the war, from September 1862 through the paper's final issue, dated February 4, 1865—the *Southern Illustrated News* maintained its political focus, as well as the literary agenda it somewhat ironically shared with its Northern counterparts: namely, to amuse, entertain, and instruct.[2] Positioning the paper as a kind of friendly neighbor, the editors say that they wish "to pay our weekly visits to thousands of homes in our sunny Southern land—homes that are lonely in the absence of loved ones in the army—and impart something of cheer to their loneliness," as well as furnish "our brave soldiers, in their summer bivouac and their winter cantonment, with a pleasant and not unprofitable companion."[3] Above all, the editors note, the *Southern Illustrated News* will "present more vividly to the reader the grand and imposing events that are happening around us."[4]

This literally becomes the function of the *Southern Illustrated News* as the paper comes to embody the nation it promotes. Springing from the rebellious South's final capital, Richmond's *Southern Illustrated News* contains within its pages the ideological, philosophical, and literary seeds of the Confederacy. As Barnum and editors of other Northern popular weeklies less defiantly and emphatically claimed, the editors of the *Southern Illustrated News* and its Southern cohorts contend that the creation and perpetuation of their nation is their central goal. As the editors of the *Southern Illustrated News* observed, "in vain shall we establish our separate nationality, if peace is to be followed by an instantaneous resumption of trade with the enemy."[5] The creation and prosperity of the Confederacy was synonymous with the initiation and success of the *Southern Illustrated News* in a much more explicit way than it was for similar periodicals produced in states still aligned with the Union. In the case of Confederacy, the nation and the print commodities that stemmed from it and attempted to define it were one and the same.

If it's true that the *Southern Illustrated News* becomes a kind of representation of Confederacy, then we can expect to find the racialized others inherent and necessary to its definition within its columns. And as is also to be expected, the African-American slave is crucial to this definition. But the slave's position in the Confederate imagination is complex, as it both affirms the racialist assumptions upon which the institution of slavery was based and reveals their contradictions. While the racialized others in the New York press that shore up Northern notions of

American identity are clearly cast beyond the borders of that American national belonging, the African-American slave of the Confederate press is less a racialized alien and more a racialized foundation for the Confederacy itself. Eugene D. Genovese has argued that slavery "made white and black southerners one people while making them two," confirming the belief of C. Vann Woodward that "white and black southerners, however different they may claim to be and in some ways are, have come to form one people in vital respects."[6] Certainly in the pages of the popular Confederate press, the slave is essential, rather than anathema to Confederate identity, helping to create a national belonging that is quite "peculiar" indeed.

The Question of Confederate Nationalism

Nationalism and the idea of a coherent Confederate identity are issues of contention in American historical scholarship. The question of whether or not a unique and distinct nation called the Confederate States of America ever actually existed within the larger borders of the United States of America is one contemporary historians still debate.[7] Gary Gallagher claims that arguments about Confederate nationalism are themselves historically situated and often revolve around the classic and enduring question of why the South lost the Civil War. According to him, "the American experience in Vietnam inspired dubious comparisons of the Confederate and North Vietnamese struggles for independence, which inevitably used the Vietnamese victory to judge Confederates wanting in national purpose."[8] Whether or not a sense of Confederate nationalism was ever actually achieved is what Steven Channing calls "one of the most venerable historical chestnuts in Southern history."[9] Part of the difficulty of even discussing the Confederacy as a historical subject is seated, according to David Potter, in the fact that a historian's feelings regarding a group's ideological schemata may influence his or her treatment of that group as a nation. In fact, as Potter notes, it can make it

> difficult for the historian to attribute nationality to movements of which he morally disapproves, since the attribution itself would imply that the movement had a kind of validity. This factor has certainly influenced the treatment of the question whether the Southern Confederacy was a nation, for the issue between the Union and the Confederacy also be-

came an issue between freedom and slavery. To ascribe nationality to the South is to validate the right of a proslavery movement to autonomy and self-determination.[10]

Obviously, as Potter indicates, this is something "few historians in the twentieth century have been willing to do."[11]

In 1988, Drew Gilpin Faust claimed that historians of the American South were little further along in understanding the creation, function, and final role of Confederate nationalism than they had been when Potter wrote his essay. Like Gallagher, she believes that the fact of the Vietnam War has made it more difficult to rely solely on the material argument that the South lost its war because of its relatively scarce supply of resources and technology. Faust instead argues that contradictions implicit in Confederate nationalist ideology may in fact have had as much bearing on the war's end at Appomatox as anything else. Gallagher, however, disputes this:

> Too often historians identify an absence of nationalism as both cause and symptom of Confederate failure. The Confederacy lost because its people never developed a true sense of nationalism—or the Confederate people never developed a true sense of nationalism; if they had their struggle would have been determined enough to achieve independence. Many works that posit an absence of Confederate nationalism overlook or minimize two salient points. First, Confederates by the thousands from all classes exhibited a strong identification with their country and ended the war still firmly committed to the idea of an independent southern nation. Second, although these people finally accepted defeat because Union armies had overrun much of their territory and compelled major southern military forces to surrender, that acceptance should not be confused with an absence of a Confederate identity.[12]

Gallagher goes on to outline what he sees as central in this nationalist imagination, drawing from a range of letters, diaries, and popular published images and written texts.[13] He overlooks, however, the narrative of Confederate identity that was so carefully sketched in the pages of the *Southern Illustrated News*.

Benedict Anderson argues that a nation is defined via its imagined community, one that establishes geographic and cultural borders outside of which members of other, adjacent nations are assumed to stay. Given this definition, the Confederate States of America surely constituted a nation. The Confederacy initiated and waged a long and bloody war; such a material act undoubtedly indicates the presence of an ideological foundation upon which such organized violence and devastation could stand. That this foundation rested squarely on a belief in the institution of slavery certainly adds a dimension of moral unacceptability, but it does not make the Confederacy any less a nation; the acceptance of slavery was not ever unique to the antebellum Southern. Moreover, many of the discursive qualities that undergirded the Confederacy's image of itself in the years of and surrounding the Civil War remain in circulation today in the South. It is for this reason, perhaps more than any other, that a study of that representation is imperative. What those elements are, how they can be identified, and how they functioned in the pages of Southern periodicals like the *Southern Illustrated News* to rhetorically create a politically, culturally, and imaginatively coherent picture of the Confederacy in the minds of its reading members is the primary goal of this chapter.

The Press and Confederate Identity

Confederate periodicals represented themselves as key players in the nationalist project of providing a cultural shape for the Confederacy. It was largely by way of these texts that a national literature would be documented, distributed, and developed—and so their editors tell us, at every possible turn. Benedict Anderson has argued that widely circulated publications like the newspaper were the vehicles that made a sense of imagined national community possible, and Alice Fahs has charted how the Civil War in part "suffused" the act of reading with "nationalistic aims," making it "less a private act than a vital part of a larger, public, patriotic culture."[14] But, as Faust points out, both the "comparatively lower levels of literacy" in the South as well as the lack of widespread technological sophistication and development inhibited the presses' abilities to create this sense of community: "if printed media enable citizens to imagine national communities, the South had a problem from the outset—a problem that intensified with each year of conflict."[15]

Southern editors had to create a sense of urgency in their readers—and potential readers—in order to gain support for their endeavors. While certainly greatly amplified by the onset of the war, the problem of acquiring and retaining subscribers and readers was an ongoing one for Southern editors engaged in a losing battle with Northern publishing houses and their readers' desires for well-produced literary texts. A decade before the war, in July of 1850, the "Editorial Department" of *De Bow's* published a long piece on "The Cause of the South," in which said cause becomes the success of *De Bow's* itself.[16] Arguing that they "have long ago thought that the duty of the people consisted more in the vigorous prosecution of their industry, resources and enterprise, than in bandying constitutional arguments with their opponents, or in rhetorical flourishes about the sanctity of the federal compact," the editors contend that it is a sense of inferiority based in an unwillingness to support their own Southern industries that holds the South in an inferior position, and that they certainly have "work before us now":[17]

> Who conducts our commerce, builds for us ships, and navigates them on the high seas? *The North!* Who spins and weaves, for our domestic use (and grows rich in doing it), the fabric which overruns our fields and not seldom fails to remunerate the labor that is bestowed upon it here? *The North.* Who supplies the material and the engineers for our railroads where we have any, gives to us books and periodicals, newspapers and authors, without any limit or end? *The North.*[18]

According to these editors, "it is not too late for hope" and in order to promote the cause of "working our [way to] a higher and better destiny for the South," they have devoted themselves to the task. Nevertheless, they have been thwarted in these attempts:

> We have preached this doctrine [of taking action on behalf of Southern commerce] on the hill-tops, from the day of our first editorial until now—through every defeat, every pecuniary loss and embarrassment, amidst every discouragement, oftentimes with faintest possible applause. The mead of praise came to us oftener from the North itself in our labors. "*Stop the Review*" was a familiar word that was heard often, often, often, from all quarters, from the highest to the lowest; "I have not time to read;" "I take too many other works;" "I am obliged to reduce expenses;" "You are now getting on too well to need my subscription;" "Perhaps next year I will subscribe;" "I admit it *is* a valuable work and should be encouraged," is denied in none of these letters. More frequently the word is "*refused*," as the number comes back, saddled with postage.[19]

Not only are *DeBow's* Southern readers slacking off in their responsibility to support Southern industry, but the journal itself is ironically depicted as more likely to receive "praise" from the North than it is the South.

A month before the war, the *Southern Literary Messenger* published a humorous, fictional piece called "The Mother of Eleven Children," which

begins with the conventional apologia of the woman writer who proclaims to write only to support her children.[20] This mother starts off
playing with the conventional authorial intrusion—"You may be gentle, dear reader, or ungentle . . . it matters but little to me which"—then
makes her case, despite her numerous children who continually distract
her throughout the article:[21]

> I know how to work, and if my children only gave me opportunity to
> work in the manner I like, I could soon be independent—provided you
> would do your duty.
> Surprised eh! Don't see what you've got to do with it.
> Oh! no, you don't see that Southern authors have to run North with
> their contributions, and sell them at half price to Northern magazines.
> That Southern books have to sail a thousand or fifteen hundred miles
> away from home, trembling for fear the great Mogul of Northern criti-
> cism, will kick them back into oblivion. Oh, no, of course you've got
> nothing to do with that. That's not your affair.[22]

The mother-author goes on to parody the hypocritical patriotism of the
Southern reader, arguing that "you are ready to do battle for your country and bathe it with your heart's best blood, but a country don't need a
national literature. Cotton is king, everybody knows the country's full of
genius—not worth while to publish it."[23] The "sin" lies "at your door,"
this mother tells her reader, offering the remedy of subscribing to Southern magazines so that the South "will soon have one of the brightest lit-
eratures of any land and [be] the greatest country on the earth."[24]

A similar argument appears in Augusta, Georgia's *Southern Field and
Fireside*.[25] Its first issue, appearing in May of 1859, opens with a "Salu-
tory" by editor James Gardner claiming that the paper will furnish "the
Southern farmer information useful in every field he cultivates, and the
Southern family choice literature, the offspring of Southern intellect, worthy of welcome at every fireside."[26] The paper's staff members "share—
what intelligent observer does not?—this belief of Mr. Gardner in the
existence abundantly at the South of the literary elements: and we feel
with him—what patriotic Southerner does not?—the humiliation and
the evils of our accepted dependence upon another section—a dependence only the more mortifying in that it is not necessary."[27] "Salutatory"
pleads for "emancipation" from this position of dependence: "Intelligent individual enterprise, supported with liberality and firmness by the
Southern public, would speedily effect our emancipation, and convert

sneering contempt for 'Southern literature' and Southern literary ability, into a cordial respect."[28] A story entitled "Getting Married" that appeared in an early issue of the *Southern Illustrated News* also uses the idea of consumer-loyalty to identify its adventuring protagonist as both bachelor and Confederate: "I had no more idea when I started of getting married," says the character, "than Gen. Lee has of giving up to McClellan, or you have of ever subscribing again to a Yankee newspaper."[29] Patriotism in these papers is evidenced by consumption; if the future of the Confederacy lies in part in its literary productions, then the success of that future rests in the hands of those who will—or won't—buy and pay for it.

The *Southern Illustrated News* highlights the obstacles that their writers and editors believe have inhibited the success of Southern-produced and identified literature and culture. During the war, these impediments range from the distractions the war itself creates, to the continued demand for Northern publications among Southern readers. "Salutatory" acknowledges the necessarily diminished interest in things literary when more immediate and pressing concerns are at hand—"when the wolf is at the door, the family cannot enjoy the 'Cotter's Saturday night'"—the reduced number of writers due to their active involvement in the war— "some of our writers, like Cervantes in the heroic and Korner in the utilitarian age, have laid down the pen for the sword"—and finally, the limited supply of print materials due to the blockade.[30] Depicting the paper as a kind of war-time companion, the editors paint their purpose in simultaneously personal and nationalistic terms:

> We wish to pay our weekly visits to thousands of homes in our sunny
> Southern land—homes that are lonely in the absence of loved ones in
> the army—and impart something of cheer to their loneliness. We shall
> send, far and wide, throughout our borders, carefully executed portraits
> of our distinguished leaders, that the people may know what manner of
> men they are, in bodily likeness, in the council and the field. And we
> shall count, with something of confidence, upon furnishing our brave
> soldiers, in their summer bivouac and their winter cantonment, with a
> pleasant and not unprofitable companion.[31]

Like its compatriot papers, the *Southern Illustrated News* exhorts its readers to repudiate Yankee publications. In the paper's third issue, the editors ask

> What Southern man again wishes the periodicals of the North circulated
> throughout the length and breadth of our beloved confederacy? Should

the people of the South ever again encourage and aid them in sowing the seeds of fanaticism and abolitionism in our land—in instilling in the minds of our young the doctrines of Free-Loveism, Mormonism, and the thousand of other corrupting isms that weekly have their birth in the cess-pools of iniquity scattered thick throughout the whole of Yankeedom? We do not believe that the people of the South will ever again welcome a Northern periodical into their households—we cannot for a moment believe they are so devoid of interest for the welfare of the rising generation—so lost to all reason and honor—and it is for the purpose of filling the hiatus created by the expulsion of these worthless sheets, and to supply them with a good literary journal, that we have started upon the present undertaking.[32]

Here, the *News*'s editorial staff delineates not only what makes "Yankee-dom" so problematic—the "corrupting isms" of illicit sexual behavior—but how its readers can continue to support and contribute to the Confederate cause by providing the journal "their hearty support."[33]

In keeping with this attempt to draw a distinction between themselves and the papers of the Northern press from which Southern publishers tried to wean their readers, the *Southern Illustrated News* and its compatriot periodicals routinely denounce all things "Yankee."[34] This is particularly evident in a piece in the *News* appearing in its first issue entitled "Yankee Literature" in which Northern writing is attacked for its lack of originality—"Yankee literature is a very bad imitation of the most indifferent class of English literature"—the Northern mind, for the same—"imitation, in fact, forms the substratum of the Yankee mind. The Yankee is, to an uncommon extent, an imitative animal"—and the North's corruption of the language—"they are not content with murdering [the Queen's English] outright. They subject it to all manner of degradation before they put it to death."[35] Noting that the Confederacy can not yet be said to have a literary culture of its own, the editors argue that "a Southern literature will come in due time, and when it does, it will in no way resemble the Yankee abortion."[36] Yankee engravings will likewise not be duplicated in the pages of the *News,* according to its editors: "We cannot engage to give pictures of victories that were never won, or to sketch the taking of capitals that never surrendered, as have the illustrated weeklies of Yankeedom."[37] Neither will the *News* "attempt to make one engraved head serve as a portrait for 'poet, statesman, fiddler and buffoon'—passing off the likeness of a British orator for an American divine, and bringing it out again, upon occasion, for a new major-general."[38] Even the style of the literary submissions the editors receive is apparently corrupted by Northern writing: "If the mind is crammed with sensation trash, such as is usually found in Yankee novels, you will, of course, form a flat, silly style."[39]

Near the close of the war, writers for the *Southern Illustrated News* reflected more specifically on the press's relationship to the events of the battlefield. In an article entitled simply "War," one writer outlined this connection for the paper's readers:

> Liberty came not in the old revolution in America until the press grew into a power.... How much of the tramp of the thousands of martial feet, as they move from point to point, is but the echo of the printing press.... The children of a new nationality should not grow up in ignorance; the men of the future should be men in mind as well as in physical structure, the better to guard against those dangers of ignorance and passion which so soon beset this once proud republic and have ended in its destruction.[40]

Here, in the war's final months, readers could take comfort in the fact that, as readers, they were contributing to the Confederate cause by reading newspapers. Without such "education," say these writers, "war accomplishes nothing good."[41] The commonplace injunction to inform and instruct readers, under which periodicals like the *Southern Illustrated News* operated, here takes on a much more overtly nationalist form. But not only will the *Southern Illustrated News* instruct its readers in the nation's history and philosophical foundations. It will in fact become for them metonymic of the war's effect on the Confederacy and its citizens itself.

On the event of the completion of the first volume of the *Southern Illustrated News*, editors marked the occasion by celebrating the paper's very survival—something worth noting in 1863, with Gettysburg just days away. It is here that the paper begins to figure for the nation itself, enduring in its writing, publication, and printing, the same losses and hardships Confederate citizens have:

> We were then, as now, in a condition of blockade; there was most inadequate supply of paper in the country; artists, we had none; the class of literary workmen had been scattered by the exigencies of the war, and all things seemed to promise that the journal would add but another name to that long list of failures in literature which belong to the intellectual history of the Southern States. But energy and enterprise have overcome all these seemingly insurmountable difficulties.[42]

More than a year of war later, the paper's editors again describe weeklies like their own as illustrative of an indomitable Confederate spirit. Noting that "evil genius" born of the fourth year of war has been trying to "kill" Confederate weeklies, the editors here contend that while fighting against the odds, these papers have managed to survive:

> By spasms, . . . they have burst out into the light, enfeebled, it is true, at times by the absence of most of their respective corps—contributors, printers, engravers, editors—delving in the mud of the trenches or standing guard around the prisons and bridges of this devoted city. Here and there, through Spring, Summer and Fall, we get a glimpse of transitory evidence that they did not quite expire under the blight of the cold, wanton and arbitrary curse which come on their heads that bright May day. . . . they appear once more, after a very long suspension, and it pleases us.[43]

Despite the loss of their workers or their press "corps," these papers have managed to survive and this survival connotes another—the survival of the Confederacy itself. More than simply reflecting the Confederacy, or even contributing to its construction, the *Southern Illustrated News* here actually embodies it.

Slavery and Confederate Identity

Drew Gilpin Faust argues that in the discourses that emerge in the development and promotion of a Confederate nationalism, the Confederacy is often situated as a kind of jeremiad or agent of nationalist Christian evangelical reform. Confederate writers added to this mix an advocacy and embrace of Republicanism—complete with a highly popular harkening back to the Revolution as the best analogy for the Confederacy's part in the Civil War—to inscribe their claim to Americanness.[44] Rather than extricate the idea of the Confederacy from American history, Confederate writers argued that the South's fight for autonomy from the North actually represented a continuation of the struggle of 1776. The South, they insisted, was the legitimate heir of American revolutionary tradition. Betrayed by Yankees who had perverted the "true" meaning of the Constitution, this revolutionary heritage could be preserved only by secession. Southerners therefore portrayed their independence as the fulfillment of the most basic tenets of American nationalism.[45]

Such comparisons are common in the *Southern Illustrated News*. The lead article for the September 20, 1862 issue on General John H. Morgan carefully indicates that this Morgan is "a lineal descendent of Morgan of Revolutionary fame" and Mary A. M'Crimon's "A Night's Experience in Camp" that appeared a few months later notes that Confederate General Hardee shares with General Washington the tendency to laugh— when he does so—"uncontrollably."[46] The most obvious example of this claim to Revolutionary heritage and history in the *Southern Illustrated News* appears in the April 11 issue of 1863 in an article incredulously entitled "Washington a Yankee!"[47] Written in response to the assertion made by "the Yankee ambassador at the Court of Saint James" that "had Washington been living, he would have been a Yankee," the article includes the following remarks in its concluding paragraph:

> Washington was a Southern man in all his feelings. He was, indeed, the very model of a Southern man. He was the owner of immense estates, and a vast number of slaves. He was one of the most successful managers of slave property that has ever lived in the South.[48]

Republicanism was particularly suited to the aristocratic landholders of the South who had no wish to lose their political prowess to nonland- and nonslaveholding whites in the Confederacy; Republicanism allowed for a system of governance seemingly democratic in tone yet elitist in practice. But as this sketch of Washington shows, it also depended upon and promoted an assumed stance on slavery. Washington, this most potent of American figures, owned "a vast number of slaves," and gains additional distinction because he "was one of the most successful managers of slave property that has ever lived in the South." Faust shows that beyond any doubt, "in public discussion of both the war's origins and its purposes, southerners repeatedly cited slavery as a fundamental source of sectional conflict and a foundation for their peculiar national identity."[49]

The Southern and Confederate press printed all versions of the pro-slavery argument—and did so frequently. The Christian case that relied on the mention and treatment of "servitude" in the Bible appears in *De Bow's Review of the Southern and Western States* in the year that saw a considerable increase in the printed debate over slavery over all—1850. An anonymous author claims that "we find, then, that both the Old and New Testaments speak of slavery—that they do not condemn the relation, but, on the contrary, expressly allow it or create it; and they give commands and exhortations, which are based upon its legality and propriety. It can not, then, be wrong."[50] Other popular discussions include the injunction to "civilize," as is promoted in this discussion penned by "Bland," Attorney General J. Randolph Tucker in the *Southern Literary Messenger* in 1861. Prefaced as covering a "hackneyed topic," the editors present the following in the hope, as they say, that it may still be helpful. Look at the slave, freed, says Tucker:

> In the West Indies, he wanders back to savage life. He needs the continuing pupillage of slavery to keep him from falling into barbarism. In the North—here among us—as a class—the slave is infinitely more moral than the free black. Freed from the restraining influence of a superior's discipline, the negro relapses into vice. American slavery elevates the African above what he was in his native land, or what he can be, freed here. The moral effect upon the master is equally great. The great Educator at last is responsibility. It necessitates thought and self-discipline. . . . I can but suggest these views, but it could be fully shown that, *morally,* slavery is essential to the highest development of both races. Destroy it, and the slave sinks to savage life; and the master loses those great qualities which have so marked the men of the South in all our history.[51]

Both slaves and masters are here affected by slavery and both are crucial to the definition and functioning of the culture that embraces it. Rather than exclude the slave from its national and ideological borders, Confederate thought and propaganda worked to pull the slave more resolutely into the nation's definition.

The slave appears as both a contrasting other and key figure within the confines of Confederate nationality in the visual imagery contained in the *Southern Field and Fireside* and the *Southern Illustrated News* periodicals. The masthead of the antebellum *Southern Field and Fireside* includes those scenes that will come to mythologically constitute the Confederacy—a field being plowed to the left, a group of women and friends frolicking by the waterside to the right, and a "true" family circle in the center, mother holding a baby, other children sitting nearby, and father reading that week's *Fireside*. The people working the field to the left are, of course, slaves, and are rendered both as backdrop to and foundation for the other scenes depicted. The masthead of the *Southern Illustrated News* that appeared at the end of the war positions the slave quite differently (see Figure 16).[52] In the right hand side of this image, a white Confederate couple stands, the woman in hoop skirts and the man outfitted for battle; both have a hand on the rifle the soldier will obvi-

Figure 16. Masthead of the *Southern Illustrated News* (14 January 1865). Reprinted by permission of the Houghton Library, Harvard University.

ously take with him. On the left is a slave couple, the woman holding a freshly filled basket of cotton and the man, an ear of corn. Neither pair is necessarily privileged; both are literally central to the image and consequently, the nation here under construction. The scenes on either side of these couples are war scenes—the battle of Fort Sumter on the left and the ironclad *Virginia*'s victory at Hampton Roads. War situates and defines the couples in the middle, but their sharing of the space in the center indicates the necessity of both to the Confederate's understanding of him or herself as a Confederate. The editors of the *Southern Illustrated Weekly* confirm this idea in the description of the masthead they include the week following its initial appearance:

> The medallion in the foreground pictures a volunteer about to depart for the war, who finds
> "Parting is such sorrow,"
> that he lingers to rehearse the oft-repeated vows. To the left we see negroes in their happiest sphere, 'mid the cotton bloom and sugar cane.[53]

Given their centrality to Confederate self-definition, it's no wonder that slaves appear frequently in the pages of the *Southern Illustrated News,* usually as background characters serving the needs of the white characters that appear opposite them and those of the white writers who utilize them in their narratives. "Getting Married," a two-part story written anonymously by "An Artist" indicates the kind of bifurcated and contradictory quality inherent in the Confederate discourse on slavery.[54] The story unfolds by explaining how the narrator meets and wins his wife. The character upon whom the story's key action depends is Uncle Phil Jones, an old slave that the narrator insists was "'a colored gentleman,' if ever I saw one."[55] Nevertheless, the narrator's attitude toward Uncle Phil is complicated and contradictory. Uncle Phil inadvertently becomes the reason the narrator's beloved turns her eye his way, but this only happens because the narrator accidentally kills the old slave when he runs into him while riding a trail in the dark. The horse recovers to get fat and well, but Uncle Phil does not. It is the narrator's subsequent kindness toward the dead man's wife, in the form of a gift of guilt—a portrait of Uncle Phil drawn by the narrator—that wins the affections of his soon-to-be fiancée. In order to get to this place, though, the narrator's attitude about slaves must be transformed. At the story's outset, the narrator contends that the trouble with current matchmaking practices is that Southerners have dropped their ritual of "courting by proxies, . . . sending our 'head-man'" to the household of the object of marital interest (4). On one hand, the narrator holds that a return to this method of courtship could only be an improvement; under the current system, "our modern young ladies hold their noses so high, and so many excellent young men so often get horribly kicked," making an unfortunate reference to what will ultimately happen to Uncle Phil (4). Yet, as the narrator then admits, "I doubt if I would altogether relish the appearance in my parlor of an aged gentleman from Africa, charged with a respectable but preemptory demand from his master for my daughter, offering to pay me so many head of cattle for the same" (4). The notion of a slave offering to "buy" the daughter of the speaker is depicted as a cultural affront not only because property cannot itself "buy" property, even representationally, but because of the racial affront such a potentially possible transaction—black man bartering for white woman— simultaneously suggests. Despite the narrator's eventual conciliatory gesture toward Uncle Phil's wife and his future fiancée's slave, he believes that slaves are not always to be trusted. When considering which slaves would be most likely to leave their masters if the "Yankees were to get in the neighborhood," the narrator comments that "it is not the mean-looking negroes that go soonest, as many masters have found to their cost,—for the very chaps most relied on for their fidelity have been the first to 'skedaddle'" (5).

But the narrator, an "Artist," must ultimately undergo an emotional transformation in terms of how he thinks of slaves in general, and Uncle Phil, in particular. While first impressing himself on the narrator as a "gentleman," Uncle Phil soon becomes the focus of the narrator's attack when he interrupts the Artist in a moment of self-pity. Uncle Phil inquires if the Artist is "distrested in yo' mine 'bout sumthin nuther or ruther" (5). "Seeing he was a negro," the narrator tells us, "I broke loose upon him: 'You impertinent old scoundrel, if you open your lips to me again, I'll knock your brains out!' "(5) But the Artist is a good master in the making and he feels instant regret for his outburst and concern over the impression Uncle Phil must have of him. It is here that the narrator spills over with praise for the "well-bred, intelligent old negro house-servant": "I can hardly tell you how such a servant impresses me. I love him, I honor him. He makes me feel that there is something innately right, something really beautiful, in our 'peculiar' Southern 'institution,' for which we are so reviled by all the world" (5). Even though Uncle Phil has to die in order for this story of marriage and union to occur, what is evident is how the Artist's interactions with and response to a slave are constitutive of his own moral development and standing. The fact that the Artist is so "kind" to Uncle Phil's wife Aunt Abby is in fact the very reason his wife agrees to marry him:

> "Well, Aunt Abby is my 'mammy,' you know, and I always promised her to marry the man she chose. After you gave her Uncle Phil's likeness, her heart softened toward you. She told me of the visits you had made to her, and of the kindness and goodness of heart you had shown. Then she talked to me about you, and I got to thinking about you, and then— then—"[56]

The illusion that Aunt Abby actually has a "choice" in who her white charge will marry—and who will therefore be her master as well— highlights the way in which Confederate discourse reiterated the moral effect slavery supposedly had on its masters. The facts that the narrator could, if he desired, "knock the brains out" of Uncle Phil to punish his assuming impudence, or that he can, with complete impunity, kill Uncle Phil, are unconsidered complications of the Christianizing influence slaveholders believed slavery had on everyone living in the South.

The racism that both predicated and justified slavery is, of course, frequently displayed in the pages of the *Southern Illustrated News* as well as other Southern periodicals. "Nights on the Rapidan," a dialogue between a colonel and a physician, is prefaced by the heavily accented speech of Hannibal, a slave the doctor prizes more than "the four best horses between the Potomac and the Susquehanna."[57] After Hannibal explains how—and why—he "escaped" from the abolitionists of Pennsylvania, the two white men settle in for discussion over a "tin cup of Confederate coffee."[58] The Colonel inquires whether the doctor agrees that the "existence of that African race amongst us, and the intimate relation they bear to us and our children . . . this great broad feature of our Southern life sufficient of itself to color our modes of thought and of expression; and is not that the chief element of a distinct national literature" (68). The Doctor heartily disagrees:

> No; the existence of African slaves amongst us is essential to the production of cotton and rice, but its only effect upon our language has been to corrupt it by negro idioms and sounds which are scarcely human. . . . the presence of the negroes who are naturally, necessarily and eternally lower in the scales of creation can have no spiritualizing action upon our social life. (68)

The Doctor concedes that the effect on the white masters of caring for these slaves "instead of inviting them, by free competition, as in Europe, to eat one another's heads off" is "wholesome, humanizing and noble," but he does not ascribe this at all to the character of the slaves in question. While not the fault of the slaves themselves—"if a dog is not a man, is he therein under a curse? Is a horse cursed in that he is not a cavalry officer?" asks the Doctor, rhetorically. For the Doctor, the fact remains that African-descended slaves are something less and other than human. In fact, he notes that, given the choice, "I should prefer white slaves" (68). In August of 1850, *De Bow's* printed a piece called "Physical Characteristics of the Negro" that reasoned that "the negro has on his head '*wool,* properly so termed,' and not *hair.* And since the white man has hair upon his head, and the negro has wool, we have no hesitancy in pronouncing that they *belong to two distinct species.*"[59]

But the existence of racialist rhetoric like this also testifies to an awareness in the culture of the contradictions and incongruities of a slaveholding system. Those contradictions are repeatedly represented in the periodicals, as two political cartoons in the *Southern Illustrated News* nicely illustrate. In the first, two slaves are shown walking in the rain (see Figure 17). Jeff asks Sambo why he isn't wearing a hat: "Golly, Sambo, what makes you walk in de rain widout your hat? You'll cotch

Figure 17. Political cartoon of "Jeff" and "Sambo" from *Southern Illustrated News* (18 April 1863): 8. Courtesy of Virginia Historical Society, Richmond, Virginia.

cold in de head, you stupid nigger."[60] Sambo replies: "Go way, nigger! Dis chile knows what he's doing. Dis head 'longs to Massa, but de hat 'longs to me! Ha! Ha!" Apparently supposed to comment on the illogic of the slave, the cartoon instead illustrates the illogic of the system itself— that the slave as a human can "own" a hat, but as a slave cannot "own" his own head. It also illustrates the slave's contempt for attending to the care of the master's interests over his own, despite the brutally ironic turn that within slavery, this also means a contempt for care of the self. In another *Southern Illustrated News* cartoon laden with overdetermined cultural meanings, a war-deprived Confederate mistress disparagingly attempts to fashion a hoop for her skirt out of what appears to be chicken wire (see Figure 18). The model for her work is a young slave girl who stands, hand on her hip, almost completely covered with the ill-shaped hoop. The cartoon, appropriately titled "A Hard Case," bears this caption: "Miss Susan, *despairingly*—'There! it's no use, Kitty; you can and take the old thing off. Was there ever such barbarity? Who but the Yankees would ever have thought of making hoop skirts contraband of war?'"[61] Ironies here abound. The contraband referred to is apparently the hoop, yet what the hoop covers, if not entirely hides, is the slave herself, who could *become* contraband if she were indeed not just to "take the thing off," but "take off" overall. Indeed, the way the cartoon is drawn leads the reader to imagine that Kitty is in fact *trying* to hide herself, perhaps for the obvious but unstated purpose of running away. The "barbarity" here is the behavior of said Yankees who have made these hoops contraband but again, it is the Yankees who have, superficially at least, made what hides *under* the hoop the most significant contraband of the war. The "Hard Case" of this cartoon is in fact to what—or whom—the title of contraband refers, as well as under whose skirt this contraband is hiding.[62] In a way, the cartoon foreshadows the greatest dilemma for the Confederacy overall—what shape their society would and will take without the support of slavery. What would the plantation aristocracy of the South be, the image suggests, without slaves like Kitty, and without slavery in general, to hold it up?

Race, Nation, and the Yankee

While texts like "A Hard Case" reveal the contradictions inherent in the pro-slavery ideology that was essential to the Confederacy's ideological constitution, other pieces that appeared in the *Southern Illustrated News* indicate the clear interconnectedness of race and nationhood in Southern writing. But who is racialized in these discourses complicates the way in which race can be understood to function in the Confederate imagination. *Southern Illustrated News* writer "Oats" proclaims "that the *baser* nature of the Yankees could not be *changed* any more than the Ethiopian's indestructible hue, or the spotted hide of the leopard."[63] This equation indicates that as much as Confederate nationalism depended upon a racialized understanding of the "inferior" position of

Figure 18. "A Hard Case," political cartoon from *Southern Illustrated News* (6 February 1864): 40. Courtesy of Virginia Historical Society, Richmond, Virginia.

the "Ethiopian" in the scale of human evolution, it likewise depended upon an alienated Yankee presence, one that was even racialized to make it more effective. Such metaphors take center stage in a two-part story published two weeks later in which slaves are ideologically and practically included within the boundaries of the Confederacy, and the morally and racially problematic Yankee is cast out.

In a Confederate answer to Northern expressions of Emancipation anxiety, one complete with the explosive and fiery images that seem always to accompany this cultural fear, "The Little Incendiary" is a story about a barn fire with suspicious origins. The anonymous author begins this tale with a qualification:

In no one thing have the Abolitionists been so completely disappointed, as in the conduct of our slaves during this war. The theory of the Northern people was, that we of the South stood on a volcano, which would burst forth into the wild excesses of a servile insurrection the moment the Union was dissolved, and the slaves felt themselves free to do as they pleased, not only without the disapproval, but with the countenance and active co-operation of "the strongest and best Government the world ever saw."

These expectations, in the realization of which the Abolitionists exulted fiendishly and openly, have not been realized. Our slaves have remained quiescent. . . . No outrages have been committed, and even arson, the most practicable of all crimes, and the one most feared, has not been indulged in. True, at the breaking out of the war, there were frequent alarms of fire in Richmond; and wild stories about a plot between the abolitionists and the negroes in that city were rife.—But these stories proved unfounded. Since then, there has been a destructive conflagration in Charleston, which was also attributed to the slave population, incited by the abolitionists. But on closer investigation, it was found that the wind was to blame, and not the darkies.[64]

While the author begins this tale with a protest that despite rumor and Northern-based predictions, slaves in the South have stayed peacefully bound to their masters, two illustrations show precisely the kind of violence the author claims has *not* resulted from the slaves' emancipatory efforts. The first bears the caption, "The Burning Barn," and the second, "The Fire at a Distance."[65] The writer explains that he is led into these remarks by the reconsideration of "a singular instance of incendiarism" that took place near his home "some years ago"(4). Barns were being burnt around Charleston at the time of John Brown's raid on Harper's Ferry and "although there was no proof, every conflagration, indeed, every event of whatsoever sort, that happened about that time, was attributed to the negroes, who, as we now know, were innocent as babes unborn" (4). The reader is clear now that whoever set this "little incendiary," it will certainly not likely be the fault of one of these "innocent as babes unborn." In fact, in the engraving of "The Burning Barn," the only person included in the picture is a white man, a hired hand the author tells us was seen lingering around when the barn of his neighbor, Appling, went up in flames.

Along with rumors of slaves uprising, Brown's raid also led to increased public suspicion of "every person who had the least taint of Yankee blood in their veins" (4). In this instance, though, the writer is not so quick to exonerate those suspected. He indicates that Appling had in fact employed a woman with suspected abolitionist leanings and his description of her is telling:

> Her name, Miss Crane, was, I thought, singularly appropriate; for she was a scrawny, scraggy old maid, with a neck almost as long as a fence rail; and, strange to say, she was proud of this neck, and wore her dress in such a way as to display it to the utmost advantage. Hateful as she was to me, with her neck and her drawling Yankee accent, she was a great favorite with Appling and his family. . . . the report was that he intended to make her his second wife. (5)

On the same page of the *Southern Illustrated News* on which this piece appears, another essay entitled "Mrs. Poynter's Reflections" considers the proper role and sphere of the Confederate woman. While certainly not advocating the overt political action of these women, "Mrs. Poynter" does encourage her female readers to embrace a public role in the events of the day, helping with the war effort by working in hospitals or making goods for the soldiers. "Mrs. Poynter" encourages her female readers to put behind them the pretensions of fashion—"do without plumed bonnets, and silk dresses, and velvet cloaks" (5). As "The Little Incendiary" tells the tale of the potential evil of women's political actions (an indirect accusation of the Appling's Yankee schoolteacher), "Mrs. Poynter's Reflections" redirects its female readers' political and material energies in support of the Confederate war effort.

In the second half of "The Little Incendiary," the writer links the theme of marriage—or, more precisely, unwise, inappropriate marital choices—to the theme of abolitionist insurrection. According to yet another neighbor, the fact that Miss Crane has been chosen by Appling to be his wife is enough to relieve her of suspicion: "the last thing she would do would be to burn down property which she expected some day to be her own."[66] The narrator confesses that this is fine logic, but "there is no accounting for the conduct of an abolitionist, and especially a female one. They are all crazy, and there is no telling what they will do. They act not from reason, but from a strange, incurable hallucination" (4). The neighbor's mother joins the conversation and when the narrator questions the wisdom of using slaves to help put down what may well be a slave uprising instigated by an abolitionist or "man who calls himself the friend of the slave," she is loudly dismissive:

"Friend indeed! They have got no better friend than me. Didn't I raise 'em like they was my own children, and don't you think they would help me to cut off the head of any meddling old fool who would come here murdering white people and trying to persuade colored folks to leave comfortable homes for a certainty of starvation at the North? Don't talk to me about abolitionists," concluded the old lady, "or about negroes; I know 'em both, and I know that a properly raised colored person has got too much self-respect to have any thing to do with them." (4)

In essence, "The Little Incendiary" pits this woman's faith in slavery against the "scrawny, scraggy" abolitionist Miss Crane who, once her betrothed's circle of suspicion grows sufficiently large to include her, leaves "for home," after "a long private interview" with Appling. Moreover, it pits the old neighbor woman's faith against the "tough disciplinary" techniques of Appling and the narrator themselves. The hired man—who originally came from the North—runs off, and the little slave boy who first announced the fire to the suspiciously unruffled Miss Crane is discovered to have acquired a range of goodies including candy and "many gewgaws and trifles" (4). According to the narrator, Appling was of the beat-first; ask-questions-later school:

The story came out under the switch very promptly and, no doubt, fully—though all the facts were never made known. The boy confessed he had bought the candy and other things with money given him by the hired man who ran away. Among his purchases he had bought several boxes of matches, and, while experimenting with them in the shed, the hay had taken fire, as he declared to the last, accidentally. (4)

This explanation hardly satisfies the narrator: "My own opinion is, that the hired man was an accomplice of Miss Crane, and my suspicion is, that both of them knew too much about John Brown" (4).

While it is unclear to the narrator—and to the reader as well—exactly what happened to Appling's shed, the final conclusions suggest a couple of things. First, the story implies that Yankee, abolitionist tendencies tend to act themselves out in violent fashion, particularly in regard to upsetting what is here depicted as the paternalistic balance of the Southern plantation. Had the slave boy not encountered the hired man, he would not have been tempted to "play with matches," as the proverb warns to which the text points. In fact, the narrator points out that the elderly neighbor woman who sustains such faith in her slaves in fact handles them with too light a touch and may well pay for her gentleness. Moreover, despite general opinion, those with Northern alliances—and Northern unions—will surely upset the Appling cart. Better to keep Yankees where they belong and a firm hand on one's slaves in order to ensure a peaceful, untroubled existence.

What's most interesting about the events in this story, though, is that they suggest that the slaves themselves are not to blame for the "trouble" caused here; the narrator takes every precaution to insure that the reader not make this assumption. It is rather the use and manipulation of those slaves—most notably, by way of possessions that technically slaves can't own anyway—by "cool" and unscrupulous Yankees that is the central threat to the continued tranquility of the Confederacy. If these two things are not kept apart, the result may indeed be incendiary. There is no question in this tale though, that slaves should stay with the Southern planters who "best" understand how to "handle" and "care for" them and that anyone of abolitionist leaning should stay far, far away—preferably, in another nation altogether.

At times, the writers of the *Southern Illustrated News* attempt to outright racialize the Yankee figure in order to further separate him/her from those Confederates attempting to create their own nation. In a rather offhand attempt at angry humor, the writers of the newsy "The Times" column include commentary on the attempts of the Confederate Congress to refuse voting privileges to anyone who has not served in the Confederate forces and been naturalized as a Confederate citizen following that service. The writers point, somewhat humorously perhaps, to the problems sure to result from a regionally specific form of miscegenation:

> ethnologists have decided that the admixture of an inferior with a
> superior race of the human species degrades the latter to the level of
> the former; and it is very certain that unless we restrain immigration
> by the most stringent laws, we shall, in a very few years after peace is
> declared, be overrun by Yankees and other foreigners, and that the next
> generation of Southerners will be the vilest of mongrels, incapable of self-
> government, and fit only to grease machinery, eat codfish, and run mad
> about spirit-rapping.[67]

In yet another dialogue between the Colonel and the Doctor in "Nights on the Rapidan," the Colonel muses that "there must be some original fundamental difference in breed and race between ourselves and those New Englanders more than the common histories of colonial settlement clearly account for"; when he broaches the question with the loquacious Doctor, he is initially disappointed.[68] According to the Doctor,

> there is more nonsense written and spoken upon this matter of races than upon any other whatsoever within the last thirty or forty years. As a general rule, every writer on the subject has taken up his own favorite race, namely; the one to which he either belongs, or imagines himself to belong, and applies himself to the task of demonstrating that the race which had the honor of producing *him,* has done most of the great things in history. Then he resolutely claims kindred with those nations which have made themselves most distinguished in the modern world, and gives his own stock credit for all they have done.[69]

While a surprising admission from a writer who has already claimed the evolutionary inferiority of the African—or "Ethiopian"—to the "Caucasian," the Doctor's reflections go on to postulate a demographic blood-mixing of various European nations in different regions of the United States, noting that, only with "much more minute and conscientious" examination of these groups and their movements could an "ethnography of the Federal and of the Confederate States" be compiled.[70] In short, the argument that Yankees constituted a different race altogether from the Confederates never seemed to hold much water, even in the Confederacy itself. But while these attempts to divide Confederates and Yankees into different races don't quite carry the day, the Yankee is undeniably the most important and visible alien in Confederate ideology, an alien that is nevertheless racialized in specific ways. Rather than biology, the Confederate press would rely on Christianity to create a clear-cut division between themselves and the Union soldiers and citizens against whom they were pitted, a discourse of heaven and hell that would clearly place all concerned exactly where they belonged.

FIVE

The Yankee, the Stump, and the Creation of a Confederate Imaginary

There is but one word in the language sufficiently comprehensive to fit their case—the word YANKEE. It has always heretofore been used as an epithet of contemptuous ridicule. Hereafter it will stand as the epitomized synonym of ingratitude, insolence, knavery, cowardice, falsehood, deceit, thievery, brutality, and cupidity; for all these vices and crimes do the Yankee people stand convicted—not by the verbal accusation of their enemies, but by their own voices and deeds.
— *Southern Illustrated News*, December 13, 1862

A good book is the Devil's worst enemy.
—William Gilmore Simms, *Paddy McGann;
or, The Demon of the Stump*

The position of the slave within the rubric of Confederate nationalism was contradictory but secure; while not in any way viewed as a full human member of the nation, the slave was nevertheless necessary to the Confederacy's understanding of itself. Slaveholders argued that both they and their slaves were morally improved by their respective places in the plantation South. Rather than ideologically cast the slave *out* of the borders of the Confederate nation then, the popular texts of the Civil War South work very hard to *maintain* the slave's presence within the Confederacy's legal and ideological bounds. But the creation of the Confederate citizen necessitated its diametrically opposed other—the Yankee. Without an ideological opposite, Confederates could not possibly know who or what they were. As Anderson has indicated, "the most messianic nationalists do not dream of a day when all the members of the human race will join their nation."[1] And messianic is precisely the way in which Confederate writers and editors depicted their new nation. According to Drew Gilpin Faust, Southern Christianity legitimized the Confederacy, providing

> a transcendent framework for southern nationalism. During the antebellum period, southerners had portrayed themselves as the most godly of Americans, and independence and civil war only reinforced this identification. . . . Secession . . . became an act of purification, a separation from the pollutions of decaying northern society, that "monstrous mass of moral disease," as the Mobile *Evening News* so vividly described it.[2]

There can be no doubt of the centrality of Christian discourse to the nationalist thought of the Confederacy. "Lines on the Proclamation Issued by the Tyrant Lincoln, April 1st 1863" printed in the *Southern Illustrated News* and attributed simply to "A Rebel," comments on Lincoln's call for a day of fasting to commemorate Emancipation. This "Rebel's" religious fury knows no bounds:

> To bend devoutly on your knees
> To mock Almighty God;
> Insult him with hypocrisy,
> And court his angry rod;
> To ask that God to be unjust
> Who rules infinite space;
> To ask Jehovah's blighting curse
> Upon his chosen race;
> To ask of God to hallow crime!
> Oh, horrid, impious thought!
> The tyrant asks—the heart replies,
> To *fast* and *pray* for what?[3]

Confederate writers argued against everything associated with the Union North using a language of sin and salvation. The way in which extortion was characterized in the Southern press is an excellent example of this. As Faust describes, the South's resistance to a free market economy that directly "challenged the system of slavery that dictated the peculiarities of the traditional southern way of life" led to a particularly vehement position against the inflation of the price of daily commodities during the war itself.[4] As a result, extortion became one of

the most potent "sins" to emerge from the wartime South. In the serialized "Thoughts of My Own Thinking," one columnist for the *Southern
Illustrated News* notes that "one of the misfortunes of the present un-
natural state of civil strife is a tendency, everywhere, to a spirit of reckless speculation and heartless extortion."[5] "Would it not be well," asks
this writer,

> to revise some of our business maxims, and pause a moment to reflect
> on the consequences of all this madness? Who now really transacts
> business on Christian principles? We hear the teachings of the Bible on
> Sunday, and pray that God would direct us in all things. We are taught
> not to oppress the poor and the weak, to do justice to all men, and then
> go straight away on Monday and drive the hardest bargains we can, and
> absolutely plume ourselves on our skill and dexterity in over-reaching
> our neighbor.[6]

While one cartoon for September 19, 1863, simply represents the burning of various extortioners at the stake (with the helpful "Recipe to Get
Rid of Extortioners—Chain them to a stake, as above; pile their ill-gotten
gains around them, and any passer-by will fire the mass"), such images
usually depict the Jew as the main culprit in this extortion.[7] In an article
entitled simply "Extortion," *Southern Illustrated News* writers argue that
Jews have "done their share in the work. At the same time, what else
could be expected from a Jew but money-getting? . . . since the time they
were driven out of the Temple until now, for them money has been
country."[8] Although not centrally blamed for the extortion the article
lambasts, it is significant that the phrase, "for them money has been
country," is used to define Jewishness here. The only kind of money-
getting sanctioned in this nationalist Confederate discourse is that associated with the planter class. In fact, in a cartoon published earlier, two
caricatured Jewish merchants smile as they attempt to charge an outra-
geous price for the cloth a mammy figure attempts to purchase (see Figure 19).[9] The caption reads: "Shameful Extortion! *Colored Lady* (loq.)—
What! dollar and half for dis ninepence Caliker, an' old fashion at dat.
Great King!" Here, not only is the slave co-opted into reproducing the
material conditions of the society that oppresses her by opposing a free
market economy, she also uses a Christian exclamation—"Great King!"—
to punctuate her own distress. The interweaving of these discourses—
one characterizing the virtues of a slave-based economy and another, an

SHAMEFUL EXTORTION! *Colored Lady* (loq.)—What! dollar and half for dis ninepence Caliker, an' ole fashion at dat. Great King!

Figure 19. "SHAMEFUL EXTORTION!" political cartoon from *Southern Illustrated News* (14 February 1863): 8. Courtesy of Virginia Historical Society, Richmond, Virginia.

evangelical Christianity—is essential to the way in which the Confederate body politic was imagined.

While Jewishness embodies the sin of extortion in this image, mercenariness is a character trait more readily attributed to the Yankee. As Fletcher M. Green notes, in the early nineteenth century in England, the word "Yankee" " 'carried with it the implication of crass commercial dealings, shrewd bargaining, and even sharp practices.' "[10] But this is hardly the worst element of Yankeeness discussed in the Southern press during the war. In fact, as the delineation of race ascribes a set of "natural" characteristics to a given group of people, so the Yankee is racialized using a language of Christian morality. This characterization and racialization effectively alienated the figure of the Yankee from the Confederate nation and therefore helped its ideological definition. Yankees are described as sharing a common set of Satanic traits inherent to their natures by virtue of the same rhetorical process used to other the Irish, the African American, the Native American, and even the Confederate in Northern versions of Americanesss. And while images of devilled Yankees fill the pages of the *Southern Illustrated News,* a story about a different demon by William Gilmore Simms will complicate the question of Confederate identity once again. As the war reaches an end, the Southern press will embrace a newly blinding whiteness in order to redefine and reassert itself.

By Any Other Name: Yankee Liars, Beasts, and Demons

References to Yankees in the *Southern Illustrated News* are incessant and consistent. Sometimes literally and at others metonymically, the Yankee is nevertheless always linked by the writers of the weekly with all things evil, Satanic, and hellish. And it is by virtue of a single trait—lying— that the *Southern Illustrated News* draws a direct link between the quintessential Yankee and the Great Liar, Satan.

In the first issue of the *Southern Illustrated News,* editors play with this idea in a poem titled simply "A Slight Variation." While McClellan's casualties rot, making "fertilizers," what McClellan himself seems to make most successfully are "fertile lies."[11] Just above this piece is a punny gloss on Yankee character: "One base the Yankees can never change,—their base natures."[12] Within the Calvinist-based doctrine to which Confederate Christianity seems most closely tied, it is natural depravity—the animalistic or "base" part of human nature—that puts humanity at the greatest distance from God and at the greatest risk of indoctrination by Satan. The Yankee's "base nature" as well as his/her inclination toward lie-telling situates him staunchly within Satan's camp, as well as explaining the discrepancies that appear in the war's coverage North and South.

In almost every edition of the *Southern Illustrated News*'s weekly news feature, "The Times," mention is made of the Yankee habit of lying about the events of the war. The first issue includes a reference to this in a comment on the kinds of engravings the editors hope to provide here. "We cannot engage to give pictures of victories that were never won," say the editors, "or to sketch the taking of capitals that never surrendered, as have the illustrated weeklies of Yankeedom."[13] The second issue of the paper includes a criticism of "Yankee" histories, something, the writer assures the readers, that should be read with a highly critical eye indeed:

> the British historian, writing even of the Napoleonic period, or of the American war of 1776, will be thought an accurate and impartial chronicler, when he shall come to be compared with the Yankee historian of the war now raging on this continent. The Yankee, indeed, has shown a boundless aptitude for lying, as a nation and as an individual, ever since the war began, and it is really difficult to determine in what class of Yankee society the most colossal and overwhelming lies have found their origin.[14]

The October 11 issue of the paper includes "a correction of the lie published upon the authority, we suppose, of McClellan himself, viz: that we sent a flag of truce to bury our dead. . . . Of course that is a lie, on its very face."[15] The October 18 "Times" column proclaims that "no man can doubt the truth of anything Gen. Lee says," while highlighting the insincerity of Union leaders: "Lying is an art, indeed, in which the Yankee generals particularly excel. No general is fit to command a Yankee army, who is not an adept in it, and no general will be tolerated, who is not such an adept."[16] According to this writer, "there is no use for lying in our army," because Confederates win the battles they say they do.[17] While mention is also made of the savage and brutish Yankee, "The Times" makes the predictable leap between lying and the uncivilized Northern nature. Apparently, the British understand that the Yankees are

> not more than half civilized, and they see that, like half civilized nations in general, the Chinese for example, they are unaccountable liars. That

is, indeed, a national characteristic of the Yankees. There are liars among all people; but with most a liar is an exception. With the Yankee, it is the general rule. . . . *Prima facie*, when told that a man is a Yankee, it is fair to conclude that he is likewise a liar.[18]

Of course, much of the emphasis placed on Yankee lying is linked to the Confederate press's impossible position of attempting to provide its readers with encouraging war news, despite the actual events of the war. According to a report printed in the March 21, 1863, issue of the *Southern Illustrated News,* the Yankees have "told a very big lie about the surrender of Fort McAllister and the capture of a mile and a half of rifle-pits. . . . Statistics recently published by the Smithsonian Institute, show that the full-blooded Yankee dies within twenty-four hours if prevented from telling his usual allowance of lies."[19] Depicting all Yankees as liars not only helped provide a racialized distinction between North and South, it also produced yet another reason to buy Confederate newspapers and stop supporting the Northern press.

According to the 1863 Valentine's Day edition of the *Southern Illustrated News,* President Lincoln's hopes for literary greatness could only come in one form, given his Yankee sensibility. "Poets have been said to succeed only in fiction," the writer informs us, "and truth is thought by some critics to be a curse to the tribe. In this view of the case, Abe Lincoln might fairly hope to win the bays. If boundless lying be a qualification for poetic excellence, then is he only surpassed by his own laureate, Seward."[20] The biggest liar of them all, Lincoln receives the most blatant representation of Yankee devilry to appear in the pages of the *News.* In a cartoon entitled "Masks and Faces," published shortly after the issuance of the Emancipation Proclamation, Lincoln stands holding his recognizable features aside as a mask while his true face—the horned visage of the devil—glares out at the reader (see Figure 20).[21] This cartoon received additional mention in a piece reprinted from the *Chattanooga Rebel* several weeks later: "the illustration of 'Masks and Faces'—representing the face of Lincoln before the proclamation, and the black-crowned visage of destruction, upon the same shoulders, after it—is particularly striking."[22] According to this Tennessee paper, the cartoon's "truth is frightfully dramatic."[23]

Another Union official to receive consistently devilish treatment in the *Southern Illustrated News* is General Benjamin F. Butler, whose epithets

Figure 20. "Masks and Faces," political cartoon from *Southern Illustrated News*
(8 November 1862): 8. Courtesy of Virginia Historical Society, Richmond, Virginia.

include the "Brute" and "the Beast." According to Merton E. Coulter, "no other Federal commander was ever to be regarded with as loathing a contempt as General Benjamin F. Butler" and "no other commander was to be awarded the special title of 'Beast.' "[24] Coulter explains that it was Butler who "with his cockeye, compressed lips, and livid complexion," issued an order that declared that "any woman who was contemptuous or insulting toward Federal soldiers should 'be regarded and held liable to be treated as a woman of the town plying her avocation.' "[25] According to Jefferson Davis, Yankees were " 'the only people on earth who do not blush to think he [Butler] wears the human form.' "[26] Referenced in poems as well as articles and news accounts, Butler is specifically and satirically condemned in a poem entitled "The Devil's Toast" in which "ye sons of darkness" are encouraged to raise their "cups of skulls with broths of hell" to him:

> His well known oaths will ring our root—
>   Welcome his old familiar snarl,
> And clatter of his cloven hoof
>   Upon the burning marl.
>
> Come, stir the damned to howl and yell—
>   Fit music for our rousing feast—
> And toss the flaming wine of hell
>   To "Butler, our brother Beast!"[27]

In a particularly graphic and uncharacteristically well-drawn cartoon, "Butler, the Beast, at Work" digs through the graves of fallen generals, looking up from his work on Albert Sydney Johnston's grave for a quick glance at the reader (see Figure 21).[28] His face is unsmiling and human, but his thin, skanky body is that of a wolf.

The powers of hell are elsewhere referenced in the paper and indirectly connected to the work of the Union armies. In the *Southern Illustrated News* column "The Times," writers argue that it was indeed the power of Satan—disguised as "Despair, in the form of a brooding Tempter, nursed and disseminated with the energy of the Prince of the Powers of Darkness"—that was responsible for the weakened Confederate resolve of the previous summer.[29] Even so, Confederate patriotism—with the help of a heavenward force—rallied: "But before the gloom could reach the zenith, . . . the national heart appears to have awakened, stirred by

BUTLER, THE BEAST, AT WORK.

Figure 21. "Butler, the Beast, at Work," political cartoon from *Southern Illustrated News* (30 April 1864): 136. Courtesy of Virginia Historical Society, Richmond, Virginia.

the voice of the gallant men in whose trust the seal of our freedom has been placed, and touched by the revivifying finger of that Providence who will yet bear us safely to success."[30]

Paddy McGann; or, The Demon of the Stump

In February 1863, the editors of the *Southern Illustrated News* announced the appearance of "an Original Novel, written expressly for this paper, by W. Gilmore Simms, Esq., and entitled 'Paddy McGann, or the Demon of the Stump.'"[31] While ranking "deservedly as the Nestor of Southern literature," Simms is also depicted as another victim of the literary forces of the North: "His long and laborious life, if it has not brought him fortune, as it would have done in a land not oppressed by Yankee tyranny, has crowned him with honor and affection."[32] *The Southern Illustrated News*'s publication of a new work by Simms—an author celebrated both North and South—represents evidence of the editors' ability to make good on their promises to "furnish a first class literary paper."[33]

The story itself was the only piece of fiction Simms published during the war, and it has received fairly little critical attention. According to Robert Bush, in the later part of the century when Simms's other work was being reprinted, *Paddy McGann* was ignored "because it dealt with themes too sectional to interest Northern publishers who might have brought it out as a book."[34] All critics who do discuss the text comment on its overtly politicized moments, but none look at the work within the context in which it originally appeared—a weekly illustrated newspaper designed to aesthetically shape a still amorphous Confederate readership. *Paddy McGann; or, The Demon of the Stump* is the story of a man haunted by a demon—the devil himself, according to Paddy. Paddy's demon follows him through a series of mishaps, including the loss of his hunting ability and the trouble he subsequently has providing for himself and his family, a shipwreck at sea, a trip to a differently demonized New York, a very bad marriage, and finally, the Civil War itself. In a paper filled with images of Yankee evil and Federal devils, *Paddy McGann's* stump demon seems perfectly at home. Concerned as he was with secession and its results, Simms certainly chose freely from a pre-existing network of popular images for his book, reshaping the conventions of Confederate discourse to create a complex quixotic and comedic novel of Confederate nationalism. *Paddy McGann* comments on the frustrations inherent in the Confederate longing to break away from a Northern-dominated market economy, a break that devastated Simms's own career as a writer. A tale of Yankee tyranny and the way in which it upsets the South's social and economic orders, *Paddy McGann* relies on the image of a demon to convey this—and one in and of "the stump." Simms's novel, in part a critique of the political plays that led to the Civil War, also inadvertently reveals the difficulties of determining the contours of American national identity in the South. Over and over, Paddy notes that he can't "see" his demon, can't tell what form or shape it takes. Paddy is disoriented in part because of his inability to see his enemy and therefore categorize it—yet another version of blinding whiteness.

Paddy McGann lives and works in the rural region of the Edisto River in South Carolina in the years immediately preceding and during the Civil War. Told as a tale within a tale, the narrator of the story is Stylus, an aristocratic writer-figure who goes to visit his "excellent old friend," Wharncliffe, a planter living on Desilla, a plantation on the Edisto. Paddy doesn't actually appear until the third chapter and Simms uses the beginning of the text, particularly this long introductory paragraph, to reminisce on the South over which the American nations were then fighting; in it, he lovingly details what all is at stake in the fight:

> It was November, and the delicious season that we call the Indian Summer; when, after two or three smart white frosts, and possibly a little ice, the cool spell passes off; the winds grow calm and modestly beseem themselves, the temperature becomes sweet and genial—neither too cold nor too warm; when, after a heavy fog each morning, the sun suddenly bursts through the vaporous sea, in a shower of golden light; when the whole circumference of heaven, and the whole broad plain of earth, the great forests and the little hills, seem to move together in concert, as at a feast or bridal; when the woods capriciously change their suits, day by day, and ever to a glorious motley; when the birds grow more elastic in the air, when the long lines of cranes are suddenly beheld trooping south; when the squirrels are every where to be seen in eager movement, plying rapidly between their groups of great green water-oaks and the neighboring cornfields, each with his mouth full of stolen fruit; when persimmons are rapidly ripening; when Cuffee, and Cudjo, and Sambo, and Caesar take out the dogs nightly—Towser, and Teaser, and Tear'em, and Take'em—for coon and possem hunt; when the hogs, having had full range of the peafield and the potato patch, are about to be driven up to the fattening pen, and when, following the good old English rule, which forbids the hunt from the *spring* of the leaf to the season of its *fall*, the hunters begin to sound horn and summon the beagles every morning for the chase, and when, briefly, the harvest being good, the season delicious, no war in the land, and plenty on every board, our country seats are everywhere glad in themselves, and with gladness welcome their city friends to the sports and hospitality of the old plantation.[35]

Simms begins his novel with nostalgia, reminiscing at prodigious length on the image of the prewar rural South as a land of plenty, full of pastoral pleasure and prosperity. In this land, everything moves in harmony and grace: "the whole broad plain of earth, the great forests and the little hills, seem to move together in concert, as at a feast or bridal." The reference to weddings and union will, of course, echo with the actualities of Paddy's story as relayed in the text, but here, all is well, all is in its place. This idea of Southern harmony is most powerfully depicted in Simms's description of servitude. Dogs and slaves are equated here, items in two parallel lists; Cuffee, Cudjo, Sambo, and Caesar are syntactically and aurally related to the hounds, Towser, Teaser, Tear'em and Take-em. This is the mythologized Old South, paradisiacal and gentrified. Here, even "city friends" are welcomed "to the sports and hospitality of the old plantation." The images projected in the prologue of Paddy's tale resonate with peace and bliss; as Stylus notes, "in such weather, through such foliage, to dash off on free-going steeds, is to feel life in every vein and artery" (216).

Wharncliffe and Stylus do just this, and as chapter 1 continues, this tremendously good feeling comes to a crashing halt when Simms enters the rhetorical realm of war. Remembering the "sacred few among our own people who loved to seek us out in our rustic solitudes," Stylus names one, Maxcy Gregg, who he notes is "doing brave service on the banks of the Potomac" as "a Brigadier of the Confederates" (219). Even as narrator Stylus exhorts Gregg to "soon return to his earlier loves, and to our simple tastes and solitudes," author Simms must interject with one of the only footnotes to the novel. "As I write the above passage," Simms explains, "but a little week, indeed, after I had written it—came the mournful tidings of the death of my noble friend on the battle field of Fredericksburg" (219). Simms includes excerpts from Gregg's final letter to him, a document that spends significant time discussing the horrors of war for those who fight it: "our poor soldiers, without tents, many of them insufficiently clad, without blankets, and some of them barefoot, bear their hardships cheerfully; but in such weather they suffer much" (219–20). Even as Simms attempts to end the footnote on an upswing, indicating the devastating losses incurred at Fredericksburg by Federal forces, his questioning of the justification behind such loss is evident. Simms adds that the papers surviving his friend include Gregg's commentary on "the army and the prospects of the war, but the matter is not yet proper for publication" (219). Why such "matter" might not be "yet proper for publication" could be due to any number of reasons, including the possible threat such commentary might pose to the resolve of still-optimistic Confederate readers. Even as the novel energetically denounces the Yankee North and all it encompasses, particularly the publishing stronghold of New York City, this authorial aside suggests that Paddy's demon will be so hard to pin down in part because it is more than simply a Yankee force. The demon resides in a stump, the conventional stand of political posturing, and the tragedy of the text and of the moment in which it appears—the war itself—for Simms, seems to be the result of this kind of demonic activity.

The pages following this intrusive footnote do then indeed turn to the war, its "raging tempests" and "unleashed war-dogs," but both the narrator and Wharncliffe transform this equally disruptive intrusion to their momentary bliss into a kind of rallying cry. Wharncliffe leaps to his feet and proclaims,

> "It is not all over—our happy life, my friend! We shall enjoy the old sports of our sweet little river once more, in communion with our noble-hearted companions. It cannot be that God will deliver us into the hands of these atrocious heathens. As between us and the Deity, there is no doubt a sad reckoning to make; but as between us and these accursed Yankees, no reproach lies at our doors, unless that single one of having too long slept within the coil of the serpent. I have faith in God, my friend.—He may punish us, and we must suffer, for this is the meed of our desert; but he will not let us sink." (221)

This paragraph completes the nationalist frame Simms constructs for his novel. Set up as a kind of nostalgic aftcasting of what the war has taken away, it likewise provides a religious context for the events to come. Simms's readers are informed that the "accursed Yankees" are also "atrocious heathens," and if the Southerner has done anything in the least to provoke this distressing turn of events, it is to have "too long slept within the coil of the serpent" (221). The serpent in this Edenic planta- tion is obviously the Union; as the novel progresses, though, the ques- tion becomes who (or "hoo hoo hoo," as the demon cries) the demon might be. It seems significant that even as Simms begins his novel with proclamations of Southern patriotism, including a firm positioning of God in the South and the Devil as serpent in the North, these pro- nouncements are visibly and emotionally undercut by the long foot- note that offers a much more debilitating view of the events at hand.

As well as framing the novel within the events of the Civil War, Simms uses his introductory chapter to argue for a kind of fictional renaissance that may in fact be one of the happy byproducts of this horrendous fighting. Wharncliffe and Stylus discuss the worth and possibilities of fancy and imagination and in the midst of their discoursing, they dis- cuss the need for attrition for creative invention in a society, attrition here used to mean the action of two energies in contact with one another. As Wharncliffe says,

> The *fiction* will come from the *friction*. The transition periods are those always most full of invention. The realm of romance is ever a debatable land. It is the unsettled empire between two great extremes, for which both parties are contending. In their conflicts they evolve the wondrous event, the daring heroism, the beautiful eccentricity, the curious custom, the wild, graceful manner, the flashing novelty, the piquant adventure, such as make the periods of Chivalry and Feudalism—periods dear to Poetry and Romance. It is the perpetual conflict between Valentine and Orson—between the ever hostile worlds of civilization and savage. It is in the transition of a people from the one confine to the other, that develops the richest materials for art in fiction. And this is also the formation of society. (225)

Wharncliffe argues that not only will "*fiction* . . . come from *friction*," but this evolution from savagery to civilization—an evolution in which he sees the South fully involved—realized within its cultural productions is likewise "the formation of society" (225). Not only does Simms cast his novel as a gloss on the project of national formation, he indicates quite clearly that such fictional productions will in fact be centrally responsible for that social and national formation overall. Like the *Southern Illustrated News* in which *Paddy McGann* appeared, Simms sees himself as actively involved in the creation of the imaginary community of the Confederacy, using his text to help define that nation's borders.

As almost every critic writing on this novel has said, Simms celebrates the comradery he felt should and could exist between members of different classes in the South in *Paddy McGann*. As Bush notes, the character of Paddy "belongs to the folk," most at home in the rural backwoods South, hunting, rafting, and fishing for his living as he does, but he is likewise "a natural aristocrat who can hold his own with the planters and the learned men who assemble to listen to the tales of his adventures."[36] In terms of his class representation, Paddy functions as a kind of Southern Everyman; belonging to the common people, Paddy is still "broad enough to embrace the gentry."[37] And the gentry embraces Paddy. As Wimsatt indicates, the two share a strong sense of community, despite their varying class positions, and share a mutually beneficial economic relationship as well; Paddy brings Wharncliffe's household fish and game while Wharncliffe reciprocates with tradable commodities and monetary loans and gifts.[38] As well as socially, Paddy is historically representative, spanning "a goodly cross-section of Southern life from solitary frontier huntsman to raft pilot in the lumber industry to innocent ambassador to the North, and finally to Confederate soldier."[39] And most poignantly for Simms, perhaps, Paddy is an aesthetic symbol. When Wharncliffe hears Paddy singing and prepares to introduce him to Stylus, he tells his friend that the raftsman is quite creatively gifted but "one of the most uneducated of our people. . . . You will find that he has not only fancy, but imagination" (228). As well as the text that bears his name, Paddy comes to figure for the broadest understanding of a Confederate national imagination.

Something must be terribly wrong with the national forces if Paddy is suddenly stripped of his hunting and fishing abilities and forced to wander the woods aimlessly while unseen voices taunt him. Driven almost to insanity and suicide, Paddy is unable to correct the unexplained malfunction of his gun or his fishing lines. A sound like an owl hooting—"hoo hoo hoo!"—haunts his every hunting step. His friend Sam Hartley urges Paddy to return to God and in fact Paddy does undertake a brief period of Bible study in order to decide for himself who—or what—haunts him. When relating the story to Wharncliffe and his cohorts, Paddy speculates on why he has been selected:

> I rayther reckon that a man must have something in him that makes it aisier for the devil to take hold of him. It may be sin and a bad conscience, or it may be the whiskey, which some people seem to think is as bad as both of them. The Good Book tells us, and so does the parson, that, when a man has sin in him, then he is more at the mercy of the devil than at any other time. Then is he nearer to the devil and further from God. Now it may be that 'tis all owing to my own sinful nather and avil dispositions that I have been put at the marcy of the etarnal inimy!—That's raisonable enough. All I am sartin sure of is that he *has* been at me, and putting it to me with tooth and horns and toenail. (253)

Why the devil—"the etarnal inimy!"—has chosen Paddy to provoke is one of the great questions posed by the text. For Paddy and Simms, though, the source of such possession is best found within. If demons are haunting Paddy—or the Confederacy—regardless of what form they take, the reason for their being must lie within the Confederacy itself.[40]

The devil harasses and abuses Paddy relentlessly and there seems to be no clear way he can stop it. More so, even, there seems to be no clear sense of who—"hoo hoo hoo!"—this "devil" actually is. Even as Paddy loses his ability to make a living, his own self-respect, and the companionship of his closest friend as a result of this harassment, the most troubling aspect of the whole affair is finally the state of ignorance in which Paddy is kept regarding the identity of his harasser. Part of the reason Paddy can't pin down his tormentor is that the form it takes keeps changing. Sometimes its presence is heralded by the owl-like hooting Paddy hears in the forest, sometimes the sound of heavy footsteps sets him off, and at still other times, the demon announces its presence by calling Paddy's name. The devilish force that haunts Paddy assumes many voices but refuses to allow itself to be seen:

> "sometimes I'd feel my arm or shoulder brushed, as ef somebody was passing by in a hurry.—now and then, a shout or yell, not thirty yards off, and nobody thar! Every day these throubles got worse and worse, 'tell I was half the time in a trimble and a rage! I got so used to it, at last, that I got desperate sassy, and would cry aloud, 'Ef you're the devil, whoever you *air,* stand out and let me look at you.' Then I'd hear a chuckle, a sort of dry, husky laugh, at my very elbow. Wheeling about, quick as a shot, I'd see nothing! And so it went on for weeks longer, ontill I fairly prayed on my bended knees, that ef it waur the Devil sent for my tormenting, he should come out boldly and look me in the face! I was desperate enough now to face any devil, no matter what the length of his horns, or the blackness of his face.
>
> "But the answer I got to the prayer was nothing but a horse laugh; so sassy, so provocating, that I fairly danced agin with the rage, that I could see nothing!" (281–82)

The significance of Paddy's inability to "see" his tormentor extends beyond the realm of this torment itself; the difficulty or impossibility of determining what constitutes Paddy's devil is akin to the frustrated attempts to name and categorize who or what threatens the Confederacy. While Wharncliffe contends that this period of conflict and its consequent development of a national identity functions as a "realm of romance," constituting a "transition of people" from "the ever hostile worlds of civilization and savage" that both "develops the richest materials for art in fiction" and forms society itself, Paddy's frustration over his demon in the stump is hardly a cause célèbre for his artistic or personal development. It's quite simply torture, of the most hellish kind. And while the devil never shows himself to Paddy, it is at least certain that he is no static figure, moving through the lives of his characters with as much ease as he does evil intent.

At the same textual moment Paddy experiences the intrusion of a devilish presence in his Edisto paradise, the *Southern Illustrated News*'s "Outlines from the Outpost" was recording the upheaval in Fairfax County caused by the influx of the war. Writer Tristan Joyeuse sounds much like Stylus himself at the beginning of *Paddy McGann* when he describes the once-quiet people and quiet streets of these small Virginia towns, places that comprised a land of "'tranquil' beauty, and smiling plenty;—of cheerful homesteads and happy people."[41] Joyeuse says that he indeed "knew Fairfax—its streets, its houses, its kindly smiling faces of true Virginians" as it once was, but now knows it also as the Yankee-transformed entity it has become, full of "sneaking watchful *Yankee* eyes and lips—eyes lurking and wary; lips simpering, guileful and 'cunning as the devil.'"[42] As "cunning" and devilish Yankee eyes have replaced the "kindly smiling faces of true Virginians," so too has something devilish moved into Paddy's home. But Paddy's demon is not so easily named, in part because of the many shapes it assumes.

Paddy's demon next appears in the form of a buck that supernaturally evades Paddy's usually infallible aim. The experience leaves Paddy wondering about the possible forms the devil can and will take and desiring, even more powerfully, to confront this force that is ruining his life:

> I was so desperate of heart that I felt sure I could face any Devil, let him be never so black! It's true, I thought I'd already seen him, plain enough, in that same old buck, but I felt agin that that warn't his *natheral* shape, tho' what that was I couldn't think. . . . it was only his Devil way of disguising himself, when he took the innocent figger of the buck. (293)

The term "buck" at this time was used primarily to refer to a black man.[43] Like the slaves in "The Little Incendiary," this "buck" is initially suspect in an evil encounter, yet finally deemed innocent. Paddy's demon is not the slave, the inherently innocent figure plantation ideology positioned as the moral charge of white slaveholders, but the Devil who can assume any number of shapes, even that of an innocent buck. But while the devil is not a buck, per se, he is still a racialized being—"I felt sure I could face any Devil," Paddy says, "let him be never so black." And it seems significant that the episode ends with a racing train engine that practically runs both Paddy and the buck down, a force evocative of the industrialized North. If the demon isn't precisely the Union and what it represents, it's certainly aligned with it.

This same issue of the *Southern Illustrated News* includes an episode in the serialized "Outlines from the Outpost" titled "My Horse, and Some Animals I Have Known."[44] The horse, named "Buck," suffers from a fear of losing all things of luxury, shying frequently because, as Joyeuse concludes, he has become "too comfortable in life."[45] Nevertheless, Buck redeems himself in battle, being "in action . . . perfectly well behaved."[46] In fact, Joyeuse claims that Buck

> does not exhibit any extraordinary emotion at the roar of the cannon. With equine inconsistency he is far more easily startled by a field mouse in a fence corner, or the sudden appearance of a hostile stump, around an angle in the road, than by the heaviest firing in battle.[47]

It seems that Buck is much more effective in battle than in a setting in which sudden intrusions to his otherwise peaceful existence—including, significantly given the piece's proximity to Simms's novel, a "hostile stump"—disrupt and disturb him. The column could easily be a comment on the ongoing conversation among Confederate leaders, as to the feasibility of enlisting slaves to fight in the war. While the idea of arming slaves was troubling enough to many Southern whites, more problematic was the likelihood that these slaves would be granted their freedom at the end of their service.[48] In any event, while both of the "bucks" represented here are in and of themselves inherently innocuous, this doesn't mean they can't be appropriated by a much more suspect source.

Paddy of course does eventually encounter his own "hostile stump," one that he fights for hours, red eyes blazing at him from deep inside it. Determined to win his battle on the second try, if not the first, Paddy notes that he "went into the fight as the Lord's soldier—a volunteer,—and though a poor sodger enough, yet I was full of faith, and I felt bold enough to say to myself that I woudn't show the white feather, even to the devil incarnate!" (332). The devilish stump eludes him, though, reappearing some time later as a log on a raft Paddy has been contracted to take "down river," full of slaves, cattle, and provisions. The raft itself functions as a kind of microcosm for the plantation-based society of the South. Paddy and the slaves have "a jolly time of it going down," living "together like a well rigilated family that hed enough; where every one knowed what he hed to do, and was willing to do it; and we had time enough for fiddling, and singing, and dancing" (338). Of course, the devil breaks up this merry band, and after a night of wild carousing, Paddy's raft is somehow cut free, and Paddy finds himself drifting out to sea. The culprit turns out to be the demon stump that then throws Paddy overboard and dives to the bottom of the ocean when Paddy tries to grab hold of it to save himself. Paddy nevertheless survives and eventually is rescued from the shipwreck by the Brigantine, *Adele* (335–70).

Captain Wilson, the *Adele*'s commander, is en route to New York, and thus begin Paddy's adventures in the North. Before they land, the Scotch captain gives Paddy a lecture on the "Amerikin charackter": "'It's a nation of rogues and swindlers. Their only idee of vartue is *smartness*, and they uses their smartness only to take a fellow in! The only difference between 'em, any whar, is that one man is a *smarter rogue* than the other" (373). Offended, Paddy tries to defend himself as an American, but here Captain Wilson makes the distinction that the Southern Paddy is "one of the *geese;* the *fox* is in your feathers!" (373). Simms uses this section of the novel to clarify what separates the North and South ideologically and culturally. The same issue of the *Southern Illustrated News* that finishes with this segment of *Paddy McGann* includes a longish letter by the mock foot-soldier, "Turkey-Foot," about the difficulty of distinguishing between Northern and Southern troops on the battlefield. "Turkey-Foot" blames the armies' mutual use of a stars and bars flag: "The union was the same, the colors were all the same, and when the flags drooped round the staff in that sultry July day, it was impossible to distinguish them."[49] In effect, this portion of *Paddy McGann* poses the same problem: as long as they are contained within the same nation, North and South cannot be recognized as the clearly separate entities Paddy will soon discover they are.

The sections of *Paddy McGann* that appear in the following issue of the *Southern Illustrated News* begin to directly address the idea of Yankee lying and its prevalence in the particularly New York Northern press. The chapters of the novel appearing in the April 25, 1863, edition of the paper include a conversation Paddy has with several New York press men who are following up sensationalized stories of Paddy's shipwreck and ocean rescue. They engage in a conversation about secession and once the reporters leave, Ellick Thompson, another Scotsman on board the *Adele,* tells Paddy that the men who edit these three papers are "three of the arrantest cowards in all New York" (381). He goes on:

> "the worst of all is, that them three newspapers are pretty much the rulers of these people. They lead 'em back and for'a'd as they please. Here are three notorious poltroons, notorious rogues, notorious liars— stock jobbers, swindlers, and leviers of black mail—everybody in New York knows it—and yet the papers make their way and rigilate the politics of thousands and thousands. They flatter the people, in every way, at the expense of the best citizens; and the people are daily tickled—to their ruin! They are jest hurrying them on to the Devil!" (382)

When a newspaper account appears reporting a con to which Paddy falls, it is coated in anti-Southern rhetoric, and the *Adele*'s Captain and Thompson reassure Paddy of both the inconsequence of such reportage and the unwiseness of any adverse public response to it. "Don't you mind it, Paddy!" they tell him, "nobody minds the newspapers here in New York. Their business is lying, that's what they goes for" (409). Arguing that the paper in which that particular article appears makes its business by lying about the South, they again advise against trying to catch the editor responsible for its printing: "Ef you was to go to his office you'd niver see him. He is only a human throat, that does nothing but vomit again the South! He's not a human at all" (410). Paddy concludes his record of the episode by saying that he indeed prayed that he might have a "chaince for a clip at the infarnal editor, who was ividently inspired by the divil" (410). As Paddy puts it, New York is "'a sort of hell on airth'" (383). "Yankeedom" in *Paddy McGann* is just that, and Simms's use of the metaphor is entirely in keeping with the images already circulating in the popular Confederate press.

This same issue of the weekly includes one of the many published calls for talented writers of Confederate literature. Claiming that future Confederate authors need to carefully select appropriate literary models for their own productions, the editors argue that "if the mind is crammed with sensation trash, such as is usually found in Yankee novels, you will, of course, form a flat, silly style. A young girl who has seen nothing of life, ... re-produces, very weakly, the style, the character, the stuff of her reading in Yankee essays, sketches, or yellow back novels."[50] It is in fact literary figures like the ones here described that Paddy will meet in New York—newspaper men as well as the authors who gather at an elite

New York literary salon Paddy attends—and who will most seem to poison the town in which Paddy suddenly finds himself. As Wharncliffe says early on in the narrative, when Paddy asks if he might borrow a copy of Sir John Froissart's *Chronicles of England, France, Spain, etc.,* "You shall have it whenever you want it, Paddy, and reading it will be apt to keep the Devil from troubling you. A good book is the Devil's worst enemy" (305). Advertisements appearing in the May 2, 1863, issue of the *Southern Illustrated News* for *The Confederate Spelling Book, with Reading and Spelling Lessons for the Young* reiterate the significance of such "good books" in the Confederacy's configuration.[51] Simms's novel ultimately reinscribes the notion that Confederate editors worked very hard to impress upon their readers; namely, that Confederate newspapers and books were essential not only to the nationalist project of asserting Confederate autonomy from a Northern-controlled print culture, but to the spiritualized and militarized project of casting out the demons of Yankeedom. But a Confederate readership was not quick to respond to such calls. As Alice Fahs notes, Simms himself was quite bitter about the turn his career took during the war. Mourning his sudden lack of opportunity, Simms lamented that his occupation was "utterly gone, in this wretched state of war & confusion," and that he no longer found "refuge in my wonted employments."[52] "Nobody reads nowadays, and no one prints," Simms wrote, "my desks are already filled with MS.S. Why add to the number?"[53] Who was to blame for this "wretched state of war and confusion," however, remains a question to be answered, much like the one surrounding the identity of Paddy's demon.

Paddy's adventures in New York continue, leading him into observations on the black population of the city (406), the New York literati he encounters (422–32), and the carefully detailed, if brief, mention of the dishonorable way in which women are treated in the Northern city (438–40).[54] All of his experiences in New York only further convince him of the ungodliness of the North and the Yankee sensibility bred there. But given the "hell on airth" New York obviously already is, it seems odd that Paddy's demon wouldn't bother him there. Only once in New York does Paddy hear the "hoo! hoo! hoo!" sound that marks the demon's presence: when he is celebrating with a group of Southern-minded friends. The core of this demon, as Paddy himself notes, seems to lie within Paddy himself.

Once Paddy and the narrative return to South Carolina, the conversation turns to Paddy's bachelorhood. Paddy's mother joins forces with the wife of his friend, Sam Hartley, and the two put all their energy into convincing Paddy to marry. But Paddy is very particular about the conditions under which such a union would be favorable to him. When a couple that can "speak to each other's thinking, and to each other's feeling, though, perhaps, with niver a word to say on either side," marries,

> "living together in one house, having the same ockypations day by day, the same interests, and heving the care of the same things, the two hands working together, and not in cross-grain, agin each other, it's supprising how much good work is done, and how pleasant it is in the doing. It's this pleasant working together, onder one law, that makes marriage such a pleasant sitvation and condition; and, ef this working together be wanting, then all its other pleasures are only so much husk and shuck, that burns up in a rush, and gives out no good heat, and lasts but for a minute." (465–66)

Unfortunately, the marriage Paddy eventually makes to Susan Pogson is of this latter kind, and the events and the consequences of this unhappy joining—Susan turns out to be the dreaded "fool" Paddy claims earlier he would not marry, and her family, rapacious and trashy—occupy the novel's final pages. Paddy receives several supernatural warnings of the ill-effects of his particular union, one from a friend speaking beyond the grave and another from the demon himself who appears just as Paddy undresses in front of the mirror on his wedding night. The red eyes appear in the window of his nuptial bedroom and a voice cries and moans, terrifying Paddy's new bride. Finally the voice speaks:

> "'So, Paddy, you've gone and done it, and I'm done with you! I'll trouble you no more; and now you'll find, ould fellow, you're in worse hands than mine iver waur!'
>
> "With that the window was slammed to; and then I haird the crying and moaning agin, getting softer and softer, as ef 'twas going off; and in a leetle while I haird nothing more! And I've niver haird it sense; and for two years I've been free of all trouble in the swamp, and on the river, and in the woods; and my luck has come back to me; and I kin shoot as well as iver; and ef 'twant for one thing I'd be the happiest man in all creation!"
>
> "What's that one thing, Paddy?'" I asked.

"I'm MARRIED, Stylus and oh! Lord, gentlemen, very good friends
and masters, after all my kear, and painstaking, and watching, and
inquiring, I MARRIED A FOOL! A FOOL! A FOOL! A FOOL! (490)

With these words, Paddy drops out of the narrative, leaving, as we soon
discover, to fight in the war not long thereafter.

Wharncliffe finishes Paddy's tale for him, indicating the horrendous
marital situation in which Paddy finds himself. (The Pogson family into
which Paddy has married turns out to be completely void of any honor
or financial independence, and before long, while Paddy is providing
for his new wife's whole family, they attempt to take over Paddy's estate
and turn his mother out of her house.) Wharncliffe tells his friends that
it is clear that Paddy needs a divorce; unfortunately, the laws would
favor his wife: "Nothing short of entire escape from such a connection
could prove remedial; and our laws afforded opportunity for the victim" (502). In the end, the only form of escape Paddy is able to take is—
significantly—the war. In Wharncliffe's words:

Paddy, as you perceive, has volunteered for the war. What the poor fellow
will do when it is over, is a problem; meanwhile, he suffers much more
than he shows, and is so wretched when he thinks of his condition, that
I verily believe he will cheerfully seek and encounter more risks in battle
than are required for any degree of bravery. He keenly realizes, in his
domestic experience, how far inferior is the grief and misery of being
haunted by the Devil, than of being married to a Fool! (505)

If readers had been convinced that Simms's depiction of his demon in
the stump correlated simply with the Yankee devils found elsewhere on
the pages of the *Southern Illustrated Newspaper,* this ending may have
given them pause. Although there is significant argument against reading
this section of the text as an allegorical injunction against the union of
North and South—a couple that certainly does *not* share ideas and work
tasks in the way Paddy argues a correctly joined pair must—an ill-devised
marriage that could only be left by going to war would surely have hit a
chord with Confederate readers.[55] But if Paddy's marriage was to a fool,
and the demon that haunts him is now happy to discharge him to those
"worse hands," then Paddy's possession must have other possible meanings. In fact, particularly given the position in which Simms and other
writers found themselves, Paddy's demon could in fact represent the
situation in which Confederates now found themselves: seceded, at war,
underresourced, and undersupported. While certainly intertextually

drawing upon the multifarious images in the press of other demons and devils linked to Abraham Lincoln and the North, Simms's demon of the stump is finally less simplistic and pointed than these. The fact that this demon is never fully comprehended, never conclusively defined, never even clearly seen, points to the final problem, perhaps, of Confederate nationalism itself—namely, the contradictions and ambiguities that attended the attempts of its cultural agents, trying to define this peculiar identity.

"Traitor or True?" or, Who's Fighting Who?

As Appomatox approached and a peace-seeking Confederate commission worked in Washington, D.C., editors of the paper busied themselves with speculation: "it is said that Lincoln is co-operating with the malcontents in the Confederacy, who are determined to end the war on any terms, however humiliating."[56] The lack of certainty evidenced here about what would happen once the war was over certainly characterizes the cloudy, doubtful atmosphere of this moment. If the Confederacy was at its end, how would editors of magazines and weeklies like the *Southern Illustrated News* reconceptualize who they were and what they were doing? In fact, the murky nature of Confederate identity and its possible slippages is an issue already apparent in the fiction published in the paper.

The February 27 issue of the 1864 *Southern Illustrated News* includes a tale of the daring escape of one Confederate scout from a Yankee stronghold. Captured by a group of Yankee cavalrymen, the scout tries to convince a Yankee captain that he is actually a Union soldier. In order to "prove" his Federal loyalty, he leads them to his picket post but eventually shoots his way free of the battalion before his true identity is discovered. According to the paper, the episode illustrates the "daring character of our scouts, and the ease with which a resolute and assured demeanor imposes on the cowardly foe," but it also demonstrates the slipperiness of these national distinctions.[57] The problematic fluidity of Confederate identity becomes the focus of another story to appear in the *News*.

"Traitor or True?" is a narrative about two Confederate soldiers who discover that they love the same woman; one will marry her while the other will die of fever. The story opens when the two meet on the road, but Harry Lyme and Irvin Fendall spend the first full segment of this serialized story just trying to decide if they are fighting for the same side or not. The narrator informs us that neither man is willing to reveal his identity for fear of lethal repercussions; "they were on the Debatable Grounds," says the narrator, "and it was hard to tell friend from foe."[58] The sheer number of names by which these characters are "known"— Lyme is at once Harry, Lyme, Mr. Jenkins, and Blue Jacket, while Fendall is simultaneously Fendall, Fenn, Irvin, and Mr. Smith—indicates the instability of identity that creates the primary tension in the tale. Lyme and Irvin watch each other closely in order to catch every discernable clue about the other's possible national alignment, but they come to no conclusions until they encounter "a darkey on a mule."[59] Lyme—here referred to as "Blue Jacket"—asks if the slave has seen soldiers about.

> The negro grinned, and seemed indisposed to answer. "What kind of sogers you want me to tell you is about here, sah?"
>
> It was so ludicrous to see the negro as noncommittal as themselves, that both the travelers burst out laughing, in which the negro joined, without knowing, probably, what it was about.
>
> "Any kind, old man," said Blue Jacket, after he had restrained his risibles. "It don't make any difference to us which kind they are."
>
> "But ef dey catch you, it gwine to make a difference wid you, cause dey gwine take you off certain, ef you don't belong to dere side."[60]

Eventually the slave tells them he's seen Union soldiers "swearin' dey was gwine to root out all de rebels about dese parts," and Blue Jacket/ Lyme threatens him with a pistol for calling his "masters" rebels.[61] Blue Jacket/Lyme's angry response to the slave is apparently enough to indicate his Confederate leanings to Smith/Irvin but later Lyme will doubt Irvin's Confederate loyalty because of his patience with the slave.

The incident here is telling. While neither white man is willing to reveal his identity to the other, it is via their interactions with the black slave that the white men come to understand each other—to in fact *know* each other. Although they laugh to see the "negro as noncommittal as themselves," in fact it is the slave who best understands the centrality of relativity in determining identity in a white world. This finally hostile encounter with a black man is the incident that ultimately reveals who the white men are. They argue—falsely—that it doesn't matter to them "which kind" of soldier the slave has seen, yet it is not the identity of these other soldiers that determines the identity of the main characters, but rather their treatment of and interaction with the black man. When

Irvin remarks that Lyme shouldn't have been so hard on the man, Lyme retorts that Irvin shows "*your* colors, sir," meaning that his patience with the black man could indicate abolitionist leanings.[62] In effect, it is by virtue of the slave's blackness that Irvin's own "colors" are known.

As the two men spot a group of horsemen in the distance at the end of this first section, they consider the dangers that lie both in front and behind them:

> [Lyme] argued that there was no use in going back, as they were fleeing from danger behind; and it was now both 'fore and aft,' as he expressed it, and there was no chance in turning off from the road, as that involved being lost and bewildered in the mountains, they had as well face the danger in front as it was on their way, and trust to good fortune to get through. His companion was not long in coming to the same conclusion, and they re-commenced their journey, not only weary in body, but harassed in mind at the obstacle which presented itself, and the doubt as to their future movements.[63]

This seems as fitting a description of what the Confederate citizen faced after the war as any contained in the pages of the *Southern Illustrated News*. Certainly, the future of those who had defined themselves in this way was in great question and constituted an obstacle not seen before in the United States. While the story seems to resolve this conflict of identity, readers would have noted that the issue of who identifies with whom arises again at the end of "Traitor or True?" when in a dying delirium, Lyme accuses Fendall once more of being a traitor. The story unravels its tapestry of Confederateness much more quickly and easily than it knits it. "'I know you,'" yells Harry, "'traitor that you are!'"[64] As present-day readers, we thought this issue was resolved. Confederate readers, on the other hand, would have been close to realizing that it was unlikely it ever would be.

As the war crawled to its end, cartoons representing blacks in the North appeared with greater frequency in the *Southern Illustrated News*. The issue of February 20, 1864, includes a cartoon captioned "The Yankee Soldiers' Nightmare. A Vision of the Black-Horse Cavalry," which depicts a black man with a bit in his mouth and a whipping Yankee on his back; the image is intended as a satiric jab at Union efforts to bring freed blacks onto the battlefield.[65] The June 11, 1864, issue includes a similar cartoon, entitled, "An Illustration of the New Yankee Doctrine about the Darkey." It shows a wide-eyed black soldier running from the battlefield while a white officer tries to stop him, saber held high. In the caption, "Cuffee" tells the white officer: " 'No, sah! can't go back dar—dis chile too 'motional for dat sorter thing."[66] By moving the black man northward, the *Southern Illustrated News* indicates a new designation for the Yankee: the new caretaker of the black, one who will crack the whip to make the former slave do *his* bidding. Taking the slave north transforms the Yankee into an inept and cruel slaveholder. In both cases, at the war's end and in the period that followed it, it was neither the Confederate nor the Yankee who would, however inadequately, determine the identity of the other. Rather, the African American would once again become the re-racialized casualty of a whiteness that blinds.

SIX

What the Railroad Brought:
The "Heathen Chinee" and a Nation in the West

Then I looked up at Nye,
    And he gazed upon me;
And he rose with a sigh,
    And said, "Can this be?
We are ruined by Chinese cheap labor"—
    And he went for that heathen Chinee.
                    —Bret Harte, "Plain Language from Truthful James"

Eastern cranberries are coming over the railroad.
                    —*Golden Era,* November 14, 1869

As the former Confederacy entered the Reconstruction period and white Southerners fought against federal forces in an effort to reinstate their economic, political, and racial supremacy in that region, Westerners found themselves pulled by the steadily chugging locomotive "inexorably... into the capitalist orbit" of the postwar North.[1] In the May 1, 1869, issue of San Francisco's weekly story paper *The Golden Era,* one enthusiastic writer sings the praises of "the now daily expected completion of the great continental railroad which is not only to unite but with bonds of iron to draw us towards the older Eastern states":

> The feeling of isolation that has hitherto oppressed us has almost vanished. We feel that we are now indeed one of the great family of equal States that compose this great nation, and no longer a mere colony or outside dependency, owned by the nation of which we were too distant from the centre to form an actual part.[2]

In the May 15, 1869, issue, writers for the *Golden Era* note that the celebratory ceremonies for the much-anticipated joining of the Central and Union Pacific railroads had been held the preceding Monday, May 10, at Promontory Point. But this description carries with it a cynicism implicitly critical of the market forces at work that day:

> Two trains, one from the East, the other from the West, approached. The Chinamen laid all but the last rail, and all except the last tie. This was put in position by the Superintendents of construction of the two roads. Several distinguished gentlemen then drove spikes that fastened the last rail in place. . . . After the conclusion of the ceremony, the fancy "last tie" and spikes were torn up again and hacked into fragments by the crowd, to keep as mementoes, while ordinary ones were put in their places by Chinamen in the usual manner. *Viva la Humbug!*[3]

Even as the line's completion was hailed as the greatest technological achievement of the United States to that date, its significance for California's residents was complex and contradictory. The accessibility afforded by the railroad line would draw California more resolutely into the nation's economy; this meant both the possibility of greater economic development for the West and a lessening of control over that economy by Californians themselves, this last also a potential threat to a budding sense of Western American identity.[4] As Confederate editors prompted their readers to stop buying Northern-produced periodicals, so Californian editors urged their readers to support their region's literary productions and help fund the creation of a Western Americanness.[5] Eric Foner notes that as the network of the transcontinental railroad grew and subsumed the autonomy of individual farmers, merchants, and citizens, "the railroad increasingly appeared less an embodiment of progress than an alien intrusive force that disrupted traditional economic arrangements and channels of commerce and threatened the independence of individuals and local communities."[6] In 1869, the railroad became one of the most crucial and visible sites of cultural and economic conflict in the popular Western press.

At the same time the railroad is complicating and potentially threatening the idea of admittedly nascent Western Americanness, the Chinese emerge as an equally contradictory element in the California press, functioning as the region's central racialized other and the best illustration of the dilemma of American freedom and economic possibility. Western periodicals like the *Golden Era* decry the increase in visibility and political movement of the Chinese, a situation that is also always linked to the larger shifts in American identity occurring as a result of the passage of constitutional Amendments 13 through 15, arguing in favor of a nonviolent, but nevertheless disenfranchising, course of action in relation to the Chinese. This was also the moment in which Bret Harte became a nationwide household name because of his parodically poetic articulation of the position of the Chinese in the American imagination. As Gary Scharnhorst and other scholars have noted, Harte's "Plain Language from Truthful James" or "The Heathen Chinee," the nickname the poem received and the title by which it was better known, gained a popularity previously unknown in the realm of American literature.[7] According to Ronald Takaki, that popularity had an obvious link to the events at Promontory Point:

> The publication of Harte's poem was timely.... thousands of Chinese, released from railroad employment, were moving into the cities and becoming very visible.... By the end of 1870, there were three workers— two white and one Chinese—for every job in San Francisco. But fear of Chinese labor competition was no longer confined to the West, for Chinese laborers had begun working in a New England shoe factory three months before Harte's poem reverberated in the print media. The poem helped to crystallize and focus anti-Chinese anxieties and paranoia, its rhymes evoking from white America a nervous chuckle.[8]

The two papers to which Harte contributed—the San Francisco weekly *The Golden Era* and the more self-consciously literary *Overland Monthly*—both include dozens of references to the Chinese in their issues for 1869, the year that both anticipated and saw the joining of the Union and Central Pacific railroads.[9] References to African Americans, Native Americans, and Mexicans also appear, but never with the frequency or consistency of the references to the Chinese. By the early 1870s, as a result of "their rapid demise due to military annihilation, malnutrition, and disease," Native Americans in California were "no longer perceived as obstacles to Anglo civilization."[10] And although California racists did not forget the African American, "white Californians were never drawn into the same frenzied competition with blacks as they were with the thousands of Chinese immigrants who also immigrated into the state during the goldrush period."[11] The sheer number of Chinese immigrants in the state—in 1860, 34,935 of the 146,528 foreign-born California residents and in 1880, more than 75,000 at their highest point—in part ensured their position as the region's most visible, exploitable, and consequently threatening cultural other. The Chinaman or so-called "Chinee" becomes metaphoric for the loss of economic control that accompanies the transcontinental railroad's finished presence in California. The editors and publishers of these journals see themselves as harbingers of the true future of the United States, figuring the East of both the Chinese and the United States as representatives of a corrupt past of which California wants no part. The image of the Easterner and the Chinese of the Far East begin to blur in their appearances in the press, a slide that reveals a deep cultural anxiety over market control and regional identity spurred by the railway's joining of the eastern and western United States.

Whenever the railroad is discussed in the *Golden Era,* it spawns a series of repeated concerns. The editorial page for the July 24, 1869, issue includes articles that discuss the issue of women's rights, the recent Republican State Convention where the Fifteenth Amendment's implications for the citizenship and suffrage of the Chinese were discussed, and the problematic benefits accompanying the Union-Pacific Railroad. All three issues occur again in the September 19 issue. "Women and Marriage" argues that advocates of the women's rights movement "either take ground openly against marriage or seek by covert sneers to weaken its hold upon the public mind"; "Where the Money Goes" explains that money not going into the Californian economy is not necessarily being sent back to China by the Chinese laborers who earn it, but is actually being invested in Eastern manufacturing because of a dearth of products manufactured on the West coast; and "The Southern Pacific Railroad" offers an update on the beginning of the San Diego and Gila Railroad.[12] The railroad never rides alone in the California press. While it seems to promise greater opportunities for exporting goods, it also promises a greater market for Eastern goods and potentially devastating changes in California business practices overall. Its construction relied heavily on foreign immigrant labor—namely that of the Irish and Chinese—but such an immigrant population, now freed from this work by the railroad's completion and newly related to the nation by the Fifteenth Amendment, represented yet another "crisis" in American identity, one exacerbated by the movement of women into the public economic sphere. This chapter will focus on the first two of these issues—the way in which the transcontinental railroad fueled an anxiety over Western

Americanness, an anxiety typically figured in the press by the Far Eastern Chinese—leaving the question of the role of women's rights in the making of Californian identity to chapter 7.

What the Engines Said

In her work on the railroad's role in transforming American life in the late nineteenth- and early twentieth-centuries, Sarah H. Gordon argues that national unity and a stronger sense of national identity both resulted from the growth and expansion of the railroad in America.[13] She notes that the increased mobility for citizens made possible by the railroad lessened the import of local and regional institutions on those who came and went via the train throughout their jurisdictions.[14] While the secession of Southern states and the advent of the Civil War halted the laying of track and construction of railways in the South, the Pacific Railroad Act, signed into law by President Lincoln on July 1, 1862, chartered the Union Pacific Railroad Company and launched the first wide-sweeping attempt to reach the West via rail.[15] After the war, dominant Northern interests dictated the resumption of such construction: "Northerners tended to abide by William Seward's dictum . . . that the entire country had to have the same economic system. Local and regional differences could not be allowed to stand in the way of national unity based on commerce."[16] This last point—that to the policymakers of the North, the idea of national unity was based in commerce—is key to understanding the events following the completion of the transcontinental line. The Civil War itself had made apparent the benefits of a wide-reaching, fast, reliable system of transportation that could cart supplies, weapons, ammunition, and troops to needed areas. The railway hospital cars that picked up, cared for, and carried the wounded to safety even laid the imaginative groundwork for the Pullman sleeping car.[17] But it was the standardization and unification of the economy across the country that most motivated the railroad's Northern and Eastern backers.

As Gordon indicates, the expansion of the railroad in America was always fraught with conflict of some kind. Even while the push for profit led to the inevitable (and desirable, for those seeking to gain from that profit) consolidation of the nation's individual regions and parts, that unification had a cost. "Trade was based on competition," Gordon says, and

the idea of union was based on cooperation. The two forces never coexisted peacefully, and the rail service became an amalgam of both:

the network of rails that brought distant communities together, and the agent of cutthroat competition that drained the public purse (through state bonds and other considerations) for private gain. And even while distant communities came into contact with each other, common interest was not always the result.[18]

The train directly benefited Northeastern business and a centralized national government that was also based in the Northeast. The attempt to bring the country together with the railroad—an act that would further profit these institutions and the regions where they were centrally located—opened a Pandora's box of social, political, legal, and economic conflict:

> The railroad's need for legal help became legendary as townspeople and farmers fought to preserve their land and their own safety from the loud, dangerous, and apparently unstoppable steam engines. . . . Different towns passed different laws, creating a patchwork of regulation without uniformity or consistency. . . . Train travel uprooted people from all regions and generated the crowds that became a new and permanent feature of the American social order, eclipsing the old bulwarks of community, family, and church. . . . Efforts by the railroads to eliminate competition concentrated the ownership of the roads under a few men from the major urban centers of the North. Crowds of travelers swamped the cities, drawn to the centers of the greatest wealth. The cities quickly grew to unprecedented and unmanageable proportions just as the population and wealth of smaller towns began to stagnate. Cities welcomed the crowds, which translated into profits for stores, restaurants, theaters, and hotels, but they did little to control crowd behavior or protect the weak from the strong in crowds of strangers. . . . Thus the centralization of wealth and services advanced the national economy but left behind many individuals, towns, and even states. . . . In the drive for national unity and prosperity, some were left behind and unable to go home.[19]

Gordon's retrospective view of the railroads' effect and influence ends on a contradictory note, at once progressive and gloomy. And the California press will echo this dichotomy, although before the railroad is finished, writers for the *Golden Era* laud the "progressive" and racialized work it will certainly do.

In early 1860, nine years before the completion of the transcontinental railroad, the *Era* remarks that even if Congress and the press have forgotten the Pacific Railroad, white Western Americans have not:

The case is no longer that of a single community pressing for an avenue
through vast tracts of uninhabited wildernesses, to a tenantless harbor
upon the unpeopled coast, but that of the united longings of two great
communities, composed of the people of the same blood, race and origin,
bound together by a national tie and linked in a common destiny.[20]

Here the railroad promises to help "settle" the country and give it "form,"
as well as "inhabitants."[21] Ignoring the existing populations in California, this *Era* writer contends that the West will now no longer be a "tenantless harbor" and with the railroad's completion will come "the establishment of large, enterprising and wealthy communities upon the
shores of the Pacific."[22] The communities calling for this linkage are
racially coded: the railroad will serve those "people of the same blood,
race and origin, bound together by a national tie and linked in a common destiny."

As we might expect, early references to the railroad in the *Era* are op-
timistic and largely so in terms of the "waves of immigration" the cars
promise to carry: "The first waves of the great stream of immigration,
that once fairly started is to sweep over and fill with a hardy, industrious
and enterprising population the entire coast of the Pacific, have already
reached us, and their influence is felt from one end of the State to the
other," the *Era* claims; "We have talked and prayed for the good time
that was coming. . . . Let every one be awake to the fact and improve the
golden opportunities the present affords."[23] A little more than two months
before the completion of the transcontinental railroad, when anticipa-
tion of the railroad's beneficial effects ran high in the California press,
an article entitled "Commerce" by "Rev. J. Gierlow" ran on the front
page of the *Golden Era.* "Commerce" argues that commercial enterprise
and a liberal, strong government were necessary bedfellows. "It can
scarcely be denied," says Gierlow, "that commerce is intimately connected with the free institutions of government—the only soil in which
it is raised and nurtured to perfection."[24] Commerce breeds liberty and
visa versa for Gierlow: "the pure air of liberty is necessary to the existence of commerce, as the favoring breeze, which wafts the vessel to the
haven where she would be, and steady laws, administered upon settled
principles, indispensable as the compass by which she is steered."[25] Gierlow's readers would have interpreted his article as an affirmation of
the increased economic development of California that the railroad

promised, and an increase in the very freedom possible in the far western state as a result.

A piece in the *Era* recording the thrill attending the ceremonies at Promontory Point that was written prior to the actual celebrations ends up being a false prediction. The writer of "The Present" fairly sings in the "report":

> as the hammer fell, the electric spark flashed over plain, mountain and valley to either ocean, and instantly a thousand cannons belched forth their joyful thunders, bells rang out their merry peals, and the flag of our country, now more than ever united, was flung to the breeze amid the rejoicings of young and old.[26]

But this writer wrote too soon. A short follow-up piece to the article, joyously entitled "To-Day!" explains that "a bridge or two upon the Union Pacific Railroads had been carried away by freshets," delaying the arrival at Promontory Point of some of the event's dignitaries, causing the proceedings to be postponed. "Our readers may therefore," requests the *Era*, "please postpone the reading of the foregoing for a couple of days, when it will be alright."[27] The great unification of the nation promised by the joining of the Union and Pacific lines, is nothing more than a fantasy here—and potentially a terrible disappointment.

The page of the *Golden Era* that actually commemorates the completion of the railroad—the fourth editorial page—also includes a segment of the continuing "Soliloquies of Betsy Barnes," a series of reflections of a young, single, California-emigrated woman by the pseudonymous "Nancy Nettle." The May 15, 1869, column, entitled, "She Attends the Railroad Celebration," criticizes the effect of the railroad on Californian society, showing that despite the public acclaim for the unification of the nation the line enables, individual happiness may well be its cost. Betsy bemoans the "bluster" of the celebration: "It's nothing but jam and push and crowd all the time. . . . didn't hear one word, nor see a soul that I know, or ever shall know, and lost my pocket handkerchief that was trimmed with lace. I've carried that handkerchief six year."[28] Betsy reports being "squeezed to death in the crowd," and claims that she hopes this "iron wedding, as they've called it, or the wedding of the East and West" won't fall apart in six months "because they have found their *real* affinities somewhere else. They will probably get up too much steam occasionally, and run off the track, but I don't think a divorce should be

granted even for that."[29] Despite the crush of people around her, a crowd
that causes Betsy to lament the ruin of her silk dress—someone in the
crowd spits tobacco juice on it—Betsy's real concerns lie with her own
singularity: "What will become of me, anyway?" Betsy asks, "here I stay,
cooped up, don't know anybody that I care for or cares for me, and
might die here, for all I see."[30] Betsy's story—printed side-by-side with
the joyous descriptions of the end of the railroad's construction—offers a valuable counterpoint to what was celebrated in popular rhetoric
as the "wedding" of the century. Betsy explains that she came to California after her father died and her family situation became intolerable;
after a period in the Lowell mills, she ventured west. But Betsy's Eastern
demeanor doesn't help her much in California. "Women who have been
here so long are so bold, they aren't afraid to face anything; I know it
never would be so with me, never!" she says, and even though she insists that "nice, modest, fresh women, just from the States, are thought a
great deal more of than these old stagers," unlike the rail line itself, Betsy
just can't seem to connect with anyone.[31] She came west, as she explains
elsewhere, to find a rich husband; what she's found instead are isolation, poverty, and loneliness. The market "marriage" and commercial
unification promised by the railroad obviously comes in part at the cost
of individual lives.

Betsy's narrative is bordered by a guest column by Eastern writer Ned
Buntline, in which he muses on the effects of the railroad's completion.[32]
Buntline did not emigrate to the West, but visited the region as a paid
correspondent and representative of the Grand Division of the Sons and
Daughters of Temperance—essentially, the 'tourist' Gordon discusses
who experienced a very different California than did emigrants like the
fictionalized Betsy Barnes.[33] According to him, California now can

> begin to be understood, to be valued and she will take her merited place
> among the states. With ample resources to employ and subsist outside of
> her minds, in fruit and grain cultivation, from eight to ten millions of
> people, with the noblest forests the eye ever looked upon—the healthi-
> est and most varied gradation of climate that can be found in the world,
> she must and will fill up with a population worthy of her and her
> institutions.[34]

Not only does Buntline ignore the native and nonwhite populations
currently residing in California when he calls for the railroad to bring
to California a population "worthy of her and her institutions," but he

also overlooks people like Betsy Barnes who, despite their unquestioned whiteness, have limited access to the profit incurred by those ample resources.

In the November 7 issue of the same year, another writer for the *Era* argues that anxiety regarding the future economic and political health of the state is groundless:

> Last week we chanced to pick up a paper professing devotion to the interests of the laboring classes, in which all sorts of gloomy predictions were made. Had we been a new-comer, unacquainted with the State and the character of the sheet, we should have purchased a return ticket without unnecessary delay. We were told that the leading and most influential bank in this State is about to fall; that Chinese are soon to supersede whites in nearly all departments of labor; that all the land in the State is in the hands of speculators, and can be bought only at ruinous prices; in a word, that California is about the worst place a poor man can find.[35]

But when a collision on the Alameda Railroad line occurs in November of 1869, it sparks hot criticism in the *Era* regarding the responsibilities of this new institution. "When railroad companies know they will have to pay roundly for slaughtered men and women, they will place some value on their lives," one commentator remarks. "Corry S. Pondent" writes into the *Era* to say that *someone* must be at fault for the deaths: "Probably [the Western Pacific Railroad] can answer for this switchman's sins, as, 'in the nature of things,' they will mostly be required to do, in way of exemplary damages."[36] Here what is "gloomy" in the shifting landscape of California's new railroad culture is the dwindling value of a human life. The lead editorial in 1869's final issue of the *Era* claims that the year has provided Californians with "more than ordinary prosperity," and that, despite the drop in business traffic, "the people of this State have no cause to complain.... If old Californians cannot come down to the methods of business that elsewhere prevail, new Californians will take their places. The country in itself has resources that will compel it to advance."[37] What national membership meant at the end of 1869 as spurred by the Union-Pacific Railroad's "iron wedding" seems to be an acceleration of industrial progress, of the distribution and marketing of regionalized goods, and a willingness to embark on a journey that privileged a national economic health over the individual well-being of its citizens—an economic system based in the centers of wealth in the Northeast.

The frontispiece for the more genteel literary organ, the *Overland Monthly*, includes a small engraving of a bear stepping onto a railroad track with the caption, "Devoted to the Development of the Country" (see Figure 22). In his introduction to the journal and his explanation of this image, editor Bret Harte encapsulates a desire for cultural exchange and a hope not to be overrun in the process:

> Here creeps the railroad, each day drawing the West and East closer together. Do you think, O owner of Oakland and San Francisco lots, that the vast current soon to pour along this narrow channel will be always kept within the bounds you have made for it? . . . Will the trains be freighted only with merchandize, and shall we exchange nothing but goods? Will not our civilization gain by the subtle inflowing current of Eastern refinement, and shall we not, by the same channel, throw into Eastern exclusiveness something of our own breadth and liberality? And if so, what could be more appropriate for the title of a literary magazine than to call it after this broad highway?[38]

Harte's emphasis on the mutual "inflowing" of things other than "goods" is largely realized in the *Overland Monthly*'s attempts to explore and demystify cultural anomalies like the Chinese in its lengthy, carefully detailed features. But when Harte discusses the emblem of the bear on the frontispiece, his anxiety about the repercussions of this become apparent:

> The bear who adorns the cover may be "an ill-favored" beast whom "women cannot abide," but he is honest withal. Take him if you please as the symbol of local primitive barbarism. He is crossing the track of the Pacific Railroad, and has paused a moment to look at the coming engine of civilization and progress—which moves like a good many other engines of civilization and progress with a prodigious shrieking and puffing—and apparently recognizes his rival and his doom. . . . Look at him well, for he is passing away. Fifty years and he will be as extinct as the dodo or dinorinis.[39]

Harte lingers on the positive attributes of the bear, a symbol for "our San Francisco climate," and mourns his inevitable passing in the wake of the progress afforded by the railroad and represented in the *Overland Monthly*'s title image. The *Golden Era*'s masthead features an Indian looking off into the setting sun, alluding in part to "his" extinction as well

THE

Overland Monthly

DEVOTED TO

THE DEVELOPMENT OF THE COUNTRY.

VOLUME I.

SAN FRANCISCO:

A. ROMAN & COMPANY.

1868.

Figure 22. Frontispiece for the *Overland Monthly* 1, no. 1 (July 1868). Courtesy of California Historical Society; FN-36028.

Figure 23. Masthead for the *Golden Era* (6 July 1862). Courtesy of California Historical Society, North Baker Research Library; FN-36019.

(see Figure 23).[40] While both papers incorporate progress into their signature images, the *Overland Monthly*'s representation of the bear crossing a set of railroad tracks lends an air of tension to the picture.

In "What the Railroad Will Bring Us," published in the *Overland Monthly* in October of 1868, Henry George attempts to offer a similarly balanced speculation on the effects of the railroad's completion. Highlighting the fact that an increase in the state's wealth and prosperity will *not* mean an equitable distribution of that wealth, George explains that the great benefits promised by this accomplishment will most likely be most enjoyed by a select portion of the population. "Those who have lands, mines, established businesses, special abilities of certain kinds, will become richer for it and find increased opportunities; those who have only their own labor will become poorer, and find it harder to get ahead," he explains carefully.[41] Noting that "one millionaire involves the existence of just so many proletarians," George claims that what has truly been the essence of California is a liberality of feeling—"a certain freedom and breadth of common thought and feeling"—resulting from the state's unique history and its many different human sources.[42] Yet when imagining the problematic changes to come, George notes that already one negative shift has occurred: "the 'honest miner' of the placers has passed away.... the Chinaman, the millowner and his laborers, the mine superintendent and his gang, are his successors."[43] The primary threat to Californian uniqueness is this loss of personal control over one's labor, a loss prompted and perpetuated by the railroad, but symbolized by the replacement of the "honest miner" with the "Chinaman."

The appearance of the Chinese in the San Francisco press shows how the repercussions of the Fourteenth Amendment of 1868—granting citizenship to all native-born persons, primarily former slaves—and the perceived repercussions of the impending Fifteenth Amendment to be ratified in 1870—ensuring the vote for all American citizens, despite "race, color, or previous condition of servitude"—were experienced in California where the most significant and visible racialized alien was the Chinese. Despite attention to the racial violence and persecution directed toward the Chinese, and various attempts to demystify them, the San Francisco press continued to maintain distinctions that kept the Chinese well beyond the boundaries of American national belonging. At crucial moments, though, the Chinese begin to be confused or collapsed into a different Easterner—a Northeastern. This conflation holds California up as a locus of future national possibility rather than an extension of a necessarily corrupt Eastern past. While seen as a threat to free labor policies and white domination of financial resources and jobs, the Chinese also come to represent larger fears in the West among white Californians about a loss of regional economic control that is inevitably tied to the railroad's completion.

"The Heathen Chinee"

Just as the California press represents the railroad and its implications in highly contradictory ways, so too does it represent the Chinese population that was so vital to, yet maligned in, the region.[44] As Ronald Takaki has observed, Harte's most popular and focused pieces concerning the Chinese in California are often ambiguous in their racial categorizations.[45] According to Takaki, while "Plain Language from Truthful James" "negatively stereotypes the Chinese" in the person of "Ah Sin," the cheating, crafty Chinese euchre player, it also portrays Bill Nye, the "American" card player, as brutally violent, equally dishonest, and not nearly as intelligent or successful as Ah Sin.[46] Takaki argues that "while [Harte] protested against the injustices committed against them, he perpetuated anti-Chinese racism through his images of them as 'heathens' and threats to white America."[47] Harte's 1863 contribution to the "Bohemian Papers" column of the *Golden Era* is a typically conflicted example of his writing regarding the Chinese. "John Chinaman" seems in fact to be the basis for Harte's longer story, "Wan Lee, the Pagan" to which Takaki also refers.[48] When noting that "John Chinaman" "cut marvelous imitation roses from carrots for his little friend," Harte adds that he is "inclined to think that the few roses strewn in John's path were such scentless imitations."[49] And although Harte expresses sympathy

for the persecution the Chinese endure, he nevertheless himself stereotypes the Chinese man in his story as "John Chinaman." This John Chinaman, with whom Harte conducts "weekly interviews involving the ad-
justment of the washing accounts" is effectively infantilized as "generally
honest, faithful, simple and painstaking." It is John's simplicity that most
occupies Harte's attention as he relays a story about the "sad and civil"
Chinaman who takes Harte literally when Harte wryly remarks to him
that, rather than just partially, he'd just as soon have the buttons of his
laundered shirts completely torn off. When John returns the clean shirts
the next week, he brings them "with a look of intelligence, and the buttons carefully and totally erased."[50] It's not clear if this is part of Harte's
ironic sense of humor, if he intends to expose his own stupidity at under-
estimating the intelligence of John Chinaman who turns Harte's sarcasm against him, or if he indeed blames the mishap on the laundry
boy's inability to understand such irony. The message regarding John
Chinaman's craftiness versus his "faithfulness" and "honesty" is finally
unclear.

But the *Golden Era* in general exhibits internal conflict in its depictions of the Chinese. In the January 16, 1869, issue, a note appears regarding an incident that occurred in Unionville, Nevada:

THE WHITE PEOPLE of Unionville, Nevada, have just driven away the
Chinese who had taken up their residence at that place. It was feared that
the superior industry and intelligence of the Chinese would effect a
monopoly of trade and labor in that locality.[51]

The classification of "whiteness" here is unexpectedly defined in ironic
contrast to the "superior industry and intelligence of the Chinese." This
racially coded conflict takes place in a town named for the newly celebrated, if fragile union of, American states. While it is clear that the
Chinese of Unionville cannot hope to consider themselves part of the
American Union, given their not-white racial categorization, the end of
the note seems self-consciously accusatory. The Chinese are *not* driven
out because of their savagery, but because of the fear that their labor
would eclipse that of the whites in Unionville and consequently "effect a
monopoly" of Chinese trade there. The note is, perhaps not surprisingly, tucked away on the eighth page of the paper, one dedicated not to
news, but to advertising.

In "Imitation," a piece published on the *Era*'s editorial page on November 28, 1868, one writer notes that the Chinese in America are in fact learning to imitate Western behavior and are doing so by virtue of their use of the popular press. The article notes that some American-based Chinese are circulating stories in the Chinese popular press regarding injustices enacted upon their countrymen in China at the hand of American missionaries; apparently, American magazines and newspapers have done the same in regard to the Chinese in this country. Officials in China responded to the perceived threat against American missionaries, the writer insinuates, as have their American counterparts in this country:

> The Police Judge, probably, remarked that his business was to punish violence, not to prevent it—a very natural remark when his sympathies were all for his own people, and not with the "disgusting foreigners." The people could not remain quiet while Chinese babies were being boiled for medicine, and rose and mobbed the missionaries, very much in the same style as we have mobbed Chinamen here occasionally. They broke into their houses and destroyed all their property. They beat and bruised the ladies connected with the mission, and set fire to the house and tried to burn the inmates with it. The ladies were compelled to throw their children from the upper windows and jump after them to escape from the flames with their lives. One of the ladies was within a month of her confinement. The Rev. Mr. Reid had his eyes so badly injured that [sic] is doubtful whether he will not lose his sight. No arrests were made.[52]

The writer turns up the sarcasm at the end of the piece when he rhetorically asks "who shall say the Chinese are not rapidly adopting the ways of western civilization?" and adds that, while the example of the missionaries in China had its own impact on attitudes toward America, "the example of the Americans in their own country was by far more powerful and had its effect."[53]

Certainly such an editorial is an unqualified attack on the behavior of racist Americans, particularly Californians, who openly persecute the Chinese by way of false rumor and circulated bad press. But the beginning of the piece cagily reminds readers of a remark made earlier in the paper that the Chinese in this country are assuredly clipping the articles in American newspapers that spread false and damaging rumors regarding their behavior "to draw upon the politicians hereafter, all the illiberal assertions and arguments made use of against his countrymen, when after their naturalization as American citizens under the new treaty, they appeal to them for their votes."[54] In other words, the real danger here is one yet to be realized, when the American-based Chinese use the scathing commentary provided by American newspapers to their own political advantage once they are granted suffrage and legal membership in the American national community. While the editorial argues against persecution of the Chinese in this country, the reasoning behind it seems to stem from a fear tied to the passage and expected passage of the Fourteenth and Fifteenth Amendments and their repercussions for California politics.

Other articles and stories are more overtly racist in their depictions of the Chinese. Ned Buntline, writing under his pen name, "Colonel Judson," begins writing for the *Golden Era* in early 1869, and his pieces range from short fiction to travel narrative to personal commentary. A story entitled "Sacrilege, or a Story about Valley Rest" tells the tale of the return of a California girl, "Dream Elmore," to her once-happy childhood home, Valley Rest, with her paramour, "George R." Valley Rest has been corrupted by a range of unsavory types, including a band of Chinese:

> On a little further, and the cottage, once so white, except where covered with vines and flowers, was in sight. No flowers or vines were there now—old mats and rags hung on its roof and walls, and they were black with smoke and dirt. Leeks and cabbages grew where poor Dream's lovely roses had blossomed.
>
> "Oh, this is sacrilege!" she murmured, as tears came in her dark, hazel eyes. "All that was so beautiful is destroyed—my arbors are torn down—the very birds have fled!"
>
> George drove on. A crowd of dirty, opaque-eyed Chinamen looked up from their labor and grinned like ring-tailed baboons as they gazed at their carriage and their occupants.
>
> "Where shall we stop for our pic-nic?" asked George R.
>
> "Anywhere but here. It is madness to think what Valley Rest once was and is now! sacrilege! sacrilege!" cried Dream. "Oh I would give everything but my immortal soul to own it, so that I could drive these Vandals away and make it beautiful once more!"[55]

George R. promises Dream that she "*shall* possess it!" and when Dream looks up into his determined eyes, she whispers to herself that she has "met my destiny" and adds that, "if I ever do possess it, these Vandals will be taken with a sudden desire for travel."[56] Once George R. and his

Dream return and reclaim the land, "the streams ran clear once more, the flowers bloomed, the birds returned and all was beautiful again."[57] The "dirty Vandals"—the simian-featured, "opaque-eyed" Chinese— have literally blackened Valley Rest, a place that in Dream's memory was once "so white."

Buntline makes no bones about his feelings regarding the Chinese elsewhere in the *Era*. In his "Traveling Editorial Correspondence," he laments what he depicts as the Chinese tendency to lessen the "dignity and value of labor." Such a comment calls up visions of an endangered free labor system coded white and offers a good example of the way racializing the Chinese as alien contributed to the project of free-labor advocates who "believed that social mobility and economic independence were only achievable in a capitalist society unthreatened by non-white populations and the degrading labor systems associated with them."[58] The Chinese are "pagan creatures," completely culturally alien and morally compromised: "no trust can be placed in them—the quarters they inhabit reek with filth—they drink to great excess, smoke and eat opium to madness—gamble and quarrel more than any other class, and nowhere win respect by any line of good conduct."[59] All of this is something Buntline claims to have only recently come to understand:

> One thing strikes me—and it is striking me more and more as I travel over the State, and in this town more than perhaps anywhere I have been—that the Chinese are getting too strong a foothold. I was prejudiced in their favor from what I had read before I came to California. Now the prejudice is all the other way.[60]

For Buntline, sympathy with the plight and situation of the Chinese is an Eastern property, much in the same way the Western press of Minnesota depicted sympathy with the Dakota as being confined to the Northeast in 1862 and 1863. Aligning the United States Easterner with the Far Eastern Chinese is a telling affiliation, one that will reveal another possible back story for this racialized anxiety and a different manifestation of blinding whiteness.[61]

Elsewhere in the *Golden Era* there is clear distrust of Eastern United States interests in a discussion of a proposed colonizing project utilizing the Chinese. An untitled news brief appears on the same page as Ned Buntline's story, "Sacrilege," detailing the terms of a grant made by the Mexican government to "an eastern American company... energetically engaged in the scheme of colonizing that region ["Lower California"] with Chinese emigrants."[62] According to the article, the grant allows for a range of protected freedoms for the Chinese emigrants: the establishment of an autonomous system of government and taxation, religious freedom, the ability to import—duty-free—a range of goods for ten years, and finally and most important the right "to have conveyed to them such lands as they may require or desire . . . at a trifling advance on the cost of said lands to the Company, together with mining and fishing privileges."[63] The final sentence of the piece reads: "It is asserted by the Company that the enterprise will recive [sic] the sanction and encouragement of the United States Government, and that Minister Browne, formerly their agent in this country, will use all his power, in his official capacity, to aid the scheme."[64] The Chinese indeed pose a danger, this article seems to suggest, but it's not necessarily a savage one; rather, it is the danger of invasion, of redefining the notion of American identity which itself has historically been defined by way of property ownership. While another, albeit less racially alien group—the Mexican government—is behind this project, the supposed "sanction" offered it by the U.S. government is the most chilling chord struck for the writer of this piece. The question of whose interests the federal government will represent—white Californians or a foreign body like the Chinese—problematizes California's actual inclusion into the nation at large. Considering who is portrayed as standing *behind* the Chinese may begin to show the way in which the Chinese of the Far East and the Easterner of the "other" American coast become theoretically and linguistically aligned.

"The Only Spot Fit for a White Man to Live"

In "What The Engines Said," a poem published in the *Overland Monthly*'s editorial column "Etc." a month after the completion of the transcontinental railroad, Bret Harte sweeps away "the popular rhetoric in regard to 'indissoluble ties,' 'wedding of the East to the West,' etc.," and provides a poetic rendering of what the two locomotives themselves *really* "said" when "their pilots rubbed together, symbolic of the friendly salute of their respective owners" at the laying of the line's final tie.[65] According to Harte, the onlookers for this event wildly misinterpreted this gesture. The locomotive "from the WEST" brags that it has crossed "Sierra's crest" while the "Engine from the EAST" claims to have "chased the flying sun," seeing "all he looked upon."[66] But the Western engine argues that what constitutes the East is somewhat misleading here:

"Come now, really that's the oddest
Talk for one so very modest—
You brag of your East! *You* do?
Why, *I* bring the East to *you!*
All the Orient—all Cathay—
Find through me the shortest way.
And the sun you follow here,
Rises in my hemisphere.
Really—if one must be rude—
Length, my friend, ain't longitude."[67]

Who will define what the East—and what America—means is a matter of contention, as is the issue of who will import that Eastness where. Harte's Western engine poses the very threat that would capture the attention of many more readers when "Plain Language from Truthful James" was published. If the East means the Orient, then the East also means the Chinese; to tell the United States Easterners that this engine will be bringing "all the Orient" to them is both a promise and a threat. Harte's poem plays with the idea that the connection of America's coastlines via the railroad further destabilizes what that Americanness—East *or* West—might mean. Of course, this conflict masks a cultural fear, one realized in Dr. J. D. B. Stillman's report on the finishing celebrations for the line's completion in his "The Last Tie." In his witnessing of the event, Stillman reveals the truly invasive force in this scenario. "We Californians were too few to make much noise," he tells his reader. "We did the best we knew; but we were swallowed up in the multitude that came up from the East."[68]

The alignment of the Chinese with the Eastern sector of the American nation happens on other, more obvious levels. In the August 14, 1869, issue of the *Era*, a "Free Discussion" about the persecution of the Chinese finally concludes that anti-Chinese action will only result in a draining of Eastern sympathy for the West. The writer argues that the Eastern centers of American government and business are indeed envisioning a West that meets their needs and they "will have their way."[69] The Chinese will not only be encouraged to come west in even greater numbers (something of which the writer is clearly not in support), but, as universal suffrage is at present the universal panacea for all our ills, John Chinaman will soon be made a citizen, and neither National nor State Constitutions or legislation will be allowed to stand in the way of so great and desirable a result, as our Eastern friends now view it. To do this, the ideas of those who consider the interests of California opposed to those of other sections of the country will be laughed at, or despised and disregarded, and California will be forced to take John Chinaman as a man and a brother, whether he is welcome or not.[70]

Again, as Ned Buntline argued, Eastern sympathy for the Chinese is a force with which Californians must contend, but this writer goes further, arguing that the concerns of the Chinese and the (North)eastern centers of American power are practically indistinguishable. While not going so far as to racialize as alien these residents of the Northeastern United States, this writer points to the fact that "the interests of California" are "opposed to those of other sections of the country," and that this fact is one for which its believers will be "laughed at, or despised and disregarded." Although not nearly as confrontational, Rev. A. W. Loomis's "The Old East in the New West," published in the *Overland Monthly* in October of 1868, also forces the image of the California Chinese into a semiotically slippery zone. Promoting California as a place where Americans can experience the farthest corners of the world (an alienness most vividly embodied in the persons of the Chinese), Loomis's article inadvertently uses the term "East" in an increasingly overdetermined way. Juxtaposing the youth and rebelliousness of California to the rest of America, Loomis's "East" comes to symbolize both the ancient cultures of China and the oldest, most tradition-laden region of the United States. The absorption of the Chinese resident into Western American society parallels the similar absorption of the Easterner into a supposedly less traditional, less fixed cultural and social environment in the American West.

Loomis begins by pointing to the contrast contained within the state itself: "Here, where the Occident exchanges salutations across the waters with the Orient, the youngest born of states is brought into near neighborhood with the oldest survivor of the sisterhood of nations."[71] Noting that what distinguishes California is its "strange mingling of elements," Loomis paints a picture of San Francisco street life where convention and tradition are abandoned: "The independent Californian dresses as he pleases; he dares to wear a hat that suits himself, whether Paris and

London, New York and Boston, approve his taste or not."[72] The Californian is unique and unfettered by a need for cultural validation; it is significant that those from whom he does *not* need approval are in part his peers in New York and Boston. A "visitor from the East" materializes in the essay only to passively observe the activity around him from his "luxurious" rail car. According to Loomis, what California has to offer such a tourist is a scene he would otherwise have to travel to the ends of the globe to see, but Loomis's placement of the traveler in an isolated and contained railway car highlights *his* otherness in this scene, *his* inability to be a part of it.

The essay returns then to the issue of the Chinese, including a brief explanation of the characteristic Chinese respect for and obedience to family elders. Loomis tells the story of one wayward Chinese prodigal son in the West (whose crime was largely to set aside his "national costume" and cut off his queue) who is brought into line swiftly and painfully by an older male relative. This kind of familial relationship, notes Loomis, would be an anomaly in the American West: "The docility of these youth, their respect for age, and the cheerfulness with which they usually submit to the control of those of superior age, stand out in strong relief as compared with Young America."[73] California's strength lies in its "newness," its youth, and its daring and dashing away with convention. As far as the Chinese are concerned, though, even these customs will pass away in time: "as the years roll on, the power of home influences will weaken, and national superstitions, national prejudices, and national fashions, will all loosen, and by degrees be forsaken and forgotten altogether."[74] Even the Chinese, undeniably alien as they are, will assimilate and lose their "national superstitions, national prejudices, and national fashions" once California exerts her steady and determined influence.

Loomis's essay continues to privilege youthful attitudes over age-bound traditions. San Francisco's Chinese schools are termed unfavorably "ancient" in comparison to the newer American versions, institutions that have suddenly cropped up in the West like the glorious mansions of self-made men to which Loomis refers in the essay's first paragraph. "We need not stop," Loomis says, with a figurative sweep of the hand, "to point out the difference between these ancient schools imported from the shores of the old world, and . . . the magnificent school buildings of our young city and state."[75] Loomis ends the article with a call to newness, a call to catch the latest waves of American possibility and make what is possible to make of them:

> Surely the old things are passing away, and passing faster than most people are aware. Nothing can resist the rushing tide of reform. Better that we adjust ourselves to the circumstances of the times. He who is alert to improve the turning tide, and to catch the first favoring breeze, is wise; while he who would attempt to beat back the current and to still the winds, because the best likes the quiet waters and the calm, is insane.[76]

While in part anticipating public resistance to the changes the railroad will bring, Loomis here directs his reproach to those not already identified as Californians. The call to the future, Loomis says, is in the West; the East is antiquated, tradition-bound, corrupt. But who exactly embodies the East is tricky here; the Far Eastern Chinese will—and are—adapting to life in California in ways that, as Loomis says, will soon show those "home influences" to be forgotten. The Easterner less likely to adapt and the one more reluctant to jump on the future-bound West-coast train is the Eastern resident of the United States. Clearly, Loomis's West is no transplanted East, but rather a new America yet to be realized, one composed of rebels and outcasts. The question is not whether the West will be "civilized" by the East, but whether the Easterner can get off of that train, cast his tourist garb aside, and "catch the first favoring breeze" of his own Western future. The figure of the Chinese in this essay functions less as a racialized alien and more as a metaphor for the American East from which Californians will even more resolutely have to distinguish themselves.

Certainly the control of California government and business centers by the Northeast was a real issue for Western Americans and it is therefore not surprising that a racialized language would be common in these conversations, whether they involved the Chinese or not. "First Impressions of the East, by a Returned Californian" appeared in the *Overland Monthly*'s October 1870 issue and was written by James T. Watkins. The essay records the impressions, indicated in the title, of the narrator's first trip east in fifteen years. Watkins uses a racialized language to privilege the Americanness of the West; calling himself a "representative Californian," Watkins's narrator proudly and defensively refers to his belief that California is "the only spot fit for a White Man to live in."[77] Given the cultural gulf between West and East, as well as Watkins' undying loyalty to all things Californian (what Watkins calls the "White-fitness" of California stems as much from the state's climate and the all-season strawberry than anything else), the central tension in the piece is whether or not Watkins will "like" the East at all (352). In fact, the article ends in an indeterminacy: when asked whether or not his "First Impressions" of the East "are favorable," he replies, "perhaps they are," and when asked whether or not "I am disposed to rather like it," Watkins hedges with "possibly I am" (361). The article certainly plays up this ambiguity, at once asserting the majesty and prosperity of the great Eastern cities of New York and Boston while simultaneously offering equally unattractive descriptions of Eastern manufacturing and architecture.

While Watkins praises the evidence of the "so much work done" by the "great numbers of peoples—of millions of peoples" that he scans from his spyglass as he moves up the New Jersey coast, he consistently indicates an inability to grasp "in a compact and complete way, the idea of this population" (356). It is quite literally more than he can handle, and as he continues to explore the New York region, Watkins's descriptions begin to emphasize how overwhelming and overbearing this East is. Traveling by the mansions along the Long Branch coast, Watkins notes that "these vast caravansaries are for the accommodation of a small portion of that minute portion of the swarming population of New York" (356). Not just overwhelming, Watkins's East is as impenetrable and impervious as the unbroken brick line of New York's coast:

> Solid. No gaps, no vacant spots, no scattering outskirts in sight; there is no boundary at all in sight; to the right, the vast red sheet rolls over the Brooklyn hills out of sight, and directly before us is spread away as far as the vision ranges, until it sinks behind its own thickness. Solid. Miles. I do not know how far... you can follow it rolling away over the Brooklyn Heights, but it is miles. Also, it is piled up—six stories, five stories, seven stories, wherever your eye rests, it appears that the city is piled up; it is as a building upon a building. It was thus that the great city came upon me, and stagged me; and it was thus, as I looked at it, that its features—the characteristics new to the Californian—impressed themselves upon me. It was Red, Solid, Piled-up, Miles. (358)

Oppressive in its stolid, red nature, New York causes Watkins to feel "diminished," as he compares himself and San Francisco to the world he now experiences on the East Coast (359). Speaking of his unfashionable clothes, Watkins notes that he was afraid his "appearance was disrespect-

ful to people whom I might meet.... I stood an embodied indecorum"
(359). Claiming over and over again to find this East Coast fascinating,
Watkins's descriptions nevertheless reveal it to be relentless, engulfing,
and overpowering. He feels diminished, his home city shrunk in his
imagination, his senses of wealth and size all knocked out of propor-
tion. He is humbled by the East, he says, and finds in it a truism, a "moral
which all these things have borne for me, the Californian":

> from the red light of furnaces, from the huge, black piles of building,
> from the sign-boards of the towns—every thing has spoken to me of
> Manufacturing. The old first principle that Wealth is concrete Labor, has
> come upon me with something of a more vital meaning: I have seen it in
> application in a large way; the night's ride has spoken of laboring arms
> and busy hands by the thousand and ten thousand; I have seen how one
> great natural resource, admitting of cultivation, is Muscle. (361)

This revelation links a sense of national longing to an East-based economic power, to "concrete Labor" and "busy hands by the thousand and
ten thousand" that result in a tremendous, but tremendously ill-portioned,
wealth. The unspoken fear seems to be that Watkins will become simply
another set of those "busy hands," absorbed into this body of "Manufacturing," and lose the whiteness he has so clearly ascribed to California in the bargain. As the Chinese workers in the West threaten a racialist understanding of free labor, here the East and its representation of
the national body of the United States threatens the very core of Watkins' Californian identity, even to the point of subsuming him in a
Northeastern body of "Manufacturing." But Watkins's descriptions, evi-
dentiary of a powerful Eastern American force as they may be, are nevertheless hardly life-changing for him; his response to his own epiphany is
to fall asleep (361). Despite the wonder Watkins feels at the sights he sees,
he remains finally a "Californian," something less determined and possibly less technologically muscular than the Eastern powers he has witnessed, but also less stifling, less suffocating and invasive than the Eastern edifices that threaten to overwhelm him. Californians' tentative
embrace of the railroad and what it forecast for Western Americanness
was mediated by their own blinding whiteness, one that strove to establish a sense of racial superiority over groups like the Chinese while
struggling to maintain viability in relation to the Eastern centers of U.S.
commerce and politics. And while white Californians were ideologically
shielding their Western whiteness, they needed the practical support

and physical production of new Californians by their female counterparts in order to maintain their presence in this racial system. It is the
part played by white women in this system of white Western Americanness and the discussion regarding their rights in the California press to
which I now turn.

SEVEN

The Woman Question, Coast to Coast

"Good Lord, Jim, I can't tell it, or at least depict its horrors; for
I dreamed that the day of Woman's Suffrage had come."
— *Golden Era*, August 14, 1869

... the crime of infanticide, which includes foeticide, is so commonly
practiced that in American families the average number of children
has been reduced in little more than a generation of time, from
seven or eight to three or four.
— *Golden Era*, January 9, 1869

OUR FEMALE SLANDERER. MRS. FRANK LESLIE'S BOOK
SCANDALIZING THE FAMILIES OF VIRGINIA CITY — THE
HISTORY OF THE AUTHORESS — A LIFE DRAMA OF CRIME AND
LICENTIOUSNESS — STARTLING DEVELOPMENTS.
— *Daily Territorial Enterprise*, July 14, 1878

While Bret Harte may have gained national fame with the poem, "Plain
Language from Truthful James," his more lasting literary reputation rested
on his short stories; "Miggles" is one of these, appearing in the *Overland
Monthly* in June of 1869.[1] The story of a self-exiled prostitute who spends
her days caring for an incapacitated customer named Jim and hosts the
stranded travelers who tell this particular tale, "Miggles" can be read as
an allegory of California, one that depicts the problems that result when
Eastern ideas are imported to the West as a result of the railroad's cultural exchange. A "bright-eyed, full-throated young woman, whose wet
gown of coarse blue stuff could not hide the beauty of the feminine

curves to which it clung," Miggles is iconoclastic and something other than definitively "civilized" (125). Her clothes are often a blend of men's and women's garb (along with her "wet gown," Miggles greets the storm-stranded stage coach party in "a man's oil-skin sou'wester"), she is a former prostitute living with a former customer without the social bene-fits of marriage, and her other roommates include a talking magpie and a grizzly bear named Joaquin (125). An unconventional yet ultimately moral figure, Miggles becomes a kind of embodiment of California it—or her—self. She lives outside of the law and traditional codes of socially sanctioned "civilized" behavior; while lonely, she is apparently less so since she "picked up Joaquin in the woods yonder one day, when he wasn't so high, and taught him to beg for his dinner" (132). The fact that Miggles has made a best friend out of a grizzly bear solidifies her symbolic con-nection to the state. First appearing in 1846 on a flag for the Mexican-independent California Republic, the grizzly bear eventually became the key symbol for the California state flag.[2] The animal was chosen, of course, to grace the title page of Harte's *Overland Monthly,* and its appearance in this story as another creature for which Miggles cares suggests Miggles's role as a kind of nurturer for the state itself and the values associated with it. Beautiful, with a flashing smile and stunning dark eyes, Miggles embodies the kind of hybrid personality Harte depicts as inherently Californian.

But the arrival of the stage coach party threatens to upset Miggles' contentedness in a couple of ways. The party may contain men who have "known" her and would now bother her further or—perhaps worse—deny knowing her. Even more than the men, though, the women of the party could destroy Miggles's life's careful balance by their disapproval of her, shunning her or denying her very womanliness—both of which they do. While Miggles says that the women in the area "are kind and don't call," the two women who show up on Miggles' door are encircled by a restrictive definition of womanhood, one that does not extend to include Miggles (132). Harte notes that in the company of Miggles, "a chillness radiated from the two lady passengers that no pine-boughs brought in by Yuba Bill and cast upon the hearth could wholly over-come" (129). Despite Miggles's hospitality, the women—one French and the other from Virginia City who "had long since lost all individuality in a wild confusion of ribbons, veils, furs and shawls"—do not "partic-ipate in the general masculine admiration" of her (121, 127). This feminized disapproval deeply affects Miggles. When she is emotionally pushed out of the room where these icons of feminine respectability are sleeping, "her eyes were downcast, and as she hesitated for a moment on the threshold, with a blanket on her arm, she seemed to have left behind her the frank fearlessness which had charmed us a moment before" (130). In this respect alone, Miggles very much resembles California, a romantically idiosyncratic and morally unconventional entity that is also endangered by the visitors the train will bring to its home.

But despite what the reader learns about Miggles by way of this disappointing interaction with a civilized sense of femininity to which she cannot and will not subscribe, how different is she really from a conventional Victorian woman? While she may once have been, she is no longer sexually available; while not a conventional one, she is still a mother to her "baby" and former john, Jim, who apparently suffered a stroke on her "sofy" some years before (130). As Miggles herself explains, "perhaps it was that I never had a baby," but she is moved to sell her business, take her "baby" Jim, and move to "this yer place, because it was sort of out of the way of travel" (131). By the end of the story, the "Judge" of the company leads a toast "to *Miggles*—GOD BLESS HER!" (134). Harte's Miggles, her very body figuring as a site for California's own determination, hints at the way in which conventional notions of white womanhood, particularly the institutionalized control of white women's bodies, are unexpectedly reinvigorated in the California popular press at this time.

Despite the relatively low number of women living in the state—in 1850, just 8 percent of the total population, in 1860 still less than 30 percent, and in 1870 only 37 percent—there is a disproportionately sizeable conversation that takes place in the pages of the weekly *Golden Era* about women's rights.[3] The numerous references in the paper to women's rights indicate the crucial part played by white women in the rhetorical struggle of white men to establish racial supremacy in the West. Not a racialized other herself, the white woman in the popular California press is nevertheless contained within Western nationalist discourse in a way analogous to the containment of the slave in popular Confederate discourse. This is not to say that Anglo/European women are metaphorically enslaved in California—Chinese women were, in fact, often literal slaves in the state—but that they figure similarly and in similarly essential ways to the development of that region's sense of Americanness.

Not granted full membership in a Western America, white women in the West were nevertheless key to its definition. The white woman's body—in particular, its ability to bear and rear children—is seen as one solution to an endangered sense of white Americanness in the West. And this becomes even more apparent when a woman from the East—Mrs. Miriam Frank Leslie, wife of the publishing magnate, Frank Leslie, and New York-based editor, writer, and publisher in her own right—comes West to view what lay beyond New York's environs, publishing her account as the 1877 *California: A Pleasure Trip from Gotham to the Golden Gate*. Both Miriam Frank Leslie and her eventually controversial text represent quite clearly the threat an independent white woman could pose to white Western American identity once she moved beyond the strict social limitations papers like the *Golden Era* advocated.

"The Bounds of Sex and Color": Race, Women's Rights, and Reproductive Freedom

When the issue of women's rights is raised in the *Golden Era,* it is typically ridiculed and attacked by the weekly's writers. Women's rights advocate and lecturer Anna Dickinson came to San Francisco in the late summer of 1869 and the *Era* was quick to comment on the event. The writer of the commentary "Miss Dickinson's Lectures" argues against using slavery to describe women's status in American society, thereby softening the sense of oppression that metaphor suggests: "Is woman a slave? ... We all know that women are not bought and sold in the market. If a man wants a woman for a companion he has to approach her with due deference and win her consent to occupy that position. The wealth of Vanderbilt or Astor would not secure the possession of the most obscure woman in the land against her own will."[4] Although making a reasonable point regarding a problematic feature of women's rights rhetoric, this writer by his/her tone suggests a tired annoyance with American courtship rituals, implying that they are overly elaborate for what they achieve. S/he also conveniently ignores the very real slavery in which the majority of Chinese women in San Francisco lived. Another editorial, published the following week, claims that "the Woman's Rights movement is practically an anti-marriage movement. Its advocates almost without exception either take ground openly against marriage or seek by covert sneers to weaken its hold upon the public mind."[5] The loosening of the social and legal dictates of conventional marriage became the central concern for women's rights deterrents as well as what was most threatening to the racial supremacy white Californians sought to establish.

The discrepancies between a happy marriage and the pursuit of women's rights become the central topic of the prolonged spoof, "'Woman's Rights' at Goose Egg Hollow," signed by the popular *Golden Era* correspondent and sketch-writer "Nancy Nettle." The satire's main character, Mrs. Collins, is significantly described as a neglectful, not-very-bright mother and wife. Mrs. Collins attempts to achieve fame with her poorly penned verses that never seem to see the light of newspaper publication, and she falls prey to the cons of two men posing as supporters of the movement; one even dresses in drag to masquerade as a lecturer on the women's rights circuit itself. Depicted not only as a bad mother, but also an overly pampered wife and homemaker, Mrs. Collins has named her children for various statesmen, a fact that demonstrates her obsession with all things political. She doesn't understand the significance of the names her children bear, though, highlighting the absurd aspect of women attempting any type of politicized action. In the following description, which opens the second installment of the piece, Nettle points to the neglect that necessarily seems to attend any effort women make to reach for public acknowledgment, as well as the ill-use their hard-working husbands suffer at their wives' rights-grabbing hands:

> With half bent form and tottering steps our heroine entered her costly furnished but untidy apartment, designated as parlor, but which often served as a play-room for her uncultivated children, whose sticky, greasy finger marks were visible on windows and pier table, on rich damask and beautiful rosewood. Mr. Collins was a man of taste and refinement, who among the earliest settlers of California had reaped a rich fortune from the golden hills of his adopted State, and then looked around him upon the few women of which California could then boast, and without much wooing took for better or worse the woman—we will not say lady—who has already introduced herself to the attention of the reader.[6]

Not only does Mrs. Collins neglect the upbringing of her "uncultivated" and "greasy" children, she also neglects the beautiful furnishings her "tasteful" and "refined" husband, the sadly unappreciated Mr. Collins, has procured for her. His plight is one born out of the scarcity in California of possible available mates, but it is exacerbated by what is here depicted as the completely fraudulent project of the women's rights movement. The story ends on a depressing note. Once Mrs. Collins has failed in her attempt to rob her husband's office in order to fund her flight with the fake-lecturer's cohort in con, she confesses and suffers the disillusionment of every quixotic character. The last paragraph focuses on the fate of her outdone husband:

> In a few weeks after the events related, Mr. Collins closed up his business at a great sacrifice, and started for the White Pine mines, a heartsick and discouraged man, having first removed his family to another town. We will not disclose the name of the place, for if any of the readers of this tale should reside there or in its vicinity, we fear they will be peering with curiosity into the face of every talented looking lady they meet who wears short hair, wondering if they have not the honor of beholding our heroine, or at least a "Woman's rights Woman."[7]

One wonders to whom this story is directed; the woman of San Francisco who may be entertaining thoughts of a future political freedom, or her male counterpart who has, for one reason or another, not succeeded in the ways of love and family. Either way, the villains are clear: those agitating for greater political visibility and agency for women in the United States.

Regular *Era* correspondents "Occasia Owen" and "Dorothea" do offer counter voices to satires like "'Woman's Rights' at Goose Egg Hollow." In the October 28, 1860, issue, for instance, the predictably conservative article "Woman, the Friend and Benefactress of the World," is prefaced by the editor's comment that

> the object of her essay is to prove undeniably that when woman forsakes the quiet of her home to "vote, hold office or to lecture;" or to do anything but that which can be done quietly, sweetly and unostentatiously at home, she is unsuccessful; and we are sure no one can read the following without being fully convinced of the fact.[8]

Practically taunted into responding, Dorothea responds in the following issue with a sarcastic affirmation of her lofty mothering duties:

> Then to think of being the mother of one's own children. Inspiring thought! How I reproach myself for ever calling my precious infants little plagues! Do I not see now how it is my mission to instill in my Johnny's youthful mind the lofty and ennobling thoughts "that will strengthen the domestic and political prosperity of these United States." And let me here express a hope that the dear little child's predisposition to influenza will not be a detriment to his brilliant career. And my Polly!

E'er long she will be a woman. And what an awful responsibility rests
with me to train and qualify her to exercise that beneficial influence over
the opposite sex; and to eradicate any tendency she may have for traveling, and for political and literary pursuits.[9]

The logic against which Dorothea responds concludes that facilitating
women's movement out of the private realm of mothering and into the
public sphere can only lead to the destruction of the domestic and political prosperity of the United States. But the role race plays in this prosperity is hardly insignificant or ignored.

Regular *Era* correspondent Occasia Owen draws the parallel between
the plight of women and African Americans, highlighting the part of
sexuality in the management of race and American national membership. Not long after the announcement of the Emancipation Proclamation, she notes that

there is a new era dawning. Darkies are to be free. Next turn of the revolutionary wheel and woman will have her rights. . . . I am determined to
do my duty to my country; though, I suppose, strictly speaking, women
and niggers have none.[10]

In another column later this same year, Occasia again links race and
gender in the question of American freedom. "In this enlightened age,"
she says, "particularly in this enlightened country, progress has reached
its ultimatum. Freedom has found its legitimate bounds, the bounds of
sex and color. Let us cry, Amen!"[11] As Kathleen Diffley has noted, the
repercussions of Emancipation were making themselves widely felt and
Occasia's observations on her country's "enlightenment" points to the
connections statesmen and voters alike were making between the suffrage of members of nonwhite groups—the freed African American and
the Chinese immigrant, in particular—and the suffrage of women.

The connection between race and sex in American political thought
is apocalyptically portrayed by other writers commenting on the problems of women's rights. The appropriately pen-named "Nitro Glycerine"
paints a portrait of women's rights activists that depicts them in graphically sexual positions with African Americans. "All A Dream" recounts
an explosive vision of the "day of Women's Suffrage," one in which "Wen-
dell Phillips and a band of ferocious looking negroes . . . were throwing
water upon the throne which got so heated by the rays of the sun that
the woman upon it could not sit still."[12] The woman is Lucy Stone and

she occupies herself by fending off countless other women who want her throne as well. The men in the dream nurse babies and suffer the endless divorces obtained by their newly liberated wives while the children, "ragged, half-famished," run around unattended and motherless. One little girl swears freely because "she had as good a right to swear as the boys had, for men could no longer deprive women of the rights which they claimed for themselves."[13] The women declare war on the men and massacre them all save for "those of color, for the niggers were all obedient and willing to obey the powers that be."[14] Once the young women start lamenting that they are certain to be old maids now that the men are all dead, someone suggests that they marry the black men they have spared. The narrator suddenly sees

> my fair Julia, leading a great, black grinning nigger to the altar, and although she was smoking a cigar and appeared slightly intoxicated, still the old love for her was in my heart, and I rushed forth to rescue her, and as I did so I stumbled against the great brass throne and tipped it over, Lucy Stone and all.[15]

Somehow the world explodes then, rolling its fragments into "one huge woman who filled the whole universe," and the narrator wakes up with a voice screeching in his ear, "'Will you yield to the powers that be?'"[16] Obviously the threat the women's movement poses is one in which every aspect of social order in the United States will be, literally, blown apart. The racial categories that define American identity will be completely destroyed, once black men are granted citizenship and women move beyond the private sphere and into the realm of public political action.

While these texts in the *Era* paint the domestic sphere and the institution of marriage as those areas of American society most endangered by the women's movement, other female voices in the paper's columns mourn their inability to enter precisely this space. Nancy Nettle's long-running column, "Soliloquies of Betsy Barnes," circles the question of Betsy's domestic future like a bird unable to perch. Betsy is a single woman who left her Massachusetts mill job and came to California, as she tells us, to get a rich husband. "Fudge!" Betsy exclaims, "talk about girls going to California to get married. Here I have been nearly three months without getting acquainted with a soul that any girl would marry, unless she was in a great strait, and didn't think of anything else."[17] Betsy is low on funds, low on friends, and just low in general. She advertises for a potential husband, but this brings her nothing but more disappointment. There is nothing rosy or romantic about Betsy's condition; she is unable to wander around the city or explore California because of her gender and beliefs, and she doesn't meet anyone who might be appropriate for her to marry, so she is dreadfully lonely as well. Part of the reason her movements are circumscribed is that she is poorly paid and isn't often able to attend the functions she might like to in the city; "Sunday evening I will go to Dr. Benton's lecture that I see advertised. Won't that be splendid! I hadn't ought to pay the two bits, either, when I can go to church for nothing."[18] While comical in her desperation, the situations that Betsy describes must have seemed real enough to her similarly frustrated female readers.

Juxtaposed on the page to Betsy's complaints is Ned Buntline's account of "A Snow Storm in the Sierras." Rather than trapped in a lonely, impoverished home, Buntline says he has "witnessed many a time, with the wild exultation of a free untrammeled nature, the grandeur of storms at sea."[19] Proclaiming that the experience he had of a snow storm in the California mountains filled his "soul with thoughts of grandeur and sublimity hard indeed to describe," Buntline clearly does not live in the boring, claustrophobic, financially insecure world Betsy describes.[20] The fact that these two pieces are set side by side only highlights the world of difference between them—something of which the editors certainly must have been aware. In fact, as Betsy herself notes, the newspaper offers perhaps her only ticket to a romantic future given its marital advertisements and announcements of social and cultural events to which Betsy otherwise would not be privy.

Other texts more overtly suggest that the real threat posed by the push for women's rights and the call to participate in the public, nondomestic sphere, is the loss of an institutionalized control of women's reproduction. This is evidenced most obviously in the *Era*'s disturbing and disturbed discussions of the growing incidence of infanticide and abortion, particularly as they relate to the decreasing birthrates of the white U.S. population. Rather than generate sympathy for dead and not-to-be-born children, these pieces focus on the dropping birth rates of whites in the United States. That this would appear and reappear as a staple concern in the weekly in part helps explain the opposition to women moving beyond the domestic sphere, an example of social progress elsewhere celebrated in the abstract and as characteristic of the freedom-loving, unconventional Californian. Western American identity was about to be greatly unsettled by an influx of Easterners like Anna Dickinson who refused to perform their maternal duties; if white women were not having as many babies, what chance would whiteness have in the struggle to settle the state?

An *Era* article dated January 9, 1860, unabashedly denounces the "right" of women not willing to reproduce to participate in the democratic process:

> in many communities the number of births has been brought below that of deaths, among the strictly American population, it must be conceded that a prompt and energetic execution of the penalties of the law has become a terrible necessity, and especially that such mothers as these, who would come to the ballot-box, the jury bench and the judge's seat with their own hands reeking with the blood of the slain, could not fitly make laws, nor equitably dispense justice to others who should be arraigned before them for a crime which, they have succeeded in persuading themselves, is only a peccadillo.[21]

According to this writer, "the crime of willful destruction of human life is murder; and human life begins with the first instant of foetal existence"; women who would have less than "seven or eight" children can't be expected to have the rights of other Americans if they refuse to fulfill this first, most basic national duty. With so many other stories—Betsy Barnes's among them—focused on the quest for love and its happy conclusion in marriage and childbearing, the woman who wishes an occupation other than that of motherhood simply does not deserve American rights and responsibilities.

The racialized aspect of this discussion is frequently highlighted. A report published in the February 13 issue of the *Era* for 1869 laments the changes in the growth of the white American population. In Massachusetts,

> the number of children has increased of late years, but that increase is limited wholly to the foreign population. Thus it appears that if it were not for foreign immigration the population of Maine, Massachusetts, and doubtless of a few other New England States, would gradually become extinct. The opinion in which the ablest physicians generally coincide is that this result is caused chiefly by the crime of foeticide, which is far less practiced among the foreign than the native population of the United States, especially in the largest cities and in the extreme Eastern States.[22]

The fear that nonwhite groups would reproduce at greater rates than whites probably at least partially influenced public attitudes and policies toward Chinese women in California. While an extraordinarily tiny percentage of the total Chinese population in San Francisco (in 1852, only seven out of the total 11,794 Chinese immigrants there were women), the vast majority of these women worked as prostitutes (in 1860, 85 percent of the total Chinese female population listed on the San Francisco census, and in 1870, 71 percent or a total of 1,426).[23] While these women were more often than not sold into slavery in China or via the Chinese "tong" societies in California, they posed a theoretically significant enough threat to the dominant white population that between 1866 and 1905, "at least eight California laws were passed designed to restrict the importation of Chinese women for prostitution or to suppress the Chinese brothel business."[24] As Tomás Almaguer comments, "it appears that Chinese women in this industry were perceived as constituting a more damning influence on white men than were white female prostitutes."[25] One imagines that this anxiety had to have had as much to do with the danger racial mixing posed to the California quest for white racial dominance as anything else. And certainly the need to establish a racially hierarchical California made the part of white childbearing women extremely important, as it did anything or anyone who might upset the position of white women in the consolidation of a Western American identity.

One such threat did appear in the form of a book written by a white woman from the East. Mrs. Miriam Frank Leslie, wife of the successful and vivacious Frank Leslie, editor of *Frank Leslie's Chimney Corner,* writer for a number of Leslie publications, and eventually major endower of the movement for women's suffrage, published *California: A Pleasure Trip from Gotham to the Golden Gate* in 1877. Miriam Leslie's travelogue was the result of a highly publicized two-month tour taken in a Pullman car especially designed to carry the group of Leslie's reporters, artists, and editors. In her book, Miriam very much destabilizes conventional understandings of American women's roles in the culture and the social limitations placed on a woman's physical movement in the nation, the first and most obvious being the feasibility of a woman taking such a landmark cross-country trip. More than this, though, Miriam Leslie denies having any kind of naturalized maternal instinct, voices a researched respect for the isolated, unconventional, and ideologically alienated Mormon community, and lambasts those practices and laws that oppress the Chinese and facilitate the use of Chinese women as prostitutes and slaves. In other words, Miriam Frank Leslie imports, via her own physical being and her written abstracted one, those "horrors" the *Golden Era* character said would come with "the day of Women's Suffrage." And when she does import this dream of gender equity into the actual world of the West itself, Miriam is met with a devastating media assault, one that uses her own history as a "sullied woman" to discredit her.

Mrs. Frank Leslie's *California: A Pleasure Trip from Gotham to the Golden Gate*

The history of Miriam Frank Leslie and her book *California: A Pleasure Trip* is a concrete example of what was likely to happen when an Eastern woman spoke too freely and beyond the limits of masculine control about the West. A book full of unorthodox opinions told in a gracious and companionable voice, *California: A Pleasure Trip* gently guides its reader through Miriam Leslie's often foiled expectations of what she found in the nation contained between its East and West coasts. At least as important as the text itself—an often ironic, elegantly written book peppered with carefully drawn illustrations of settlers' cabins, California Sequoias, and Chinese opium dens—is the perception the nineteenth-century reading public had of its author. And by 1877, the public was well acquainted with Miriam Leslie.

Born in New Orleans in 1836, Miriam Florence Follin was schooled in Cincinnati and New York, and published her first piece of journalistic prose in the *New York Herald* when she had barely turned fourteen. Carefully grooming Miriam in matters of culture and intellect, her parents apparently never legalized their union—an issue that would crop up inconveniently at various times in her life, including the period following the publication of *California: A Pleasure Trip*. Not surprisingly, Miriam became someone who managed to fly in the face of social convention while appearing to uphold traditional standards for women's behavior in nineteenth-century America. Her first marriage was to a jeweler who lent her her first diamonds when she was seventeen; Miriam's mother forced the man, David Peacock, to marry Miriam, then swiftly had the marriage annulled. Miriam's next husband was Ephraim George Squier, an archaeologist and later writer and editor for *Frank Leslie's Illustrated Newspaper,* who lost his sanity along with his wife when they separated years later.[26] Their divorce left Miriam free to marry the vivacious and successful Frank Leslie in 1874. By this time, she was editing three of the Leslie titles herself: *Frank Leslie's Lady's Magazine, Frank Leslie's Lady's Journal*, and *Frank Leslie's Chimney Corner*. Sometime after Leslie's death, Miriam married for the last time: to Oscar Wilde's alcoholic brother, Willie, whom she divorced within two years.

By the end of the century, Miriam was one of the most famous women in America. Not only had she defied the conventional constraints of nineteenth-century American marriage by using divorce to her own advantage, she was also one of the most successful publishers of her time. She went so far as to legally assume the full name of her third husband— Frank Leslie—when he pointedly left it to her in his will after winning a lawsuit that barred his estranged son from using the Leslie name in his own publishing ventures. Along with his name, Miriam inherited Leslie's crippling debts, but by capitalizing on the events surrounding the shooting of President James Garfield, she was able to save *Frank Leslie's Illustrated Newspaper* and the rest of the Leslie establishment from bankruptcy. Miriam saw the Leslie publishing house into the twentieth century, rescuing it from ruin one more time in 1898; her involvement with *Frank Leslie's Popular Monthly* was completely finished in 1905. By the time she died on September 18, 1914, Miriam Florence Follin Peacock Squier Leslie Wilde had taken on yet another name and identity, if not another husband. Renaming and refashioning herself as "the Baroness de Bazus," this once queen of Publishers' Row left almost two million dollars to "Mrs. Carrie Chapman Catt . . . to the furtherance of the cause of Woman's Suffrage." Word of the controversial legacy joined that of the war in Europe on the front pages of New York's newspapers.[27]

Described as "matchless fair" in a poem by Western poet Joaquin Miller, Miriam Frank Leslie had clearly established herself as a professional woman on the frontlines of periodical publishing by the time she and her then husband, Frank Leslie, took their highly publicized Western tour.[28] Their entourage included writers, artists, and photographers affiliated with Leslie's publications, as well as W. K. Rice, son of the Governor of Massachusetts, and Follette, Miriam Leslie's Skye terrier.[29] Riding in a lavishly outfitted Wagner Palace railway car renamed the "Frank Leslie," Miriam and her cohorts were treated to the most luxurious and lavish accommodations then available. They traveled to and through Chicago, Omaha, the Platte Valley, Cheyenne, the Great Plains, Carson City, Sacramento, and finally San Francisco—the "Golden Gate" of the title.

Throughout the trip, Miriam records her experiences and the group's perspectives on the people and places they encounter, but her drive to physically experience as much as she can during the trip often conflicts with conventional notions of appropriate feminine behavior. As she once responded in *Frank Leslie's Chimney Corner* to a correspondent who inquired about the feasibility of a woman traveling alone in the Adirondacks, there could be no "serious obstacle" to women undertaking such travel, "provided they can make up their minds to leave crinolines and furbelows at home."[30] In many ways, it is Miriam's sense of propriety she must leave at home in order to make this trip, something that will return later to haunt her.

From the very beginning of the text, Miriam makes it clear that *California: A Pleasure Trip* is written from a "feminine" perspective, encoding its very means and methods of communication as intimate and "womanly." Rather than a book, Miriam contends, "this work of mine is a vehicle, through which, with feminine longing for sympathy, I convey to you my pleasures, annoyances, and experience in the journey it narrates."[31] Miriam appeals to her critics who may feel tempted to "anatomize the vapory visions of a woman's memory" rather than "remember that in all courtesy you should deal gently and generously with a work proclaiming itself from the outset not so much a book as a long gossipy letter to one's friends" (6). If the critics cannot accept the narrative for what itself proclaims to be, then the author reminds them that "to competently judge a woman's letter or a woman's book, one must have learned to read between the lines" (6). Miriam slyly acknowledges, then disrupts, the masculinized social control under which she as a woman, and particularly a woman writer, labors. From the very outset, Miriam Leslie simultaneously pays homage to and shrugs off a set of patriarchal assumptions, assumptions that include both the way critics read and the purpose behind writing at all. She will continue this pattern throughout the book.

Even though Miriam Leslie travels with her powerful husband, (a man to whom she even refers as "Chief"), she hardly travels under his wing. As is evident throughout the text, Miriam refuses to allow Leslie or any of the other authoritative masculine figures they encounter to usurp her opportunity to fully experience her trip. With her typically light touch, Miriam notes upon the party's leave-taking a "word to my long-suffering sex bound upon voyaging, near or far":

do not consent to share bag or valise with any man unless you wish to find collars, cuffs, and ruffles crushed into a corner beneath a pair of boots, your tooth-brush saturated with liquid blacking, and the contents of your powder-box distributed throughout the whole, ready to fly out at any moment, proving that even your complexion is not a right that anybody is bound to respect! (23)

Miriam's makes the startled yet comical observation that even her "complexion" is not considered a "right"; traveling into the West will further complicate this most naturalized and seemingly inherent of traits, including the racial designation it implies.

Beyond helpful hints to other traveling women, Miriam repeatedly indicates her unwillingness to be corralled in any way during their voyage due to her gender. When the party arrives in Cheyenne and is preparing to begin their exploration of this "H—ll on Wheels," as Miriam notes it is popularly known by its inhabitants, their conductor advises against "any night exploration, at least by the ladies of the party," due to Cheyenne's mining and desperado populations, "all utterly reckless in the use of the bowie-knife and pistol; or, at the very least, in the practice of language quite unfit for ears polite" (45). This advice certainly does decide the matter, but not in the way the conductor expects: "the three ladies, as one man, declared fear was a word unknown in their vocabulary, that purchases essential to their comfort were to be made, and that exercise was absolutely necessary to their health" (45). When the men of the party agree to accompany them and arm themselves in order to act as bodyguards, Miriam notes that the women "huddled together, far more affrighted at their friends than their enemies" (46). When men act in a clearly gendered, masculinized way, they end up acting absurd *and* dangerous. But elsewhere danger is exactly what Miriam craves. While staying at the Palace Hotel in San Francisco, the party visits the Board of Brokers where a cache of mining stocks were to be sold at historically low prices. The scene, according to Miriam, "was one of the wildest excitement, reminding the young lady of a gladiatorial arena, the Sultana of a flock of hungry chickens, to whom some corn had been thrown, and myself of the fact that I was only a woman, and could never hope to join in such a soul-stirring combat. . . . the excitement was contagious, and the writer would have given worlds to be six feet high, deepen her voice to a baritone, and be in the midst of it all!" (138).

Perhaps the most brazen example of Miriam's attempts to reach beyond conventional gender constraints is when she claims her turn to interview the venerable and mysterious Mormon leader, Brigham Young, a man with whom Miriam is fascinated. The "Chief" is speaking with Young when Miriam approaches and asks to "change places with him as we had some information to ask of the President" (97):

> The Chief rose with suspicious alacrity, and for the first time a gleam of interest shone in Brigham's pale blue eyes as he turned them upon the bold intruder, whose first question was:
> "Do you suppose, Mr. President, that I came all the way to Salt Lake City to hear that it was a fine day?"
> "I am sure you need not, my dear," was the ready response of this cavalier of seventy-six years, "for it must be fine weather wherever you are!"
> The conversation established after this method went upon velvet, and, as the rest of the party began to talk among themselves, presently assumed a confidential and interesting turn, and we felt that what Mr. Young said upon matters of Mormon faith and Mormon practice he said with a sincerity and earnestness not always felt in a man's more public and general utterances. (97)

One of the most intriguing sections of the text, this particular episode shows the "womanly" discourse Miriam utilizes. Evident in the "cavalier" and sexualized interest with which Young obviously responds to her, as well as the intimacy and privacy such conversation permits, Miriam's feminized rhetoric here proves to be much more effective in gathering candid information than that used by her esteemed journalist husband. It's also important to note that this husband is "suspicious" of what Miriam is about to do, indicating what is clearly her pattern—an assumption of control and authority in a situation not in keeping with a highly feminized woman. Miriam's portrayal of the success of her approach is also clearly gendered; the conversation that follows her takeover of it "went upon velvet," and causes Young to reveal information he ordinarily would not. Given Miriam's description of the book as a whole as a "gossipy letter," we can see here how much she privileges—and has perfected—the art of confidentiality, a discourse coded feminine, but that assumes a professionally assertive agency.

During a visit to a Chinese opium den in San Francisco, the detective escorting the group through this shady environment offers to show them "as strange and tough a sight as you want to see, if you like to risk it, for the ladies" (162). In the following chapter, entitled "Worse Than Death," the detective stops before the door of a "dark and dismal court, whose odors seemed even more sickening and deadly than those we had breathed before" (163). Say the word, he tells them, "and I will take you in": the word is, as Miriam perfunctorily notes, "said," and they enter a Chinese brothel. Miriam has much to say about what she sees here:

> The women were mostly without beauty or grace, and usually dressed in dingy blue sacks with huge sleeves, their hair drawn back and curiously puffed, coiled or plaited behind. They all wore the mechanical smile which seems part of the national character; but their faces were thin and haggard, and the paint did not disguise the wan weariness which was eating away their lives. These poor creatures are most of them bred to evil from infancy by parents who make merchandise of them in early girlhood. Sometimes the wretched creature sacrifices herself, signing a contract and receiving a certain sum in advance for services during a term of years or for life; the larger part of which sum goes to the broker or intermediary. These slaves—for they are so considered, and, as a general thing, are very harshly and penuriously treated—receive only a maintenance and coarse clothing during their brief period of health, and when overtaken by sickness are turned out to die in any hole they can creep into. (165–66)

In probably her most politicized section of the book and one that redefines the political nature of the kind of "gossip" Miriam shares, Miriam here notes that this treatment of Chinese women forms "a terrible satire upon the hecatomb of the best lives of our own country sacrificed in the late way to abolish Negro Slavery!" (166). She ends the chapter with an accusation and a "HUMILIATING CONFESSION" (167). She notes that Chinese men have few inducements to bring wives with them to the United States, in part because of "our own people, who permit ruffians infesting San Francisco to rob, insult and maltreat the Chinaman at every turn, revenging upon him, as is the habit of degraded natures, the galling sense of their own baseness and inferiority" (167). And she completes the chapter with a revelation she depicts as shocking: "We were informed that the most beautiful and accomplished imported Traviatas in China Town were intended for and maintained by white gentlemen exclusively" (167). While clearly repulsed by the traffic in women carried out by these Chinese slave traders, the most "painful" part of this subject for Miriam is the role "white gentlemen" play in perpetuating the practice. Rather than blinded by whiteness and its influence, here Miriam reveals the all-important link between the operations of race and gender in oppression such as she sees with the Chinese prostitutes.[32]

Miriam's interest in the Chinese prostitutes indicates her tendency to gauge a society's economic, political, and social liberty by the freedom of movement enjoyed by its women. While she is frequently appalled at the condition and treatment of all the Chinese in San Francisco, the oppression felt by the city's Chinese women is the most damning of the white-male-dominated culture there. It's no surprise then that Miriam would enter the Mormon community of Salt Lake City with a curiosity and inquisitiveness hard to satisfy. Members of the Mormon faith in nineteenth-century America were a cultural oddity, considered resoundingly other and disturbingly exotic. This outsider status, at least in part, was perpetuated (and/or prompted) by the separatist and self-isolating tendencies of the church's community itself. But like other alienated groups, the Mormons were often the subject of local persecution and abuse. The key trait that set the Mormons at odds with mainstream nineteenth-century culture was, of course, their espousal of polygamy as a religious duty. Such sexual and marital deviance was not only a felony in other parts of the country, it was even depicted by surgeon Roberts Bartholow as the driving force behind the physical abnormalities that characterized what he determined to be this "race" of Mormon polygamists. In a presentation given in 1861 by Samuel A. Cartwright and C. G. Forshey at the New Orleans Academy of Sciences, Mormons are racialized as alien by virtue of the physical traits polygamy supposedly propagated: "The yellow, sunken, cadaverous visage; the greenish-colored eyes; the thick, protuberant lip; the low forehead; the light, yellowish hair; and the lank, angular person, constitute an appearance so characteristic of the new race, the production of polygamy, as to distinguish them at a glance."[33] Polygamy at its core threatened monogamous marriage, an institution increasingly depicted at this time as the basis for an essentially moral and democratic American society. In 1860, an anti-polygamy bill proposed in Congress called the sanction of polygamy under the auspices of religious freedom a "latitudinous interpretation of our Constitution" and claimed that "the whole civilized world regards the marriage of one man to one woman as being alone authorized by the law of God."[34] But having been through several, Miriam had a less than stellar impression of conventional marriage and a vested interest in women's status in such social contracts. So while it makes perfect sense that she would have been driven to uncover what she could about polygamy's function and reality in Mormon country, many of the observations she makes and conclusions to which she comes are not what her readers might have expected at all.

Miriam is clear upon arriving in Mormon territory that she has a strong prejudice against the marital institution Mormons practice, but she is, as are her fellow travelers, immediately impressed by the irrigated "verdant fields," "neat" cottages, and well-fed women and children of their community (71). Casting the conversation within the familiar frame of civilization's gradations, Miriam notes that, on looking at the pleasant Mormon village below,

> we feel a vague doubt and bewilderment stealing over our prejudices, not to say our principles, and are disposed to murmur, "Certainly, polygamy is very wrong, but roses are better than sage-brush, and potatoes and peas preferable as diet to buffalo grass. Also school-houses, with cleanly and comfortable troops of children about them, are a symptom of more advanced civilization than lonely shanties with only fever-and-ague and whisky therein. Why is nothing quite harmonious, quite consistent, quite perfect in this world?" (71)

In spite of her modified preconceptions, though, Miriam remains focused on the issue of polygamy throughout her interactions with the Mormons. When discussing the matter with a photographer and acquaintance of Leslie who "freely admitted himself to be a Mormon," Miriam notes that, according to him, the upper-class Mormon wives are not likely to be willing to be interviewed: "'The ladies here don't like being made subjects of curiosity,' said he. 'Their homes are just as sacred to them as yours in the East are to you'" (76). Gaining an exotic flair given their almost harem-like protected existence, these Mormon women and wives become Miriam's chief object of pursuit during her time in the community. In a chance meeting with a "Miss Snow," one of Young's wives, Miriam recounts the portrait of sexual equality that Miss Snow relates: "Women, she said, had as much interest as men in the prosperity of the territory, and their rights and privileges were equal. At the two colleges of Utah the course of study was the same for male and female students, and the progress of the latter was fully equal to the former"

(79). Miriam asks how the various wives manage among themselves, and Miss Snow assures her that they get along "perfectly," and are so spiritually attuned that they have no time for "petty jealousies" (79).

Miriam's curiosity is far from satisfied, however, and in a following conversation with another Mormon gentleman, she learns polygamous marriages have actually decreased in number because of "the increased cost of living, and growing demands of the fairer sex," the latter by Miriam being somewhat humorously attributed to the railroad which "has come and brought a whole train of French milliners and fashion plates" (81, 82). Somewhat more seriously, she indicates to her Mormon acquaintance that the railroad and its importation of "harbingers of a higher civilization" will undoubtedly cause "the evil of polygamy" to "melt away as it never would have before either civil or moral legislation" (82). Her friend, "Mr. H—," more serious, questions whether it be "an evil at all" (82). Miriam finally asks Mr. H— if he would like his daughters to marry into polygamous unions; "he replied he should not seek to control their own choice in the matter. He might prefer to see them the sole wives of their husbands, but it would be as God willed and they chose" (83).

This is much the same answer Miriam receives from a "Mrs. J—" whom Miriam believes to have been the sole wife of her husband, but soon discovers she had actually been in a polygamous union. Her speech to Miriam is one of peace and goodwill and harmony—very difficult to critique indeed—but the final judgment comes when Miriam asks Mrs. J— if she would like her daughters to marry into the institution. Like "Mr. H—," Mrs. J— replies that "she should prefer to see them each the only wife of a good husband" (89). The end of all these conversations, Miriam concludes, seems to be that the institution of polygamy is ordained by the Mormon religion and "their religion enables them to bear it!" (89) It's very difficult to tell if her largely negative feelings about the institution have changed, given the mostly positive spin she puts on the interviews she conducts with these practitioners of polygamy. Having already informed her readers that nothing is "quite harmonious," Miriam can both question the advantage of polygamy for Mormon women while admiring what she sees as the conviction, intelligence, contentedness, and gender equality that the women and men she encounters seem to possess and value. Her "exposé" of Brigham Young and his flock would have been titillating, possibly shocking for many of her readers, but no less so than Miriam's own tolerance toward and even acceptance of them.

When Brigham Young dies after the trip is over, Miriam adds a thoughtful footnote to the text, saying that his death prior to the book's publication means that he will "never know how kindly and respectfully we remember him, or how honestly we regret his death. May the world deal as tenderly with his memory as we would do" (103).

Contrasted with the neat cottages and calmly wedded wives of the Mormons is a family the Leslie party encounters during a storm when they are stranded at Cold-Spring Station outside of Mariposa where the "big trees" are located. In a small cabin serving as both post office and grocery store, Miriam finds herself in a drastically less comfortable environment than the ones typically enjoyed by the group:

> It consisted of only three rooms, . . . and the flickering light from the fire
> glimmered upon raftered ceiling, unplastered walls, bare floor, two or
> three rickety chairs, and a table upon which stood a single dip candle. . . .
> a shelf crammed with old newspapers testified to the literary tastes of
> the family, consisting of two women, two tiny boys, and a baby, now in
> arms, but whose permanent resting-place was a queer high-posted crib
> covered with mosquito-netting. . . . On the floor at one end lay a heap
> of bags of flour and salt, and on these poor little Follette took refuge
> from the damp and dirt of the floor, her depressed tail, an unerring ther-
> mometer of her spirits, and general meekness of appearance, eloquently
> testifying to her appreciation of the situation. (223)

The situation is truly depressing for Miriam, who notes that "the forlornness of everything was beyond words" (224). As she contemplates a memory of a picture of a ruined Marie Antoinette, surrounded by her impoverished family and sundry store items such as Miriam and her companions now find themselves, the hostess suddenly thrusts the baby into Miriam's arms, "exclaiming: 'Here, you hold bub, and I'll get a meal of victuals!'" (225) Miriam is shocked out of her state of depression and says that it was "a pity that there was nobody to thrust a baby into Napoleon's arms at Waterloo! He would have *invented* a victory" (225). Displaying a distinctively unfeminine distaste for babies, Miriam returns the child to her hostess to make dinner herself. But by the next morning, Miriam's spirits have fallen again: "I found myself far too dejected to offer any help in getting breakfast, and was in fact so crushed that I think if the hostess had insisted upon my holding the baby she would now have found a submissive and passive victim" (229). Appalled at the thought of even holding a baby, Miriam defies her readers' expectations of conventional womanhood with her decidedly "unwomanly" response to the infant.[35]

The publication of *California: A Pleasure Trip* was greeted by a smattering of reviews describing the book as generally entertaining.[36] But not everyone who read it felt it was so innocuous. In the penultimate chapter, Miriam describes the party's brief stay in Virginia City and their tour of its gold and other mining operations. Appalled by the harsh environment of this kind of industrial process and by the city itself, she begins her description of this portion of the trip with a condemnation:

> To call a place dreary, desolate, homeless, uncomfortable, and wicked is a good deal, but to call it God-forsaken is a good deal more, and in a tolerably large experience of this world's wonders, we never found a place better deserving the title than Virginia City. (277)

According to Miriam's biographer, Madeleine B. Stern, it was this comment that ignited an explosion that ultimately blew the less socially acceptable facts of Miriam's life—her illegitimate birth, her stint as an actress in her teen years, her divorces and extramarital activities, and the unfortunate circumstances of her relationship with Squier—into the public eye by way of a full-page article published in the July 14, 1878, issue of Virginia City's *Daily Territorial Enterprise* by its irate editor, Rollin M. Daggett, one of the founding editors of the *Golden Era*.[37] While Miriam's censure of Virginia City—ironically and perhaps humorously also the home of the disapproving wife in Harte's "Miggles"—was certainly the spark for this flame, her consistent embrace in the book of the unconventional and even blatantly alien certainly had to have been the fuel that kept it burning. Her interest in women's freer social movement in the nation, her assertion of an authoritative voice in the text, her denunciation of white men for the abuse they heap on Chinese men and women, and her sympathetic portrait of a reputedly scandalous and undeniably alien religious community, all contradict the restrictions promoters of a Western white Americanness wanted placed on white women. Miriam survived the ugly media ordeal, but it nevertheless severely affected both her and her husband. After battling legal suits involving his sons and his business debts, Leslie himself died on January 10 of 1880, of an acute illness following a diagnosis of a possibly cancerous tumor in his neck.

This chain of events could have been devastating for Miriam, but characteristically, she rallied, ultimately streamlining and saving the Leslie publishing house from bankruptcy and failure through a number of keen business moves. She went on to become one of the most respected and influential businesswomen of her time, sealing that reputation in her own final will and testament when she bequeathed almost two million dollars—the vast bulk of her fortune—to Carrie Chapman Catt and the "furtherance of the cause of Women's Suffrage."[38] Catt used the money left once the will had gone through its numerous legal contests to facilitate an information and media campaign that ensured that women's suffrage, once it got on the ballot, would not be opposed by many, if any major newspapers of the time.

The impulse behind much of what Miriam Leslie did as a writer and editor was to build communities via print. This is evident in the text of *California: A Pleasure Trip* when Miriam refers to the narrative in her introductory "PREFATORY, TO THE READER" as "not so much a book as a long gossipy letter to one's friends" (6). Couched in her characteristically feminized and sentimental rhetoric, Miriam calls to her "dear five hundred friends already mine, and five hundred hundred more" to help her

> disarm criticism beforehand by assuring you that nobody could point out a fault or a shortcoming in this little book, which I do not know all about and deplore most modestly beforehand. In fact I have my doubts as to calling it a book at all, that title implying a purpose, and deliberateness, and method, which are not of my circle, although regarded by me with respectful admiration. No, let us rather say, that this work of mine is a vehicle, through which, with feminine longing for sympathy, I convey to you my pleasures, annoyances, and experiences in the journey it narrates; or, if you like better, it is a casket, enshrining the memory of many a pleasant hour made bright and indelible by your companionship, your kindness, your attention and hospitality. (5)

While certainly playing the part of the conventionally apologetic and flawed woman author, Miriam Leslie's preface nevertheless asserts what Miriam saw as the book's true purpose: to create a community both by virtue of the friends she meets during the trip and the ones she will make in its telling. Harte's Miggles makes numerous references to her loneliness and it is significant that she wallpapers her very house with the pages of illustrated weeklies, letting the reading of those pages carry her and Jim through the winter, connecting them to a larger community via the written word. "'When we're sitting alone,'" Miggles tells her stranded stage coach visitors, "'I read him those things on the wall. Why Lord! . . . I've read him that whole side of the house this winter'" (132). When played upon by editors and writers like Harte and Miriam Leslie, the desire to create community via the popular periodical begins to answer the question Morrison poses in *Playing in the Dark* as to what makes "intellectual domination" possible.[39] The desire of readers to find community in the pages of the popular nineteenth-century American press is perhaps the most grievous need that press commodified, one to which it appealed with a disarmingly loving discourse.

CONCLUSION

Consumption, Community, and
the Correspondence Column

Good morning, dear Mercury and sisters of the Promenade one
and all. I am in quest of sunshine. Where shall I find it? . . . a voice
replies: "Why, you silly girl, go to the Mercury and enter the Ladies'
Promenade."
                              —*New York Mercury,* March 26, 1859

I was inconsolable until the Chimney Corner appeared, and then—
oh, then!—I felt that I had found a kindred spirit.
                              —*Frank Leslie's Chimney Corner,* September 2, 1865

Toni Morrison explains that her desire in *Playing in the Dark* is not simply to "alter one hierarchy in order to institute another."[1] Her interest,
she says, and the question she finds far more compelling than such an
"exchange of dominations" is

> what makes intellectual domination possible; how knowledge is trans-
> formed from invasion and conquest to revelation and choice; what ignites
> and informs the literary imagination, and what forces help establish the
> parameters of criticism.[2]

In this study, I have argued that the key players in the popular American
press scene in the nineteenth century utilized a blinding sense of whiteness to consolidate a notion of Americanness that itself was a highly
malleable thing, differently constructed and differently configured in different regions of the nation. While it should be clear by now how that
whiteness circulated and to what effect it did so, there still remains the

189

question of why such an exclusive definition of national belonging—of community—would have been the compelling force it was at this point in American history. Market forces answer for much of this, as we've already seen. Just as P. T. Barnum utilized very different notions of sensationalized blackness to sell the commodities at the American Museum for which he was famous, so did the editors of the Confederate *Southern Illustrated News* and the Californian *Golden Era* utilize languages of white-belonging to encourage the sales and consumption of their regional publications in a market dominated by the Northeastern press. But understanding these motivations of the market still doesn't address the issue of why such an approach was considered so likely to sell. In Morrison's words, what in the end makes this kind of intellectual domination possible? Why did readers buy it?

For this answer, it is best to turn to the readers themselves, those actually purchasing and/or consuming these popular literary texts. But "real" nineteenth-century readers are a source both elusive and illusory. Nineteenth-century diarists, for instance, who typically constitute the primary sources for readership studies, rarely recorded their reading of miscellanies and the other ephemera on which this study has focused.[3] But the papers themselves contained records of their own readership in the form of correspondence columns, columns that printed the letters of those represented as readers of the periodical in which they appeared. Correspondence columns were common features in the weeklies, miscellanies, and story papers discussed in this study. Sometimes functioning as clearinghouses for information and advice, these columns often simply provided answers to readers' questions, questions that ranged from where one might acquire a tin lamp, to how much guano one should use per acre to grow tobacco, to whether a correspondent should inform his fiancée of his Swedish nationality. Other columns functioned simply as the place where potential writers for the periodical received the editor's yea or nay on their submitted manuscripts. Still others represented themselves as constituting what might best be described as reading clubs, groups whose existence formed a visible, if virtual body of reading membership, as well as the community such a public presence of belonging provided.

Using these letters as a historical record of "real readers" is a problematic task, given their questionable authenticity. Scholars have pointed out that one of the problems of viewing them as a reliable source of information about "real readers" is that we have no reliable way of knowing who actually wrote them; the evidence to determine this—copies of the letters themselves—are long gone. The following piece that appeared in *Saturday Night,* for example, sounds suspiciously like something an editor might pen. "Since the commencement of the new Indian story," the correspondent says, "I have got a number of new subscribers to the saturday night, . . . people that never read what they call 'story papers,' but who now say they will always read saturday night. As for myself, I would as soon go without my meals as without my saturday night."[4] The issue of the letters' authenticity becomes, in fact, part of the fabric of one installment of the *New York Mercury*'s carefully tended "Ladies' Promenade" column.[5] The editor claims that a tricky reader attempted to use her friend's doubt about the letters' authorship in order to finagle her own publication in the column:

> A nice young lady informs us that she has had a dispute with somebody—a gentleman, we believe. It is possible that a bet of candy or kisses, or some sort of sweetmeats, is pending. The gentleman insists that all the letters to the Promenade are written by the editor. We have not decided whether we ought to thank him for the compliment, or thrash him for his impertinence. But our friendly correspondent, zealously taking our part, has bet . . . that they are genuine, bona fide, and no mistake. And she proposed to test the matter in this way: If we publish her letter, she can show it to the gentleman, and triumphantly claim the forfeited sweetmeats.[6]

Editor "Mr. Mercury" pronounces this scheme "ingenious," but denies that it will answer the question of the other letters' authorship. He actually uses the rest of the column to argue that its readers' letters are bound to share stylistic similarities, given the "natural imitation" writers practice in relation to one another's works.

Whether or not real readers wrote these letters does not, however, stop the columns in which they appeared from sculpting a visible body of readership. Whether created by editors through a process of editorial selection or actually ghostwritten by the editors themselves, these columns indeed constitute bodies of readership, constructions that, imaginary or not, are always also a reflection of an imagined desire within the general population. In the case, for instance, of the *New York Mercury*'s "Ladies' Promenade" and *Frank Leslie's Chimney Corner*'s "Ladies' Conversazione," this readership tells us two things.[7] First, as we know, national identity as it was constructed in these papers was in part a market-driven phenomenon, an exclusive, excluding entity, the form of which was shaped at least in part by potential paper sales. In addition, though, the means by which readers are represented as reaching for inclusion into this body shows the powerful desire on the part of nineteenth-century readers to read themselves into any community available to them, a desire of which editors like Miriam Leslie took swift advantage. Overall, the need for such columns demonstrates a need to be a visible part of a larger community. And it is in part, I believe, this same need that drives the racializing and nationalizing done elsewhere in the pages of periodicals like the *New York Mercury* and *Frank Leslie's Chimney Corner*. The reason behind this form of intellectual domination—an antidote to isolation—becomes, finally and ironically, the cause of an even more virulent and painfully violent isolation.

In their recent writings on readership in antebellum Boston, Ronald J. Zboray and Mary Saracino Zboray return over and over again to a basic premise; namely, that the actual responses to the physical texts of the "real" readers they've studied have more to do with creating community with other readers than they do almost anything else. Books, magazines, newspapers, sermons, documents, letters—all of these texts served primarily as links between people, not as fetishized objects removed from the relationships and events of their daily lives. The Zborays note that in the numerous family collections with which they've worked (thirty in the study from which I'm about to quote), books could "convey owners' status" because of their costliness, but they often "transcended commercial value and ... offered solace, kindled memories, and, in general, helped maintain ties to loved ones."[8] In an earlier essay, Ronald J. Zboray stresses the increase in circulation and importance of the letter in American culture as a result of a related increase in transience among ambitious Americans and immigrants in the earlier part of the nineteenth century: "the personal letter had created an avenue of emotional release, a form of intimacy, in a society increasingly threatening the individual with isolation.... As the whirlwind of economic development scattered these individuals all over America they struggled vainly to preserve these former affectional networks through correspondence."[9]

Readers of the "Ladies' Promenade" column of the *New York Mercury* would have found represented there a wide cross-section of the American public, one surely wide enough to include whomever they identified

themselves to be. "Captain," or "Mr. Mercury," the editorial voice behind
the column, generally prefaces each new correspondent's letter by noting where the writer lives, a move that emphasizes the expansive embrace of the column and paper: "A letter from our Californian friend,
Lily, is first in order. . . . A young Virginienne now salutes us, and is emi-
nently welcome. . . . A Hoosieress is our next correspondent, and we see,
from her letter, that there are some 'cute folks,' as she says, out in Indiana. . . . A Baltimore maiden shall 'close the exercise' for the week."[10]
Letters appear from Ohio, Wisconsin, Michigan, Illinois, Massachusetts,
Kentucky, Delaware, Louisiana, Mississippi, Missouri, Maine, New Jersey, Connecticut, New York, Hawaii, and even somewhere deep in Indian
territory: "The following involves two curious things—the fact that the
Mercury is read in the distant land of the Cherokees, and that one of
the dusky princesses of that far-famed nation has honored the Promenade with a contribution. We insure her a most cordial welcome."[11] In
fact, publication in the "Ladies' Promenade" meant an invitation into a
space imaginatively and physically defined by those writing themselves
into it. As one writer put it:

> I am in quest of sunshine. Where shall I find it? . . . a voice replies: "Why,
> you silly girl, go to the Mercury and enter the Ladies' Promenade. . . ."
> I entered beneath its portals; and, ere the massive gate had closed be-
> hind me, the light and beauty of that charming circle burst upon my
> astonished sight, so that I thought I must be dreaming—wandering
> in the sweet fields of dreamland!
> I rubbed my eyes and looked again, but found it was no dream; for
> there, in the centre, in a conspicuous place, stood Mr. Mercury, his face
> radiant with smiles, surrounded by a bevy of fair girls.[12]

The "Ladies' Promenade" becomes a public walk of letters, and the voices
that comprise it conjure up an imaginary space of communion, peace,
sympathy—even love. Corinne writes that she "comes with both hands
extended, to receive the cordial clasp of the hands, which I know are
awaiting me."[13] Camille says she comes "to while [sic] away a lonely
hour, and beguile it of its sadness, in the dear delight of a renewal of old
acquaintanceship."[14] In 1861, this feeling of a shared harmonious space
is one "Mr. Mercury" insists will remain, despite the impending upheaval
of the Civil War: "Whatever brawls disturb the domain of politics, there
should be peace in the flowery and fragrant precincts of the Promenade.
Where sisters dwell, and brothers sometimes humbly crave admission . . .

quarrels should never come to destroy the harmony of this happy region."[15] Once the presence of the war does make its way into the "Ladies' Promenade," Mr. Mercury reminds readers that the column is the place to go to get away from it: "what a comfort to get out of the hard, weary, often heart-breaking world of fact, into a more natural, more real, and far better world of fancy! . . . Away with it all—business, politics, wars, and rumors of wars, and let us find a purer, and better and more lasting world in the domain of thought and imagination."[16] Regional differences, national differences, and political differences are submerged in the lofty walks of the *New York Mercury*, in the name of sisterhood and by way of consumption. "Mr. Mercury" assures his readers that as long as they all speak or aspire to speak the same heartfelt, sentimental, poetic prose, then they really are all members of a "sisterhood"; they can relish the knowledge that within the walks of the "Promenade," women may ignore the forces dividing their home communities and come together on the same page. Not only does the paper mimic the nation's rolls of citizenship in its expansive, inclusive representation of correspondents from all across the country, but at least one reader equates the paper with the nation itself—or at least its idealized form. According to Blanche Woodbury writing in 1859, "the Promenade is a credit to [Mr. Mercury's] republican heart. It is free. Free as the sun and air, and universe of God!"[17]

Magazine editors utilized their knowledge of readers' need for communal identification in their construction of these columns in order to expand—albeit in a small way—the significance and circulation of their periodicals overall. Readers could come to these columns to compare notes with other readers whose experiences and questions were printed there and could further extend this sense of community by publishing their own accounts of their own experiences. This push to connect with others via printed correspondence is certainly the central desire forefronted in columns specifically devoted to women's writing. The writers of the "Ladies' Promenade" spend as much print space discussing how pleased they are to be included in the column as they do delineating their loving feelings for the various other writers appearing there. Correspondents write about their loneliness and sadness, making it clear that writing—as well as reading the paper in which their letters are printed—helps them combat those feelings. "Alone," who writes regarding the problems of being an "old maid," explains that "it is a relief and pleasure for me to turn from my sad thoughts and gaze—in imagination—upon the beaming faces, and listen to the cheerful voices of the sisterhood."[18] She ends her epistle by saying, "Well, I have succeeded in writing away my melancholy; and now, as I emerge from the cloud, I'll give you a bright smile, and then farewell."[19] "M. A. L." writes into the "Ladies' Conversazione" column of Miriam Leslie's *Frank Leslie's Chimney Corner* with a tale of marital woe:

> baby is such a comforter. I sit at twilight with her in my lap, and tell her all my troubles, and she 'coo's' and 'sh's' in her soft little voice, and then I am happy. But when she is asleep it all comes back, and I wish I was lying in the graveyard opposite, with my baby in my arms. I believe, after all, that marriage is not best. I was happier before. But I have written you so long a letter, that I am afraid you will be out of patience with me.[20]

And while Ontario in a poem written to "Captain Mercury" claims that "never since this world began, / Was there a place that was free from man— / Until the ladies, with your generous aid, / Formed this beautiful 'Promenade,'" Maud Audesly tells "Mr. Editor" of the Chimney Corner's "Ladies' Conversazione" that he should

> devote a column in your journal to women in general—not to your remarks and views concerning them, be good enough to understand; you men have talked so much and so long, and never hit on the truth yet, that it is time you were silenced forever! What I want is a place where women may speak for themselves, in spite of all the slanders of you male creatures.[21]

Editors used these columns not only to heighten the joy of belonging their readers were supposed to feel in reading them, but also to point out the necessity of excluding someone else in order for that belonging to occur. Because of this exclusion, "A. Emily" can label her participation in the text a valued opportunity. "I highly appreciate our privilege," she tells him, "the privilege of conversing together in such a familiar way, through the instrumentality of the Mercury."[22]

The presence and tone of these letters make clear the importance of writing in Americans' lives as a tool for connection and creating a sense of community. They testify to these editors' understanding of Americans' deep sense of isolation and need for sympathetic identification with others depicted to be like themselves. But they also illustrate the exclusion necessary for such community-building to occur. In a less genteel way, perhaps, the push of the nineteenth-century's popular press to establish some kind of definitive national community—an oxymoron, of course, given the diverse range of Americas that were actually being constructed at this time—is much the same as Mr. Mercury's establishment of a feminized correspondence club in a column like the "Ladies' Promenade." While readers of columns like the "Ladies' Promenade" reached for a safe and sentimental union in those pages, participants in a wide range of popular entertainments likewise reached for solid footing in an America radically reshaped by war, changing definitions of citizenship, rapid industrial expansion, and shifting demographics. And reach they often did, blinded though they might have been by an imagined whiteness, the certainty of which existed only fleetingly in the pages of the periodical press and the performances of nineteenth-century popular American entertainments.

Notes

Introduction

1. Born Robert Carter, Leslie supervised the engraving department of the *London Illustrated News,* the model for most American illustrated newspapers, before coming to America. As well as Barnum, Leslie worked for Frederick Gleason on one of the first illustrated weeklies in America, the Boston-based family miscellany *Gleason's Pictorial Drawing Room Companion.* After Barnum sold the *Illustrated News* to Gleason after less than a year of publishing it under his name, Leslie went on to make his own publishing history with *Frank Leslie's Lady's Gazette of Fashion,* the first of what would be some fifty Frank Leslie titles. For more on Leslie, see Madeleine B. Stern, *Publishers for Mass Entertainment in Nineteenth-Century America* (Boston: G. K. Hall, 1980), 180–89, and Frank Luther Mott, *A History of American Magazines,* vol. 2, *1850–1865* (Cambridge: Harvard University Press, 1938), 452–65.

2. *Illustrated News* (1 January 1853): 6.

3. *Illustrated News* (8 January 1853): 1.

4. Benedict Anderson, *Imagined Communities: Reflections on the Origin and Spread of Nationalism,* rev. ed. (New York: Verso, 1991), 5–7. Anderson claims that a nation consists of an "imagined community" that is "imagined as both inherently limited and sovereign" (6); it is a community *imagined* because its members will, for the most part, never know or meet one another and one also *limited* because even the largest nation "encompassing perhaps a billion living human beings, has finite, if elastic, boundaries, beyond which lie other nations. No nation imagines itself coterminous with mankind" (7). Finally, it is "imagined as a *community,* because, regardless of the actual inequality and exploitation that may prevail in each, the nation is always conceived as a deep, horizontal comradeship. Ultimately it is this fraternity that makes it possible, over the past two centuries, for so many millions of people, not so much to kill, as willingly to die for such limited imaginings" (Anderson, 7). For more on the question of theorizing the formation of national identity, see particularly Étienne Balibar, "The Nation Form: History and Ideology," *Review* 13 (Summer 1990): 329–61, and Carroll Smith-Rosenberg, "Subject Female: Authorizing American

Identity," *American Literary History* 5 (1993): 481–511. For a good introduction to the seminal work on nationalism in general, see John Hutchinson and Anthony D. Smith, eds. *Nationalism* (New York: Oxford University Press, 1994) and Homi K. Bhabha, ed. *Nation and Narration* (New York: Routledge, 1990).

5. Toni Morrison, *Playing in the Dark: Whiteness and the Literary Imagination* (New York: Vintage, 1993), 52.

6. Homi K. Bhabha, ed. "Introduction: narrating the nation," in *Nation and Narration* (New York: Routledge, 1990), 4.

7. Morrison, *Playing in the Dark*, 33.

8. Ibid., 17.

9. Tomás Almaguer, *Racial Fault Lines: The Historical Origins of White Supremacy in California* (Berkeley: University of California Press, 1994), 21. For an excellent summary of the evolving conception of race in early America, particularly in regard to the work of George Fredrickson, see Almaguer, 19–26.

10. Matthew Frye Jacobson, *Whiteness of a Different Color: European Immigrants and the Alchemy of Race* (Cambridge: Harvard University Press, 1998), 25. As Jacobson's work goes on to show, whiteness in pre-twentieth-century America was never categorically inclusive of the European representatives to whom it is granted today; groups like the "Celts" and "Iberics," for example, that were racially coded in the nineteenth century are no longer operative in American culture. Arguing that it was in large part due to the massive waves of immigration of the latter half of the nineteenth century that whiteness became increasingly contested, Jacobson writes that "the untroubled republican equation of whiteness with fitness for self-government, which had informed colonial thinking and had reigned in the new nation since 1790,... became increasingly untenable as 'free white persons' of undreamt-of diversity and number dragged ashore in the 1840s and after" (*Whiteness of a Different Color*, 38). I would add to this list of contributing pressures exerted on this citizenship-based model of American whiteness the impending effects of Emancipation, increased tensions with Native Americans in the West, the creation of the Confederacy, and the effects of increased Western migration due to the completion of the transcontinental railroad.

11. See, for instance, Noel Ignatiev, *How the Irish Became White* (New York: Routledge, 1995); Lisa Lowe, *Immigrant Acts: On Asian American Cultural Politics* (Durham: Duke University Press, 1996); David R. Roediger, *The Wages of Whiteness: Race and the Making of the American Working Class* (New York: Verso, 1991); Alexander Saxton, *The Rise and Fall of the White Republic: Class Politics and Mass Culture in Nineteenth-Century America* (Berkeley: University of California Press, 1990); and Shelley Streeby, *American Sensations: Class, Empire, and the Production of Popular Culture* (Berkeley: University of California Press, 2002).

12. Michael Omi and Howard Winant, *Racial Formation in the United States from the 1960s to the 1980s* (New York: Routledge, 1986), 60.

13. Ibid., 61.

14. Ibid., 63.

15. Jacobson, *Whiteness of a Different Color*, 275.

16. June Namias, *White Captives: Gender and Ethnicity on the American Frontier* (Chapel Hill: University of North Carolina Press, 1993), 218.

17. I borrow the phrase "racializing as alien" from Streeby (*American Sensations*, 32), although I use it somewhat differently. For Streeby, such racializing indicates a

kind of doubling or complicating of racial codes; I use it to mean a rhetorical form of othering that borrows from racializing discourse at the same time that it contradicts it.

18. Bhabha, "Introduction," 2.

19. Morrison, *Playing in the Dark*, 8.

20. These terms—weekly, miscellany, and story paper—are not technical in any way, but rather somewhat obviously descriptive in that they represent the general nature of the works contained in them; weeklies appeared weekly, miscellanies encompassed a broad swath of popular genres, and story papers published largely fiction. Most of the periodicals with which I am concerned in this study contained a serious mix of genres and appeared on a weekly or monthly basis, making them less newspapers (despite names like *Frank Leslie's Illustrated Newspaper*) and more magazines. Libraries often have difficulty clearly categorizing these texts as they act at different times and in different ways as both daily newspapers and monthly literary magazines.

21. Mott's multivolume *A History of American Magazines* (Cambridge: Harvard University Press, 1930) and his *American Journalism: A History, 1690–1960* (New York: Macmillan, 1962) are classic, albeit flawed, guides. Edward E. Chielens, ed., *American Magazines: The Eighteenth and Nineteenth Centuries* (Westport, Conn.: Greenwood, 1986), James Playsted Wood's *Magazines in the U.S.* (New York: Ronald Press Co., 1971), Madeleine B. Stern's *Imprints on History: Book Publishers and American Frontiers* (Bloomington: Indiana University Press, 1956), and Mary Noel's *Villains Galore . . . the Hey-Day of the Popular Story Weekly* (New York: Macmillan Co., 1954) are also standard resources for periodical researchers. Academic study of periodicals has increased dramatically over recent years as the foundation of both the Research Society for American Periodicals in 1990 and its affiliated journal, *American Periodicals*, attest. While a highly select list based solely on my own idiosyncratic tastes and interests, the following are some of the texts that I have found particularly useful and intriguing: Joshua Brown, "Reconstructing Representation: Social Types, Readers, and the Pictorial Press, 1865–1877," *Radical History Review* 66 (1996): 5–38; Aleta Feinsod Cane and Susan Alves, eds., *American Women Writers and the Periodical, 1837–1916* (Iowa City: University of Iowa Press, 2001); Cathy Davidson, ed., *Reading in America: Literature and Social History* (Baltimore: The Johns Hopkins University Press, 1989); Michael Denning, *Mechanic Accents: Dime Novels and Working-Class Culture in America* (New York: Verso, 1987); Kathleen Diffley, *Where My Heart Is Turning Ever: Civil War Stories and Constitutional Reform, 1861–1876* (Athens: University of Georgia Press, 1992); Alice Fahs, *The Imagined Civil War: Popular Literature of the North and South, 1861–1865* (Chapel Hill: University of North Carolina Press, 2001); Ellen Gruber Garvey, *The Adman in the Parlor: Magazines and the Gendering of Consumer Culture, 1890s to 1910s* (New York: Oxford University Press, 1996); Charles A. Johanningsmeier, *Fiction and the American Literary Marketplace: The Role of Newspaper Syndicates in America, 1860–1900,* (New York: Cambridge University Press, 1997); Isabelle Lehuu, *Carnival on the Page: Popular Print Media in Antebellum America,* (Chapel Hill: University of North Carolina Press, 2000); Michael Lund, *America's Continuing Story: An Introduction to Serial Fiction, 1850–1900* (Detroit: Wayne State University Press, 1993); Kenneth M. Price and Susan Belasco Smith, eds., *Periodical Literature in Nineteenth-Century America* (Charlottesville: University Press of Virginia, 1995); Streeby, *American Sensations;* Ronald Zboray, *A Fictive People:*

Antebellum Economic Development and the American Reading Public (New York: Oxford University Press, 1993).

1. Roving Savages, Regionalized Americanness, and the 1862 Dakota Wars

1. In the following discussion, I will use both the words "Sioux" and "Dakota," but it is important to note the politicized implications of each term. "Sioux" was the term applied to the Dakota people by "white" Americans of European and Anglo descent. "Dakota" and "Lakota" are the names tribal members called themselves. In what follows, I attempt to use the word "Sioux" only where textually appropriate.

2. Étienne Balibar, "The Nation Form: History and Ideology," *Review* 13 (Summer 1990): 338.

3. Homi K. Bhabha, "Introduction: narrating the nation" in *Nation and Narration,* ed. Homi K. Bhabha (New York: Routledge, 1990), 2, 3.

4. See Benedict Anderson, *Imagined Communities: Reflections on the Origin and Spread of Nationalism,* rev. ed. (New York: Verso, 1991), 22–46.

5. Kirsten Belgum, *Popularizing the Nation: Audience, Representation, and the Production of Identity in Die Gartenlaube, 1853–1900* (Lincoln: University of Nebraska Press, 1998), xxii. As Belgum further argues, the Germany that attains narrative form in *Die Gartenlaube* became a commodity itself. (This becomes a functional point for Barnum in all of his institutional attempts to garner public attention. For more on Barnum's own signification of the issues of class in American nineteenth-century culture, see Bluford Adams, *E Pluribus Barnum: The Great Showman and the Making of U.S. Popular Culture* [Minneapolis: University of Minnesota Press, 1997].) Belgum's study undertakes the same overall problem mine does: If we concede that popular literature and culture contributed and helped create a sense of nationality in the nineteenth century—the great age of nation-building, according to Anderson—then how exactly do those texts do that? Belgum's study is an in-depth look at the ways in which diverse identities were co-opted in the pages of *Die Gartenlaube* to represent Germanness to its readers; its focus is one periodical, unlike this study's, and by virtue of the different historical situation in which Germany found itself at this time, draws different conclusions.

6. Marianna Torgovnick, *Gone Primitive: Savage Intellects, Modern Lives* (Chicago: University of Chicago Press, 1990), 245.

7. *Gleason's Pictorial Drawing Room Companion* was founded in 1851 by Frederick Gleason, publisher of the successful Boston story paper, *Flag of Our Union.* It was initially edited by Maturin Murray Ballou, sold for $3.00 a year, and soon garnered a circulation of more than 100,000 copies. Gleason sold it to Ballou in 1854, and Ballou ran it until 1859, when it was discontinued. See Frank Luther Mott, *A History of American Magazines 1850–1865* (Cambridge: Harvard University Press, 1938), vol. 2, 407–12.

8. *Gleason's Pictorial Drawing Room Companion* (19 April 1851): 28. Courtesy, American Antiquarian Society.

9. For an overview of the freak show's birth and decline as an American institution of popular entertainment, see Robert Bogdan's landmark *Freak Show: Presenting Human Oddities for Amusement and Profit* (Chicago: University of Chicago

Press, 1988), especially 25–68. See also Leslie Fiedler, *Freaks: Myths and Images of the Secret Self* (New York: Simon and Schuster, 1978), *Freakery: Cultural Spectacles of the Extraordinary Body*, Rosemarie Garland Thomson, ed. (New York: New York University Press, 1996), and Rachel Adams, *Sideshow U.S.A.: Freaks and the American Cultural Imagination* (Chicago: University of Chicago Press, 2001).

10. Bogdan, *Freak Show*, 2. Barnum's success as a "humbug showman" of course skyrocketed with his management of the career of "General Tom Thumb." While Barnum briefly entertained himself with periodical publishing, his ties to the publishing community extended beyond his work with the *Illustrated News*. His hire of Frank Leslie as both chief engraver for the *News* and the American Museum's catalogue provided Leslie with a stepping-stone to his own editorship of the successful and numerous Frank Leslie titles and probably at least partially accounts for the fairly frequent mention of current shows running at Barnum's Museum in *Frank Leslie's Illustrated Newspaper*.

11. "Freaks of Nature" scrapbook of Nathaniel Paine. Courtesy, the American Antiquarian Society.

12. Bogdan, *Freak Show*, 136.

13. Ibid., 106.

14. Courtesy, American Antiquarian Society. For more on the case of Johnson, see James W. Cook Jr., "Of Men, Missing Links, and Nondescripts: The Strange Career of P. T. Barnum's 'What Is It?' Exhibition," in *Freakery: Cultural Spectacles of the Extraordinary Body*, Rosemarie Garland Thomson, ed. (New York: New York University Press, 1996), 139–57.

15. Courtesy, American Antiquarian Society.

16. Mott, *American Magazines*, 3.

17. Ronald Zboray, *A Fictive People: Antebellum Economic Development and the American Reading Public* (New York: Oxford University Press, 1993). Zboray argues that as publishers attempted to reach the widest group of readers possible, particularly in their publication and circulation of a fiction that was largely formulaic, readers "took on the role of creators themselves, adjusting and adapting the meanings of these new commodities, these books, to their own lives, at first in a very personal and local way, and later in partial conformance to the emergent national fictive identity.... These readers helped to devise the symbolic forms and cultural practices that would allow for the construction of a national identity applicable to a diverse people scattered over an immense and varied landscape" (193, 194). By "fictive people," Zboray, then, refers to both the fiction-reading public and the identity that emerged from that practice.

18. Ibid., 189, 191.

19. Anderson, *Imagined Communities*, 35, 33. It is this apparently random, yet typically meaningful juxtaposition, that causes Anderson to liken reading a newspaper to "reading a novel whose author has abandoned any thought of a coherent plot" (33).

20. *Harper's Weekly* was established by Fletcher Harper in 1857, less than two years after *Frank Leslie's Illustrated Newspaper*, its predominant rival. Like *Leslie's*, it featured large illustrations from wood engravings that were often double-page spreads; it billed itself as a family newspaper and printed the political discussions that *Harper's Monthly* avoided. Its circulation swelled during the years of the Civil War as readers clamored for images from the front, reaching 120,000 in 1861 and remaining over

100,000 to the end of the war. Its final issue appeared in 1916. See Mott, *American Magazines*, 469–87.

21. *Harper's Weekly* (3 January 1857): 1.

22. Other periodicals use their mastheads to directly emphasize the nationalistic interests they represent. New York's *Frank Leslie's Illustrated Newspaper* highlights its Yankee status, the letters of its masthead running over, under, and through a precisely centered, majestic drawing of the country's Capital Building. The *Southern Illustrated News*, a confederate weekly commencing in September 1862 in Richmond, arches the letters of its title, dripping with Spanish moss, over a scene of Confederate tranquility: a war memorial with a mounted soldier on the upper pedestal occupies the image's center while a riverboat pumps steam over a marshy Southern river lined by plantation mansions. The war memorial functions in several ways. While paying tribute to the war then being fought, it permits itself to be read *as* a memorial, indicating to the Southern reader the paper's optimism that the war will soon be over and the Confederacy firmly established and on its way. It also draws attention to the part the very act of making war played in the Confederacy's process of building its own national image, the war itself being, as one writer for the *Southern Illustrated News* emphasized elsewhere, what would both literally and figuratively consolidate the Confederacy as a separate nation. All of these images indicate the variety of national scenes with which these American publications struggled; asserting the presence of a nation that had come into being not yet a hundred years before, or a nation that had not yet gained recognition, or a nation that was seeking a foothold in the so-called Western frontier.

23. For a very general introduction to the Dakota Wars, see Duane Schultz, *Over the Earth I Come: The Great Sioux Uprising of 1862* (New York: St. Martin's Press, 1992). Other sources include: Gary Clayton Anderson, *Little Crow: Spokesman for the Sioux* (St. Paul: Minnesota Historical Society Press, 1986); Anderson and Alan R. Woolworth, eds., *Through Dakota Eyes: Narrative Accounts of the Minnesota Indian War of 1862* (St. Paul: Minnesota Historical Society Press, 1988); Dee A. Brown, *Bury My Heart at Wounded Knee: An Indian History of the American West* (New York: Holt, Rinehart and Winston, 1970); Charles S. Bryant and Abel B. Murch, *A History of the Great Massacre by the Sioux Indians, in Minnesota, Including the Personal Narratives of Many Who Escaped* (Cincinnati: Rickey and Carroll, 1864); Kenneth Carley, *The Sioux Uprising of 1862* (St. Paul: Minnesota Historical Society Press, 1976); Isaac V. D. Heard, *History of the Sioux War and Massacres of 1862 and 1863* (New York: Harper and Bros., 1864); June Namias, *White Captives: Gender and Ethnicity on the American Frontier* (Chapel Hill: University of North Carolina Press, 1993); Charles M. Oehler, *The Great Sioux Uprising* (New York: Oxford University Press, 1959); and Sarah F. Wakefield, *Six Weeks in the Sioux Tepees (Little Crow's Camp): A Narrative of Indian Captivity* vol. 79, *Garland Library of Narratives of North American Indian Captivities* (New York: Garland, 1977).

24. (25 October 1862): 1. *Frank Leslie's Illustrated Newspaper* first appeared in December of 1855; it was published by the charismatic Frank Leslie, the British wood engraver who took his own *nom de guerre* when he came to New York and entered the world of publishing. The paper was originally "a small folio of sixteen pages, priced at ten cents a number, or four dollars by the year" (Mott, *American Magazines*, 453). By its third year, "the paper was claiming over 100,000 circulation" (Mott, *American Magazines*, 454). It ran until 1922 and, with *Harper's Weekly*, was one of

the most widely circulated and successful illustrated weeklies in the nation. For more, see Mott, *American Magazines*, 452–65.

25. Bryant and Murch, *A History of the Great Massacre*, 46.

26. Ibid., 48–49.

27. Ibid., 1.

28. The *St. Paul Pioneer and Democrat* appeared as a daily, a weekly, and even a triweekly; it ran as a weekly from 1855 to 1865. It was published in Saint Paul and contained largely news and editorial items.

29. Carroll Smith-Rosenberg, in her treatment of the Republican subject of the eighteenth century, notes that "formal iconographic tradition . . . represented nations as women"; America was typically represented in European discourse as a naked Indian woman ("Dis-Covering the Subject of the 'Great Constitutional Discussion,' 1786–1789," *Journal of American History* 79 [1992]: 869). According to Carol Chomsky, local officials in Minnesota opted to try the captured warriors on domestic crimes rather than decide if in fact as participants in an *international* dispute, the braves' actions had broken "the customary rules of warfare" (qtd. in Shelley Streeby, *American Sensations: Class, Empire, and the Production of Popular Culture*. [Berkeley: University of California Press, 2002]: 223). As Streeby points out, such a denial of the international context of the Dakota wars enabled the state to execute a less visibly imperialistic action: "What should rightfully have been understood as an international conflict was instead legally constructed as multiple conflicts between the state and individual subjects within it who had broken its laws" (*American Sensations*, 223).

30. *St. Paul Pioneer and Democrat* (12 September 1862): 5.

31. *Harper's Weekly* (20 December 1862): 801.

32. *New York Times*, (20 December 1862): 3.

33. *St. Paul Pioneer and Democrat* (5 September 1862): 1.

34. *St. Paul Pioneer and Democrat* (12 September 1862): 5.

35. *St. Paul Pioneer and Democrat* (31 October 1862): 6.

36. Bryant and Murch, *A History of the Great Massacre*, 477.

37. *Harper's Weekly* (17 January 1863): 37; *Frank Leslie's Illustrated Newspaper* (24 January 1863): 285.

38. *Harper's Weekly* (13 September 1862): 592.

39. *Harper's Weekly* (30 August 1862): 555.

40. See Torgovnick, *Gone Primitive*, 22, regarding cannibalism's role in primitivism, and Bogdan, *Freak Show*, 179–87, for more on the "Fiji cannibals."

41. Bogdan, *Freak Show*, 179–80.

42. *Harper's Weekly*, (29 March 1862): 195.

43. *Harper's Weekly* (7 June 1862): 368. Writers for the *Southern Illustrated News* comment on these descriptions in the paper's December 13 issue of 1862: "A man named Sprague testified that the 'rebels' buried the Yankees killed at Manassas with their faces down—that they used the bones of the dead for rings, and their skulls for goblets—that they cut off the heads of officers, &c., and these hobgoblin stories are published as a set-off to their horrible cruelties—to their avowed purpose of starving the whole 'rebel' country—to their instigation of servile war, &c." (2).

44. *Frank Leslie's Illustrated Newspaper* (17 May 1862): 64.

45. Ibid.

46. P. T. Barnum, *Barnum's Own Story: The Autobiography of P. T. Barnum* (New York: Dover, 1961), 126.

47. Lydia Maria Child, *"Hobomok" and Other Writings on Indians*, Carolyn L. Karcher, ed. (New Brunswick: Rutgers University Press, 1991): 189.

48. Ibid. Carolyn L. Karcher in her introduction to *Hobomok* notes that despite her early ignorance of American injustice to Native American peoples, Child "launched a career of campaigning against Indian dispossession, crowned forty years later by her eloquent *Appeal for the Indians* (1868)" (in Child, "*Hobomok*," xxxiii). To her credit, Child also disparages the spectacle that Barnum made of the Indians she sees at the museum. In Letter 36 of *Letters from New-York*, Child claims that "it always fills me with sadness to see Indians surrounded by the false environment of civilized life; but I never felt so deep a sadness, as I did in looking upon these western warriors; for they were evidently the noblest of their dwindling race, unused to restraint, accustomed to sleep beneath the stars. And here they were, set up for a two-shilling show, with monkeys, flamingoes, dancers, and buffoons! If they understood our modes of society well enough to be aware of their degraded position, they would doubtless quit it, with burning indignation at the insult." ("*Hobomok*," 187).

49. Barnum, *Barnum's Own Story*, 334–35.

50. Ibid., 334.

51. *Frank Leslie's Illustrated Newspaper* (5 September 1863): 373; *Frank Leslie's Illustrated Newspaper* (12 September 1863): 399.

52. *Frank Leslie's Illustrated Newspaper* (24 October 1863): 67.

53. *Frank Leslie's Illustrated Newspaper* (14 November 1863): 125.

54. P. T. Barnum, *Selected Letters of P. T. Barnum*, A. H. Saxton, ed. (New York: Columbia University Press, 1983): 22.

55. Ibid.

56. *Saturday Night* was a story paper published in Philadelphia by the publishing house of Davis and Elverson from 1865 to 1901. In 1869, its price was "$3.00 PER ANNUM IN ADVANCE" [*Saturday Night* (21 August 1869): 1]. I cite from the copies of *Saturday Night* housed in the Children's Literature Research Collection at the Elmer L. Andersen Library of the University of Minnesota. I particularly want to thank Jennifer Hanson, who made possible xeroxed copies of a not-easy-to-find periodical for this Alabama scholar.

57. Ellis is simply one of the most prolific writers of the period. His pseudonyms number in the dozens, and his adventure tales and popular histories were ubiquitous in the latter half of the nineteenth century. *Red Plume* was first published in book form in 1900 by Grosset and Dunlap; it was republished again in 1902 by two different Chicago publishers—M. A. Donohue and Thompson—under the title *Red Plume; or, A Friendly Redskin*. The page counts of the novel never vary—385 pages in all cases—and my own comparison of the book marketed for boys and the clearly sensationalized tale appearing in *Saturday Night* suggests that neither Ellis, nor Ellis's publishers, made any major changes from version to version. For more on Ellis, see Bill Brown, ed., *Reading the West: An Anthology of Dime Westerns* (Boston: Bedford, 1997), 1–40 and 165–68. Streeby reads two of Ellis's earlier novels about the Dakota Wars in her study of the imperialism and the "American 1848"; see Streeby, *American Sensations*, 221–27.

58. *Saturday Night* (13 November 1869): 3.

59. Ibid.

60. Ibid.

61. *Saturday Night* (18 December 1869): 7.
62. *Saturday Night* (2 October 1869): 2.
63. *Saturday Night* (16 October 1869): 3.
64. *Saturday Night* (2 October 1869): 2. Right after he says this, he promptly grabs the arm of the faltering, exhausted, but *white* Mrs. Prescott and "almost carried her along" (3).

2. Emancipation Anxiety and the New York City Draft Riots

1. Amendment Thirteen abolished slavery, Amendment Fourteen strengthened the centrality of federal government, paving the way for future civil rights legislation, and Amendment Fifteen—although not enforced until the Civil Rights Movement of the 1960s—established the right to vote for all American citizens, regardless of "race, color, or previous condition of servitude" (*The Constitution of the United States* [Washington, D.C.: The Commission on the Bicentennial of the United States Constitution, 1992], 27).

2. Ira Berlin, Barbara J. Fields, Thavolia Glymph, Joseph P. Reidy, and Leslie S. Rowland, eds., *Freedom: A Documentary History of Emancipation, 1861–1867* (Cambridge: Cambridge University Press, 1985), xv.

3. Kathleen Diffley, *Where My Heart Is Turning Ever: Civil War Stories and Constitutional Reform, 1861–1876* (Athens: University of Georgia Press, 1992), 4.

4. As Eric Foner puts it, "the riots revealed the class and racial tensions lying just below the surface of northern life and raised troubling questions about the war's ultimate meaning. Could a society in which racial hatred ran so deep secure a modicum of justice for the former slaves?" ("Slavery, the Civil War, and Reconstruction," in *The New American History*, ed. Eric Foner [Philadelphia: Temple University Press, 1997], 95).

5. For more on the historical trends regarding Emancipation, see Eric Foner, "Slavery, the Civil War, and Reconstruction" in *The New American History* (Philadelphia: Temple University Press, 1997), 85–106.

6. Ira Berlin, "Who Freed the Slaves? Emancipation and Its Meaning" in *Union and Emancipation: Essays on Politics and Race in the Civil War Era*, David W. Blight and Brooks D. Simpson, eds. (Kent, OH: Kent State University Press, 1997), 107.

7. Jos. T. Wilson, *Emancipation: Its Course and Progress, from 1481 B.C. to A.D. 1875, with a Review of President Lincoln's Proclamations, the XIII Amendment, and the Progress of the Freed People Since Emancipation; with a History of the Emancipation Monument* (New York: Negro Universities Press, 1969), 186. Douglass also, though, took the liberty to critique both Lincoln's actions and the monument itself in his description of the joy he and three thousand "others not less anxious than myself" experienced at the announcement of Emancipation: "In that happy hour we forgot all delay, and forgot all tardiness, forgot that the President had bribed the rebels to lay down their arms by a promise to withhold the bolt which would smite the slave system with destruction. . . . Though Mr. Lincoln shared the prejudices of his white fellow-countrymen against the negro, it is hardly necessary to say that in his heart of hearts he loathed and hated slavery" (Wilson, *Emancipation*, 187, 188). For more on Douglass's remarks regarding the monument itself, see Kirk Savage, "The Politics

of Memory: Black Emancipation and the Civil War Monument" in *Commemorations: The Politics of National Identity,* John R. Gillis, ed. (Princeton: Princeton University Press, 1994), 140.

8. Berlin, "Who Freed the Slaves?" 112.

9. John Cimprich, *Slavery's End in Tennessee, 1861–1865* (Tuscaloosa, AL: University of Alabama Press, 1985), 98.

10. Gary B. Nash and Jean R. Soderlund, *Freedom by Degrees: Emancipation in Pennsylvania and Its Aftermath* (New York: Oxford University Press, 1991), xv.

11. Ibid.

12. Leslie A. Schwalm, *A Hard Fight for We: Women's Transition from Slavery to Freedom in South Carolina* (Urbana: University of Illinois Press, 1997), 126.

13. Victor B. Howard, *Black Liberation in Kentucky: Emancipation and Freedom, 1862–1884* (Lexington: University Press of Kentucky, 1983), 2.

14. T. Stephen Whitman, *The Price of Freedom: Slavery and Manumission in Baltimore and Early National Maryland* (Lexington: University Press of Kentucky, 1997), 165.

15. William H. Williams, *Slavery and Freedom in Delaware, 1639–1865* (Wilmington, DE: Scholarly Resources, 1996), 176; Patience Essah, *A House Divided: Slavery and Emancipation in Delaware, 1638–1865* (Charlottesville: University Press of Virginia, 1996), 189.

16. Berlin, "Who Freed the Slaves?" 120.

17. *Frank Leslie's Illustrated Newspaper* (17 January 1863), 258.

18. Ibid.

19. Eric Foner, *Nothing But Freedom: Emancipation and Its Legacy* (Baton Rouge: University of Louisiana Press, 1983), 10–11.

20. Ibid., 11.

21. Foner suggests that this failed aspect of the Haitian Revolution is perhaps best attributed to the failure to reenvision Haiti's plantation economy and the class structure it dictated between workers and landowners. The economic system Toussaint-Louverture and his successors attempted to preserve remained structurally and practically too close to that which had formerly enslaved its now-freed workers. For more on this and Foner's commentary on the ironic relationship the American military was to have with the Haitian republic in the twentieth century, see Foner, *Nothing But Freedom,* 10–14.

22. Robyn Wiegman, *American Anatomies: Theorizing Race and Gender* (Durham: Duke University Press, 1995), 91.

23. Stuart Hall, "Ethnicity: Identity and Difference," *Radical America* 23, no. 4 (Oct–Dec 1991): 15.

24. Ruth Frankenberg, *White Women, Race Matters: The Social Construction of Whiteness* (Minneapolis: University of Minnesota Press, 1993), 228–29.

25. Ibid., 231.

26. Hall, "Ethnicity," 16.

27. Wiegman, *American Anatomies,* 47.

28. Alice Fahs argues that the popular representation of African Americans in the wake of Emancipation demonstrated an embrace of "a new diversified nationalism in the public space of popular literary culture"(*The Imagined Civil War: Popular Literature of the North and South, 1861–1865* [Chapel Hill: University of North Caro-

lina Press, 2001], 194). While carefully qualifying this assertion—"that embrace was admittedly tentative, conditioned, and incomplete"—Fahs does see the mark of "a transformative moment in American cultural politics" in these representations (194). See Fahs, 150–94.

29. *Frank Leslie's Illustrated Newspaper* (5 April 1862): 336. The image of the black bird in this cartoon may have also been playing on popular conceptions of the notion of "Blackbirders," gangs of men who "roamed the heavily Irish- and Afro-American Five Points district, kidnapping free Negroes and hustling them at night onto southern-bound boats" (Noel Ignatiev, *How the Irish Became White* [New York: Routledge, 1995], 140).

30. *Frank Leslie's Illustrated Newspaper* (6 June 1863): 172.

31. *Frank Leslie's Illustrated Newspaper* (24 January 1863): 276.

32. Ibid., 275.

33. Ibid., 276. Fahs argues that the illustration actually is "notable for its relative lack of exaggerated racial stereotyping" (*Imagined Civil War*, 168). "Relative" is the key term in these observations; nevertheless, Fahs does conclude that this particular image—at once symbolically linking black soldiers with American nationality via the flag they hold, while simultaneously reinforcing the validity of minstrel show representation in its attendant text—is an example of what she calls an "ambivalent style of representation" (*Imagined Civil War*, 167). See Fahs, *Imagined Civil War*, 166–69.

34. Wiegman, *American Anatomies*, 87.

35. As Tomás Almaguer explains it, the "sanctity of free labor" has had a long history in American political thought (*Racial Fault Lines: The Historical Origins of White Supremacy in California* [Berkeley: University of California Press, 1994], 33). The "producer ethic" of Andrew Jackson privileged all occupations perceived as involved in "the honest production of goods," e.g., farmers, mechanics, etc., and defined those workers in opposition to both slaves and members of the "wealthy, propertied class" who profited from their labor (Almaguer, *Racial Fault Lines*, 33). In the antebellum period, the Radical Republicans reformulated this idea of free labor to affirm "the superiority of the social system of the North," linking the interests of those representing it with that of "competitive capitalism" (Almaguer, *Racial Fault Lines*, 34). For the definitive discussion of this later shift, see Eric Foner, *Free Soil, Free Labor, Free Men: The Ideology of the Republican Party before the Civil War* (New York: Oxford University Press, 1970).

36. For a very different use of this trope in the American minstrel show, see Eric Lott, *Love and Theft: Blackface Minstrelsy and the American Working Class* (New York: Oxford University Press, 1993), 119.

37. William Neal Cleveland, "African Servitude: What Is It, and What Is Its Moral Character?" (Southhampton, Long Island, New York, 1861): 24.

38. Samuel Sullivan Cox, "Emancipation and Its Results—Is Ohio to be Africanized?" (Washington, D.C.: 6 June 1862), 2. Cox would gain greater notoriety later with a speech he delivered before Congress in February of 1864 denouncing the ideas promoted in the pamphlet "Miscegenation: The Theory of the Blending of the Races," that was written as a hoax by two New York journalists. For more on the text, its role in the 1864 presidential election, and the public response to it, see Sidney Kaplan, "The Miscegenation Issue in the Election of 1864," *Journal of Negro History* 34,

no. 3 (July 1949): 274–343. For more on the role of miscegenation in literary history, see Elise Lemire, *Miscegenation: Making Race in America* (Philadelphia: University of Pennsylvania Press, 2002).

39. Ibid., 5.
40. Ibid., 8.
41. Ibid., 9.
42. Ibid.
43. *Frank Leslie's Illustrated Newspaper* (30 May 1863): 146.
44. Published in response to the fervor created by the 1863 pamphlet "Miscegenation: The Theory of the Blending of the Races," the broadside sold for 25 cents. For another reading of both the pamphlet and this broadside, see Lemire, *Miscegenation*.
45. *Frank Leslie's Illustrated Newspaper* (24 January 1863): 288. In his book, though, Augustin Cochin ends up reiterating a racist rhetoric in his treatise on Emancipation's outcome in Europe and elsewhere. While decidedly in favor of abolition, Cochin cannot move beyond the boundaries of a rhetoric that inscribes and reinscribes notions of racial inferiority and superiority. "The negro race is so gentle," Cochin writes, "that under the yoke it makes no resistance; free from the yoke, it commits no abuses. Liberty has not the virtue of restoring to it the faculties denied it by the Creator; alone, deprived, as at St. Domingo, of the intellect of the whites, it will return to a slothful life, and give birth to a very inferior state of society." (*The Results of Emancipation*, Mary L. Booth, trans. [Boston: Walker, Wise & Co., 1863], 303–4.)
46. One other speculation about Williams is probably fair; he most likely spent time in Germany, perhaps as a student. "The Crab Spider" is set there, as is the anti-Transcendental thriller, "The Three Existences" that appeared in the March 21, 1863, issue of *Leslie's*.
47. *Frank Leslie's Illustrated Newspaper* (28 March 1863): 5.
48. Roger D. Abrahams, ed., *Afro-American Folktales: Stories from Black Traditions in the New World* (New York: Pantheon Books, 1985), 20. See also Lawrence Levine, *Black Culture and Black Consciousness: Afro-American Folk Thought from Slavery to Freedom* (New York: Oxford University Press, 1977), especially 81–135.
49. Joel Chandler Harris, *Seven Tales of Uncle Remus*, Thomas H. English, ed. (Atlanta: The Library, Emory University, 1948), 27.
50. William Bascom, *African Folktales in the New World* (Bloomington: Indiana University Press, 1992), 51–52.
51. *Frank Leslie's Illustrated Newspaper* (28 March 1863): 6.
52. Ibid., 5.
53. Ibid.
54. Fahs talks about the way in which women's literature of the Civil War claimed women's own wounds, arguing that "war killed and wounded women on the home front . . . even if the injuries were invisible or the causes of death misunderstood" (*Imagined Civil War*, 137). The image that accompanies Sewell's "Lines on the American Struggle" is, we're told, a depiction of Columbia—the nation at large. Yet this depiction reverberates clearly with the experiences of individual women, such as are recorded in a host of other Civil War writings. See Fahs, *Imagined Civil War*, 120–49.
55. *Frank Leslie's Illustrated Newspaper* (28 March 1863): 5.
56. Ibid., 6.
57. *Frank Leslie's Illustrated Newspaper* (25 July 1863): 279.

58. Ernest A. McKay, *The Civil War and New York City* (Syracuse, NY: Syracuse University Press, 1990), 200. McKay uses his own racialized rhetoric when he refers to the Irish as a "wild horde."

59. *Frank Leslie's Illustrated Newspaper* (25 July 1863): 279.

60. Ibid.

61. *Frank Leslie's Illustrated Newspaper* (1 August 1863): 294–95.

62. Iver Bernstein, *The New York City Draft Riots: Their Significance for American Society and Politics in the Age of the Civil War* (New York: Oxford University Press, 1990), 27.

63. Ibid., 29.

64. Ibid.

65. Ibid., 29–30.

66. Martin Scorsese's 2002 film *The Gangs of New York,* for the most part, also ignores the racial element of the riots, treating them rather as a kind of male initiation rite sparked by poverty and familial honor.

67. *Frank Leslie's Illustrated Newspaper* (1 August 1863): 293, 301.

68. Ibid., 295.

69. Lott, *Love and Theft,* 237.

70. David R. Roediger, *The Wages of Whiteness: Race and the Making of the American Working Class* (New York: Verso, 1991), 175.

71. Ignatiev, *How the Irish Became White,* 88. Alexander Saxton lets the words of journalist George Wilkes speak for themselves in his discussion of the riots' place in the history of what he calls the "White Republic." Wilkes blamed Democratic leaders for the riots, charged "the Irish Catholic hierarchy with complicity" in them, and described the rioters themselves as "a 'ferocious substratum' led by criminals and Confederate agents" (*The Rise and Fall of the White Republic: Class Politics and Mass Culture in Nineteenth-Century America* [New York: Verso, 1990], 213). All of the historians I note above make complex and fascinating arguments about the way in which class both determined and was determined by racial formation, and the case of the Irish "becoming white," in Ignatiev's words, is an excellent case in point for them. But all of these scholars spend much less time discussing the New York riots than one might expect given their collective concerns; they tend to let it function in their individual studies more or less as a self-evident example of the way race and class are undeniably and explosively linked.

72. It would be interesting to compare the looting of the Irish during the riots to the actions of slaves in the thick of self-emancipation. Leslie A. Schwalm recounts what she calls the public "redistribution" of the contents of planter homes and storehouses after Emancipation, noting that "former slaves on one North Santee plantation took fifteen hundred bushels of rice, prepared for market, and were 'feeding and distributing it to the Whole River'" (*A Hard Fight,* 129). Schwalm suggests that former slave women like these "openly declared war on slavery and the ill-gotten gains derived from the exploitation of their flesh and blood. Their attacks on lowcountry rice plantations were, perhaps, acts of public redemption against the public humiliations and loss of dignity and status that slaves had endured under the domination of planter, overseer, and driver" (*A Hard Fight,* 129). It is difficult to draw such a clear line of retribution in the case of the actions of the Irish long-shoremen in New York in the summer of 1863 because of the contradictory nature

of their actions in the riots. Certainly an exploited group, the Irish involved in the riots attempted to consolidate their own precarious racial identity by lashing out against New York's black community. At the same time, though, they revolted against the decidedly more affluent and "whiter" New Yorkers that also represented—perhaps more accurately—the source of their oppression. The confusing range of the rioters' targets—blacks, wealthy New Yorkers, and government officials—seem to indicate more than anything else the equally confusing nexus of identities that establish American national belonging.

73. *Frank Leslie's Illustrated Newspaper* (15 August 1863): 327.

74. *Frank Leslie's Illustrated Newspaper* (31 October 1863): 96. For more on the racial ambiguities of the Irish in nineteenth-century America see Ignatiev, *How The Irish Became White*, as well as David Roediger, *The Wages of Whiteness: Race and the Making of the American Working Class* (New York: Verso, 1991) and Saxton, *The Rise and Fall of the White Republic* (New York: Verso, 1990).

75. McKay, *The Civil War and New York City*, 209.

76. *Frank Leslie's Illustrated Newspaper* (19 September 1863): 420.

3. The White Gaze, the Spectacle of Slavery, and the Circassian Beauty

1. *Frank Leslie's Illustrated Newspaper* (28 March 1863): 5.

2. Ibid., 6.

3. See Patrick Brantlinger, "Victorians and Africans: The Genealogy of the Myth of the Dark Continent" (*"Race," Writing, and Difference*, ed. Henry Louis Gates Jr., [Chicago: University of Chicago Press, 1986], 192) for how British discourses about slavery perpetuated this idea.

4. *Frank Leslie's Illustrated Newspaper* (24 Jan 1863), 276.

5. For more on minstrelsy, see Eric Lott, *Love and Theft: Blackface Minstrelsy and the American Working Class* (New York: Oxford University Press, 1993); Alexander Saxton, *The Rise and Fall of the White Republic: Class Politics and Mass Culture in Nineteenth-Century America* (London: Verso, 1990); and David R. Roediger, *The Wages of Whiteness: Race and the Making of the American Working Class* (London: Verso, 1991).

6. Saxton, *The Rise and Fall of the White Republic*, 178–80.

7. Ibid., 178. Saxton quotes a particularly problematic tune that has the blackface singer claiming that, if he were "a blinkin'" (Abe Lincoln), "I'd buy up all de niggers, and—sell 'em, wouldn't you?" Saxton follows with this remark: "Geographically and emotionally, it was only a block or two from a song such as this to the lynching of blacks on the sidewalks of New York during the draft riots of the same year" (Saxton, 180).

8. Lott, *Love and Theft*, 191.

9. Ibid., 190.

10. Ibid.

11. Leon F. Litwack, "The Emancipation of the Negro Abolitionist" in *Blacks in the Abolitionist Movement*, John H. Bracey Jr., August Meier, and Elliott Rudwick, eds. (Belmont, CA: Wadsworth Publishing Col, 1971), 68.

12. Ibid.

13. August Meier and Elliott Rudwick, "The Role of Blacks in the Abolitionist Movement" in *Blacks in the Abolitionist Movement*, John H. Bracey Jr., August Meier, and Elliott Rudwick, eds. (Belmont, CA: Wadsworth Publishing Col, 1971), 117.

14. Ibid., 121.

15. Like Barnum's freaks, abolitionist speakers often sold photographic images of themselves, as well as narratives of the lives of former and fugitive slaves, to further raise money for their cause. Sojourner Truth's standard caption on her *cartes de visite* read "I sell the shadow to support the substance. SOJOURNER TRUTH." See Nell Irvin Painter, *Sojourner Truth: A Life, A Symbol* (New York: Norton, 1996), 197.

16. Benjamin Reiss discusses the whole problem of Barnum's "ownership" of Heth in his full-length study of the Joice Heth case, *The Showman and the Slave: Race, Death, and Memory in Barnum's America* (Cambridge: Harvard University Press, 2001), 23–27. Reiss's book is a finely detailed and nuanced account of Barnum's use of Heth, as well as the wide range of cultural meanings inherent in their relationship. By looking carefully at what Reiss calls "the strange career of Joice Heth," he attempts to "examine the marks left by slavery on the culture of the modernizing North" (10). My mention of Heth is to provide a fuller context for our understanding of the Circassian Beauty exhibit that would follow her; see Reiss for much more on this case.

17. Bluford Adams, *E Pluribus Barnum: The Great Showman and the Making of U. S. Popular Culture* (Minneapolis: University of Minnesota Press, 1997), 2.

18. Ibid., 6–7.

19. Reiss's account of the Heth phenomenon tells a much more complicated story, particularly in relation to the way in which meanings of slavery circulating in the culture intersected with and helped determine Heth's significance. In relation to Heth's tour in Providence and its surroundings areas, Reiss says that "to watch New Englanders reacting in conflicting ways to Heth is to watch them fumble with the meanings of race" (*The Showman*, 89). For more, see Reiss, particularly his account of the way in which Barnum represented Heth as an abolitionist speaker in the "morally rigid, socially conservative" city of Providence (*The Showman*, 74).

20. In Great Britain, the most stunning example of this kind of display of black women was the exhibiting of Saartjie Baartman, billed as "The Hottentot Venus." For more on Baartman, see Bernth Lindfors, "Ethnological Show Business: Footlighting the Dark Continent," in *Freakery: Cultural Spectacles of the Extraordinary Body*, Rosemarie Garland Thomson, ed. (New York: New York University Press, 1996), 207–18, and Sander L. Gilman, "Black Bodies, White Bodies: Toward an Iconography of Female Sexuality in Late Nineteenth-Century Art, Medicine, and Literature," in *Race, Writing, and Difference*, Henry Louis Gates Jr., ed. (Chicago: University of Chicago Press, 1986), 223–61.

21. See Roediger, *The Wages of Whiteness*, 65–87.

22. Ibid., 74.

23. Ibid., 85–86.

24. Ibid., 85.

25. On March 24, 1860, Barnum would buy these properties back and, as A. H. Saxon puts it, announce "his solvency from the stage of the Museum" (introduction to *Selected Letters of P. T. Barnum*, A. H. Saxon, ed. [New York: Columbia University Press, 1983], xxx).

26. Ibid., 361.

27. Ibid., 91.

28. Ibid., 125–27.

29. Saxon discusses Barnum's contradictory attitudes and actions regarding slavery and African Americans; although Barnum eventually publicly championed the cause of the North and abolition, he also allegedly bought and sold several slaves himself while touring in the antebellum South. Saxon sums up the discussion by saying: "Let us be candid about the matter and have done with it: Barnum's opinion of blacks during the pre-Civil War era was no higher than that of most of his countrymen, whether Southerners or Northerners. They were chattels, things to be bought and sold, like any other commodity" (*P. T. Barnum: The Legend and the Man* [New York: Columbia University Press, 1989], 85). Bluford Adams goes further than this, arguing that Barnum's pursuit and commodification of his celebrity in fact steered his attitudes toward slavery: "Much of what [being a member of the American middle class] meant hinged on U.S. whites' changing attitudes toward African Americans — attitudes that inevitably found their way into Barnum's personae. If the antebellum Barnum tended to equate respectability with whiteness, the postbellum one advocated a middle-class republic whose 'joint owners' were black and white men. Barnum's celebrity was crucial to the formation of a popular culture by and for those 'joint owners.'" (*E Pluribus Barnum*, 2).

30. My concern here is with the way in which the harem dweller is represented within the image of the Circassian Beauty and the Circassian of American periodical fiction; for more on the harem itself, see Malek Alloula, *The Colonial Harem*, trans. Myran Godzich and Wlad Godzich (Minneapolis: University of Minnesota Press, 1986); Alev Lytle Croutier, *Harem: The World Behind the Veil* (New York: Abbeville Press, 1989); N. M. Penzer, *The Harem: An Account of the Institution as It Existed in the Palace of the Turkish Sultans with a History of the Grand Seraglio from Its Foundation to Modern Times* (London: Spring Books, 1936); and Leslie P. Peirce, *The Imperial Harem: Women and Sovereignty in the Ottoman Empire* (New York: Oxford University Press, 1993).

31. Robert Bodgan, *Freak Show: Presenting Human Oddities for Amusement and Profit* (Chicago: University of Chicago Press, 1988), 238.

32. Ibid., 239, 237.

33. Ibid., 237.

34. Circus press agent Dexter Fellows says the same, highlighting the role of skin color in the Circassian's presentation and performance: "The theory that Caucasians were the purest and most primitive stock of the white, or European, race gave rise to the mistaken notion that they must of necessity be either albinos or people whose extreme blondness ran to pink eyes and white hair" (Dexter Fellows and Andrew A. Freeman, *This Way to the Big Show: The Life of Dexter Fellows* [New York: Halcyon House, 1936], 292). This may in part explain why Circassians came to be represented by albinos as the freak show progressed throughout the nineteenth century.

35. P. T. Barnum, *Struggles and Triumphs; or, Forty Years' Recollection of P. T. Barnum, Written by Himself* (Buffalo: Courier, 1875), 580.

36. Ibid., 581.

37. Ibid., 580–81.

38. Ibid.

39. Edward Said, *Orientalism* (New York: Vintage, 1978), 205.

40. *Zoe Meleke: Biographical Sketch of the Circassian Girl* (New York: P. T. Barnum's Greatest Show on Earth, 1880). All further references to this text will be cited parenthetically. This is Bogdan's explanation of Zoe's odd linguistic skills; see Bogdan, *Freak Show,* 239.

41. For more on this idea and its most recent critical responses, see Cathy Davidson's preface to the special "No More Separate Spheres!" issue of *American Literature,* vol. 70, no. 3 (September 1998): 443–63.

42. This progression in the author's argument reflects what Amy Kaplan has termed "manifest domesticity." See Kaplan, "Manifest Domesticity," *American Literature* vol. 70, no.3 (September 1998): 581–606.

43. Laura Donaldson uses what she calls the Miranda Complex to explain the complexities of treating gender within a colonialist, classist, and racist discourse. Arguing that colonialism has historically done away with the notion of men's and women's gender identities as "fixed and coherent," she claims that this realization "makes it impossible to ignore the contradictory social positioning of white, middle-class women as both colonized patriarchal objects and colonizing race-privileged subjects" (*Decolonizing Feminisms: Race, Gender, and Empire-Building* [Chapel Hill: University of North Carolina Press, 1992], 6).

44. *Frank Leslie's Chimney Corner* was, according to Madeleine B. Stern, "started, planned, and edited" by Miriam Squier, later Miriam Leslie, wife of publisher Frank Leslie. A self-described family-oriented miscellany, the *Chimney Corner* ran from June 3, 1865, through November 29, 1884, and was superseded by *Frank Leslie's Fact and Fiction,* which ran not quite another year. For more, see Madeleine B. Stern, *Purple Passage: The Life of Mrs. Frank Leslie* (Norman: University of Oklahoma Press, 1953): 44–46 and 190.

45. *Frank Leslie's Chimney Corner* (20 October 1866): 325.

46. Ibid.

47. Ibid.

48. Ibid.

49. For more on Murray, see Peter Benson, "Maturin Murray Ballou," in *Publishers for Mass Entertainment in Nineteenth-Century America,* Madeleine B. Stern, ed. (Boston: G. K. Hall, 1980), 27–34.

50. "Lieutenant Murray," *The Circassian Slave: or, The Sultan's Favorite: A Story of Constantinople and the Caucasus* (Boston: F. Gleason, 1851), 9. I will continue to cite from the dime novel version of *The Circassian Slave* in my discussion below.

51. In George Fitzhugh's classic proslavery treatise, *Sociology for the South, or the Failure of Free Society* (Richmond, VA: A. Morris, 1854), he claims that "the fact that [the Negro] cannot enjoy liberty on such terms [as whites do], seems conclusive that he is only fit to be a slave" (86). See Fitzhugh, 82–95.

52. Joanna De Groot, "'Sex' and 'Race': The Construction of Language and Image in the Nineteenth Century" in *Sexuality and Subordination,* Susan Mendus and Jane Rendall, eds. (New York: Routledge, 1989), 100.

53. Ibid.

54. Said notes that one of the primary features of Orientalism is that it reflects the relationship between European (and by extension, American) and Oriental powers as one between the strong and the weak, a point that supports Said's argument

that Orientalism always has at its center the political control of the East (*Orientalism*, 40).

55. The photographs I discuss below are all housed in the Harvard Theatre Collection. Only some have identifying titles or captions, which I have included when possible.

56. Bogdan, *Freak Show*, 239.

57. Ibid., 240.

58. Ibid., 184.

59. At least one writer of the period depicted life in the Turkish harems as something more closely resembling American slavery than what writers like Murray describe. *Thirty Years in the Harem; or, The Autobiography of Melek-Hanum, Wife of H. H. Kibrizli-Mehem-Pasha* (New York: Harper and Bros., 1872) describes the life of a harem slave—and particularly that of the Circassian slave—as a truly miserable one. Melek-Hanum's account echoes African-American slave narratives such as Harriet Jacobs' *Incidents in the Life of a Slave Girl* in that the same central elements of danger appear—the violent, raping master, the jealous, murderous mistress and the ever-present possibility of sale into an even worse situation.

60. Patricia Hill Collins, *Black Feminist Thought: Knowledge, Consciousness, and the Politics of Empowerment* (New York: Routledge, 1990), 168.

61. DeGroot, "'Sex' and 'Race,'" 120.

62. Ibid., 121.

63. Fellows and Freeman, *This Way to the Big Show*, 292–93.

4. A Peculiar Identity in the Confederate *Southern Illustrated News*

1. *Southern Illustrated News* (13 September 1862): 4. Started in this issue in 1862 by editors and proprietors, Ayres and Wade, the *Southern Illustrated News* was, according to Frank Luther Mott, edited for a time by John R. Thompson (*A History of American Magazines*, vol. 2, *1850–1865* [Cambridge: Harvard University Press, 1938], 112). Like its sister paper, the *Magnolia* (one of many of this name, this particular one started also in 1862 in Richmond), the *Southern Illustrated News* was intended to replace Northern papers like *Frank Leslie's Illustrated Newspaper*. Also according to Mott, both Southern papers were "flourishing at the end of 1862" and both "lasted through 1863, raising subscription prices to $20 at the end of that year" (Mott, *History of American Magazines*, 112). The last issue of the *Southern Illustrated News* listed in the *Union List of Serials* is dated March 26, 1865.

2. As Alice Fahs notes, the Confederate press was constantly trying to distinguish itself against the very thing that gave it some kind of shape: "Even as Southerners denounced Northern literature, it remained a powerful standard against which they defined their literature" (*The Imagined Civil War: Popular Literature of the North and South, 1861–1865* [Chapel Hill: University of North Carolina Press, 2001]: 26). See Fahs, 17–41, for her discussion of Confederate Civil War literature and the *Southern Illustrated News* in particular.

3. *Southern Illustrated News* (13 September 1862): 4.

4. Ibid.

5. *Southern Illustrated News* (8 August 1863): 37.

6. Eugene D. Genovese, *Roll, Jordan, Roll: The World the Slaves Made* (New York: Pantheon, 1972), xvii and xv.

7. For more on the Confederacy in general, see: J. Cutler Andrews, *The South Reports the Civil War* (Princeton: Princeton University Press, 1970); Richard E. Beringer, Herman Hataway, Archer Jones, and William N. Still Jr., *Why the South Lost the Civil War* (Athens: University of Georgia Press, 1986); Gabor S. Boritt, ed., *Why the Confederacy Lost* (New York: Oxford University Press, 1992); E. Merton Coulter, *The Confederate States of America, 1861–1865* (Baton Rouge: Louisiana State University Press, 1950); Paul D. Escott, *After Secession: Jefferson Davis and the Failure of Confederate Nationalism,* (Baton Rouge: Louisiana State University Press, 1978); Marjorie Lyle Crandall, *Confederate Imprints: A Checklist Based Principally on the Collection of the Boston Atheneum* (Boston: Boston Atheneum, 1955); Drew Gilpin Faust, *The Creation of Confederate Nationalism: Ideology and Identity in the Civil War South* (Baton Rouge: Louisiana State University Press, 1988) and *Mothers of Invention: Women of the Slaveholding South in the American Civil War* (Chapel Hill: University of North Carolina Press, 1996); Michael Fellman, *Inside War: The Guerrilla Conflict in Missouri during the American Civil War* (New York: Oxford University Press, 1989); Gary W. Gallagher, *The Confederate War* (Cambridge, MA: Harvard University Press, 1997); Richard Barksdale Harwell, *Confederate Belles-Lettres: A Bibliography and a Finding List of the Fiction, Poetry, Drama, Songsters, and Miscellaneous Literature Published in the Confederate States of America* (Hattiesburg, MS: Book Farm, 1941); George C. Rable, *Civil Wars: Women and the Crisis of Southern Nationalism,* (Urbana: University of Illinois Press, 1989); Francis Butler Simkins and James Welch Patton, *The Women of the Confederacy* (Richmond: Garrett and Massie, 1936); Bell I. Wiley, *The Life of Johnny Reb, the Common Soldier of the Confederacy* (Indianapolis: Bobbs-Merrill, 1943); Wiley, *The Road to Appomattox* (Memphis: Memphis State College Press, 1956).

8. Gallagher, *The Confederate War,* 64.

9. Steven A. Channing, "Slavery and Confederate Nationalism" in *From the Old South to the New: Essays on the Transitional South,* Walter J. Fraser Jr. and Windred B. Moore Jr., eds., (Westport, CT: Greenwood Press, 1981): 219.

10. David M. Potter, *The South and Sectional Conflict* (Baton Rouge: Louisiana State University Press, 1968): 63.

11. Ibid.

12. Gallagher, *The Confederate War,* 71. William C. Davis adds to the scholarly fray regarding Confederate nationalism when he characterizes the Confederacy as not really much more than "a very organized insurrection or separatist movement" (*The Cause Lost: Myths and Realities of the Confederacy* [Lawrence, KS: University Press of Kansas, 1996], 179).

13. Faust looks at a range of popular materials as well, although she tends to support the idea that it was the breakdown of nationalism's development in the Confederacy that eventually led to its fall. See Faust, *Confederate Nationalism,* particularly 1–21.

14. Fahs, *Imagined Civil War,* 25.

15. Faust, *Creation of Confederate Nationalism,* 17. Fahs argues that despite the economic problems that inhibited the success of most Confederacy periodicals, the fresh perspective offered by the *Southern Illustrated News* aided its relative success. See Fahs, *Imagined Civil War,* 21–23 and 32–34.

16. Originally seated in 1845 in Charleston, by its first number, printed in January of 1846, *De Bow's Commercial Review of the South and the West* had moved to

New Orleans. Founded by James D. B. De Bow, *De Bow's* always had "far more of the South" in it than the West; by 1853, the title became simply *De Bow's Review* (Mott, *History of American Magazines*, 342). Mostly a vehicle for information regarding commerce, history, and politics, *De Bow's* was quick to affirm secession; in 1856, De Bow wrote that it was the editors' intention to "make the *Review* a repository of all the valuable papers that have been prepared on the subject of southern slavery and in vindication of the rights of the South" (Mott, *History of American Magazines*, 344). The final issue of the periodical appeared in June of 1880.

17. *DeBow's Southern and Western Review* (July 1850): 120.

18. Ibid.

19. Ibid.

20. The *Southern Literary Messenger* was begun in Richmond in 1834 by Thomas Willys White; typically a monthly, it ran until midwar in 1864. Known today primarily for its role in the career of Edgar Allan Poe, in 1861, the *Southern Literary Messenger* was edited by the politically fiery George William Bagby. In June of 1864, Mott notes that "the *Messenger's* printers were called to the defense of the city" and did not resume publication after that (Mott, *A History of American Magazines*, vol. 1, *1741–1850* [Cambridge: Harvard University Press, 1930], 656). For more, see Mott, 629–57.

21. *Southern Literary Messenger* (March 1861): 189.

22. Ibid., 190.

23. Ibid., 191.

24. Ibid., 191–92.

25. The *Southern Field and Fireside* was founded in 1859 in Augusta, Georgia, and printed articles and sketches with an emphasis on the literary and agricultural. It was edited by William W. Mann and later John R. Thompson, who joined the staff after leaving the *Southern Literary Messenger* in 1860 (Mott, *History of American Magazines*, vol. 2, 89). The *Southern Field and Fireside* ceased publication in 1864—another print casualty of the Civil War.

26. *Southern Field and Fireside* (28 May 1859): 4.

27. Ibid.

28. Ibid.

29. *Southern Illustrated News* (25 October 1862): 4.

30. *Southern Illustrated News* (13 Sept. 1862): 4

31. Ibid.

32. *Southern Illustrated News* (27 Sept. 1862): 5.

33. Ibid.

34. Fahs also comments on this, arguing that the energy Southern publishers and editors put into these "nearly universal public denunciations of 'Yankee trash,'" is evidence of the complex interdependence that existed between Southern and Northern literary cultures during the war (*Imagined Civil War*, 25).

35. *Southern Illustrated News* (13 Sept. 1862): 5.

36. Ibid.

37. Ibid., 4.

38. Ibid. Simply finding engravers, though, was a more pressing concern, and the *News* advertises for competent wood engravers later in their paper. In the November 8 issue of 1862, William B. Campbell, an engraver who began the war under the

employ of the recognized leader of American illustrated newspapers, Frank Leslie, is cheered for returning to serve in the Confederate army and taking the position of principle engraver at the *News*, what the editors note is a "labour of love" for Campbell (*Southern Illustrated News*, 3).

39. *Southern Illustrated News* (25 April 1863): 7.

40. *Southern Illustrated News* (11 June 1864): 157.

41. Ibid.

42. *Southern Illustrated News* (27 June 1863): 4.

43. *Southern Illustrated News* (5 November 1864): 232.

44. Faust also notes the way in which Confederates themselves drew these parallels; see Faust, *Confederate Nationalism,* 30–32. Gallagher reiterates this argument when he holds that the gap between military history and social history has distorted our understanding of the Civil War overall. He claims that "this gulf is especially vexing because of the obvious parallels between the roles played by George Washington and his army during the American Revolution and by Lee and his army during the Confederacy's fight for independence" (*Confederate War,* 65).

45. Faust, *Confederate Nationalism,* 14.

46. *Southern Illustrated News* (20 September 1862): 1; *Southern Illustrated News* (13 December 1862): 3.

47. *Southern Illustrated News* (11 April 1863): 2.

48. Ibid., 2, 3.

49. Faust, *Confederate Nationalism,* 58. As Eugene D. Genovese has argued, antebellum Southern intellectuals believed that slavery was the foundation of, rather than the impediment to, freedom: "They based their defense of slavery on a prior defense of freedom, which they identified as the dynamic in a world progress the cause of which they claimed as their own. Freedom, in their view, could not be extended to all, but it could be extended to increasing numbers and could be expected to result in a better life for those who remained subservient" (*The Slaveholders' Dilemma: Freedom and Progress in Southern Conservative Thought, 1820–1860* [Columbia: University of South Carolina Press, 1992], 11).

50. *DeBow's Southern and Western Review* (September 1850): 286.

51. *Southern Literary Messenger* (11 March 1861): 164.

52. *Southern Illustrated News* (14 January 1865): 1.

53. *Southern Illustrated News* (14 January 1865): 3.

54. *Southern Illustrated News* (25 October 1862): 4.

55. Ibid. Other references to this will be cited parenthetically.

56. Ibid., 6.

57. *Southern Illustrated News* (5 March 1864): 68.

58. Ibid. Other references to this will be cited parenthetically.

59. *DeBow's Southern and Western Review* (August 1850): 231.

60. *Southern Illustrated News* (18 April 1863): 8.

61. *Southern Illustrated News* (6 February 1864): 40.

62. Fahs argues that in the North, "there is every indication that the term 'contraband' caught on rapidly precisely because it provided a means for Northerners to continue thinking of escaped slaves as property, without disturbing antebellum racist preconceptions" (*Imagined Civil War,* 152).

63. *Southern Illustrated News* (11 October 1862): 6.

64. *Southern Illustrated News* (29 November 1862): 4.

65. Ibid. Other references to this installment of "The Little Incendiary" will be cited parenthetically.

66. *Southern Illustrated News* (6 December 1862): 4. Other references to this installment of "The Little Incendiary" will be cited parenthetically.

67. *Southern Illustrated News* (21 March 1863): 2.

68. *Southern Illustrated News* (12 March 1864): 76.

69. Ibid.

70. Ibid.

5. The Yankee, the Stump, and the Creation of a
Confederate Imaginary

1. Benedict Anderson, *Imagined Communities: Reflections on the Origin and Spread of Nationalism,* rev. ed. (New York: Verso, 1991), 7.

2. Drew Gilpin Faust, *The Creation of Confederate Nationalism: Ideology and Identity in the Civil War South* (Baton Rouge: Louisiana State University Press, 1988), 22, 31.

3. *Southern Illustrated News* (31 October 1863): 134.

4. Faust, *Confederate Nationalism,* 43. As Faust puts it, "slavery had profoundly inhibited the growth of market relations in the region, both by preventing the emergence of a free market in labor and by limiting the number of the section's independent consumers"(*Confederate Nationalism,* 43).

5. *Southern Illustrated News* (8 November 1862): 5.

6. Ibid.

7. *Southern Illustrated News* (19 September 1863): 88.

8. *Southern Illustrated News* (3 October 1863): 100.

9. *Southern Illustrated News* (14 February 1863): 8.

10. Fletcher M. Green, *The Role of the Yankee in the Old South* (Athens: University of Georgia Press, 1972), 2.

11. *Southern Illustrated News* (13 September 1862): 2.

12. Ibid.

13. Ibid., 4.

14. *Southern Illustrated News* (20 September 1862): 5.

15. *Southern Illustrated News* (11 October 1862): 4.

16. *Southern Illustrated News* (18 October 1862): 4.

17. Ibid.

18. *Southern Illustrated News* (13 December 1862): 2.

19. *Southern Illustrated News* (21 March 1863): 2.

20. *Southern Illustrated News* (14 February 1863): 2.

21. *Southern Illustrated News* (8 November 1862): 8.

22. *Southern Illustrated News* (29 November 1862): 4.

23. Ibid.

24. Merton E. Coulter, *The Confederate States of America, 1861–1865* (Baton Rouge: Louisiana State University Press, 1950), 368.

25. Ibid., 370.

26. Ibid.

27. *Southern Illustrated News* (13 September 1862): 6.

28. *Southern Illustrated News* (30 April 1864): 136. Confederate General Albert Sidney Johnston, a close cohort of Jefferson Davis, died early in the war at Shiloh; see Coulter, *Confederate States*, 353.

29. *Southern Illustrated News* (26 September 1863): 92.

30. Ibid.

31. *Southern Illustrated News* (14 February 1863): 3.

32. Ibid.

33. Ibid.

34. Robert Bush, "Introduction," *The Writings of William Gilmore Simms*, vol. 3. (Columbia: University of South Carolina Press, 1972), xxix. A handful of contemporary scholars have considered the text from various angles. Renée Dye argues that the novel charts the "disintegration of the idealized Southern social order centered upon paternalism and the plantation household" ("A Sociology of the Civil War: Simms's *Paddy McGann*," *Southern Literary Journal* 28.2 [Spring 1996]: 4); Linda E. McDaniel considers how the novel charts the evolution of Southern society via its folk network of devil and god figures ("American Gods and Devils in Simms's *Paddy McGann*" in *Long Years of Neglect: The Work and Reputation of William Gilmore Simms*, ed. John Caldwell Guilds [Fayetteville: University of Arkansas Press, 1988], 60–75); Kieran Quinlan discusses the question of Paddy's Irish identity in relation to Southern culture (*Strange Kin: Ireland and the American South* [Baton Rouge: Louisiana State University Press, 2005], 203–6); Charles S. Watson looks at the way in which the treatment of secession and sectionalism Simms gives in the novel fits in the pattern of his career overall (*From Nationalism to Secessionism: The Changing Fiction of William Gilmore Simms* [Westport, CT: Greenwood Press, 1993], 1–13 and 125–38); and Mary Ann Wimsatt considers the place *Paddy McGann* occupies in the genre of Southern humor in which she sees it most squarely situated ("The Evolution of Simms's Backwoods Humor" in *Long Years of Neglect: The Work and Reputation of William Gilmore Simms*, ed. John Caldwell Guilds [Fayetteville: University of Arkansas Press, 1988], 148–65).

35. William Gilmore Simms, *Paddy McGann; or, The Demon of the Stump*, in *The Writings of William Gilmore Simms*, vol. 3. (Columbia: University of South Carolina Press, 1972), 216. In the interests of both ease and scholarly uniformity, all references to *Paddy McGann* will be to this edition of the text; it is, however, vital to note that this edition has itself been based on the *Southern Illustrated News* copy of the text. In my research, I have charted where the sections of each chapter are included in the weekly in order to clearly connect the story's actual appearance with the other texts published alongside it. It is, however, more convenient to cite the reproduced text here. Reference to all other texts found in the *Southern Illustrated News* will be, of course, to the pages of the weekly.

36. Bush, "Introduction," xxix.

37. Ibid.

38. Wimsatt, "Evolution of Simms' Backwoods Humor," 204.

39. Bush, "Introduction," xxix.

40. Dye lists the different reasons critics have put forward as to why Paddy loses his hunting ability; for her, though, paying attention to this detail—one she notes too is really irresolvable as to its origins—eclipses "the implications of the narrative structure of the novel" ("A Sociology of the Civil War," 12).

41. *Southern Illustrated News* (7 March 1863): 6.
42. Ibid.
43. For a brief history of this term, see David R. Roediger, *The Wages of Whiteness: Race and the Making of the American Working Class* (New York: Verso, 1991), 99.
44. *Southern Illustrated News* (14 March 1863): 6.
45. Ibid.
46. Ibid.
47. Ibid.
48. Eugene D. Genovese, *Roll, Jordan, Roll: The World the Slaves Made* (New York: Pantheon Books, 1972), 128–30.
49. *Southern Illustrated News* (18 April 1863): 8.
50. *Southern Illustrated News* (25 April 1863): 7.
51. Ibid.
52. Alice Fahs, *The Imagined Civil War: Popular Literature of the North and South, 1861–1865* (Chapel Hill: University of North Carolina Press, 2001), 40.
53. Ibid. For more on Simms's career in general, see Mary Ann Wimsatt's "The Professional Author in the South: William Gilmore Simms and Antebellum Literary Publishing" in *The Professions of Authorship: Essays in Honor of Matthew J. Bruccoli*, eds. Richard Layman and Joel Myerson (Columbia: University of South Carolina Press, 1996), 121–34.
54. For more particularly on the very pointed satire on these New York writers in which Simms here engages, see Bush, "Introduction," xxvi-xxvii; Wimsatt, "Evolution of Simms' Backwoods Humor," 208; McDaniel, "American Gods," 66–69; and Watson, *From Nationalism*, 133–35.
55. The issues Simms weaves into his narrative regarding Paddy's marriage are, according to McDaniel, criticism regarding the governance of the Southern people by the Confederate States Congress, a reference to the end of the kind of religious principles for which Salley Hartley stands, and a nod to the evolutionary age of science the Darwinian monkey at the wedding represents. See McDaniel, "American Gods," 70–73.
56. *Southern Illustrated News* (4 February 1865): 3.
57. *Southern Illustrated News* (27 February 1864): 60.
58. *Southern Illustrated News* (24 October 1863): 122.
59. Ibid.
60. Ibid.
61. Ibid.
62. Ibid.
63. Ibid., 123.
64. *Southern Illustrated News* (28 November 1863): 167.
65. *Southern Illustrated News* (20 February 1864): 56.
66. *Southern Illustrated News* (11 June 1864): 160.

6. What the Railroad Brought

1. Eric Foner, *Reconstruction: America's Unfinished Revolution 1863–1877* (New York: Harper and Row, 1988), 463.
2. *Golden Era* (1 May 1869): 4. The *Golden Era*, more a "literary weekly than a newspaper," according to Frank Luther Mott (*A History of American Magazines 1850–*

1865, [Cambridge: Harvard University Press, 1938], 117) and full of "racy sketches of mining life and a kind of gay and reckless dramatic criticism," was founded by twenty-one-year-old J. MacDonough Foard and nineteen-year-old Rollin M. Daggett in 1852; it gained a circulation of 9,000 selling for $5.00 year (Mott, 117). Bret Harte started working for the *Era* and later wrote for it, as did Mark Twain and Charles Warren Stoddard. It was sold by its founding editors in 1860 and lasted until 1893, when it was subsumed into the San Diego-based *Western Journal of Education* (Mott, 117).

3. *Golden Era* (15 May 1869): 4.

4. For more, see William Francis Deverell, *Railroad Crossing: Californians and the Railroad, 1850–1910* (Berkeley: University of California Press, 1994).

5. In an article published in the May 29, 1869, issue of the *Golden Era,* the editors tally up the number of texts reprinted in the Northeastern press that appeared originally in Western periodicals. The argument goes that by way of its appropriation of Western-authored texts, the Eastern press has acknowledged the value of Western-authored texts; so too should the readers and consumers of California (4). W. W. Carpenter, an *Era* correspondent, argues that California readers should support California papers, particularly because Eastern papers, inferior in quality, are reprinting the work of California writers without giving credit where it's due (*Golden Era* [26 August 1860]: 4). Carpenter believes California is being "invaded" by nefarious business practices: "Friends of our glorious Pacific home:...upon you rests the stigma of supporting and encouraging that Atlantic trash; while your young, vigorous and giant-like home literature lies mouldering in the tomb of sad neglect. Californians, why in the name of all that's rational, do you not patronize your own literature, instead of importing an immeasurably inferior article?" (*Golden Era* [26 August 1860]: 4).

6. Foner, *Reconstruction,* 474.

7. Axel Nissen, Harte's most recent biographer, notes that according to the *Alta Californian,* "'no poem has appeared within the last twenty years...that has so hit the fancy of the great world of readers'" (*Bret Harte: Prince and Pauper* [Jackson: University of Mississippi, 2000], 111). Gary Scharnhorst claims that, despite Harte's apparent dislike of the poem, "by any objective measure—the frequency with which it was reprinted, the numbers of parodies it inspired, the times it was cited or set to music—Bret Harte's 'Plain Language from Truthful James'...was one of the most popular poems ever published" ("'Ways That Are Dark': Appropriations of Bret Harte's 'Plain Language from Truthful James,'" *Nineteenth-Century Literature* 51.3 [December 1996], 377). For more on the poem, see Scharnhorst's "'Ways That Are Dark'" and *Bret Harte* (New York: Twayne, 1992), 35–37. Nissen explains that Harte's popularity coincided with his return East to a lucrative business offer made by the Boston publishing firm Fields, Osgood and Company in June of 1870. According to Mark Twain, Harte "crossed the continent through such a prodigious blaze of national interest and excitement that one might have supposed he was the Viceroy of India on a progress, or Halley's comet come again after seventy-five years of lamented absence" (qtd. in Nissen, *Bret Harte,* 115).

8. Ronald Takaki, *Strangers from the Different Shore: A History of Asian Americans* (New York: Penguin, 1989), 105.

9. *The Overland Monthly* began publication in 1868 in San Francisco; Harte was its first editor but left that post in 1871 to go East. Conceptually, the periodical was modeled after such publications as the *Atlantic Monthly* and *Lippincott's;* by 1870, it

had a circulation of 10,000. Writers like Ambrose Bierce, Twain, and Jack London all appeared in the *Overland Monthly*, and in 1912 it boasted a circulation of 75,000; it survived under various titles until 1935. It was understood to be one of the top literary journals in the country during its run. For more, see Mott, *A History of American Magazines* vol. 3, 1865–1885 (Cambridge: Harvard University Press, 1938), 402–9.

10. Tomás Almaguer, *Racial Fault Lines: The Historical Origins of White Supremacy in California* (Berkeley: University of California Press, 1994), 150. Almaguer makes the excellent case that California's racial history is unique because it was framed not within a binary system of whites versus blacks, but a three-pronged order that incorporated "three new cultural groups into existing racial patterns: the Mexican, the Chinese, and Japanese populations" (1). While the focus of my study does not comment on the role of Native Americans in the California press, Almaguer clearly shows that Native Americans in California "were summarily relegated to the very bottom of the racial hierarchy" (8). Mexicans were situated above them in part because of their cultural similarities to other European Americans and because of the continued political power of the elite Californio population. Asian immigrants were seen as having "fewer redeeming qualities and group attributes" than Mexicans, and were more "unambiguously deemed nonwhite" (8).

11. Ibid., 41.

12. *Golden Era* (19 September 1869): 4.

13. For more on the transcontinental railroad's impact on American culture and life, see John Hoyt Williams, *A Great and Shining Road: The Epic Story of the Transcontinental Railroad* (New York: Times Books, 1988). Also see Barbara Young Welke, *Recasting American Liberty: Gender, Race, Law, and the Railroad Revolution, 1865–1920* (Cambridge: Cambridge University Press, 2001).

14. Sarah H. Gordon, *Passage to Union: How the Railroads Transformed American Life, 1829–1929* (Chicago: Ivan R. Dee, 1996), 46.

15. Ibid., 150–52.

16. Ibid., 126.

17. Ibid., 142–43.

18. Ibid., 24.

19. Ibid., 5–9.

20. *Golden Era* (29 January 1860): 4.

21. Jane Tompkins argues that Perry Miller in his preface to *Errand in the Wilderness* displays a similar kind of white blindness when he describes what "fascinated him as a young man about his country's history was 'the massive narrative of the movement of European culture into the vacant wilderness of America'" ("'Indians': Textualism, Morality, and the Problem of History" in *"Race," Writing and Difference*, ed. Henry Louis Gates Jr. [Chicago: University of Chicago Press, 1986], 61). Tompkins points out that, given the Native American presence in colonial New England, Miller's use of the word "vacant" is "shocking" (61).

22. *Golden Era* (29 January 1860): 4.

23. *Golden Era* (1 May 1869): 4.

24. *Golden Era* (27 March 1869): 1.

25. Ibid.

26. *Golden Era* (8 May 1869): 3.

27. Ibid.

28. *Golden Era* (15 May 1869): 4. For a fascinating account of the way in which the railroad increased women's vulnerability to physical injury in a way distinctly different than men's, see Welke, 43–80.

29. Ibid.

30. *Golden Era* (15 May 1869): 4.

31. Ibid.

32. According to Roger A. Hall, "Buntline had lived what might charitably be called a checkered life," including a Navy resignation, bankruptcy, a duel in which he killed a jealous husband and was almost lynched as a result, several lawsuits for everything from divorce to bigamy to slander, jail sentences for his part in the Astor Place Riot and his desertion from his unit in the Civil War, as well as leadership in the American "Know-Nothing" Party (*Performing the American Frontier, 1870–1906* [Cambridge: Cambridge University Press, 2001], 51). Buntline was the first author in the famous "Buffalo Bill" Cody dime novel series published by the Beadle publishing firm. For more on Buntline, see Hall, Albert Johannsen, *The House of Beadle and Adams and Its Dime and Nickle Novels: The Story of a Vanished Literature* (Norman: University of Oklahoma Press, 1950), and Jay Monaghan, *The Great Rascal: The Life and Adventures of Ned Buntline* (Boston: Little, Brown and Company, 1952).

33. Monaghan, 253; Gordon, 154–65. According to Monaghan, Buntline spent a year in California, arriving in San Francisco in 1868 and leaving after the railway line was completed the summer following (252–56). His success in California as a recruiter for temperance and a local writer was minimal, and Monaghan's description of Buntline's misfit status in the region is intriguing for its reliance on an implicit understanding of a distinct California identity: "To be frank, California was no place for Ned Buntline and his moral lectures. Perhaps the population felt more sophisticated than people back East. Country men out West had not come from nearby parochial communities, and they were not confused and dismayed by mushrooming industrial cities. California immigrants differed from Easterners who had gone from the farm to nearby mill towns and commercial metropolises. Moreover, the cosmopolitan Californians did not favor abstinence" (255–56).

34. *Golden Era* (15 May 1869): 4.

35. *Golden Era* (7 November 1869): 4.

36. *Golden Era* (21 November 1869): 5.

37. *Golden Era* (26 December 1869): 4.

38. *Overland Monthly* (July 1868): 99.

39. Ibid., 99–100.

40. In California, though, this Indian image would have conjured up more thoughts of conflict than finality. The bear's unfortunate habit of scalping with his fore paw, is, according to Harte, "the result of contact with the degraded aborigine, and the effect of bad example on the untutored ursine mind" (*Overland Monthly* [July 1868]: 100). It's interesting to note the similarity of the *Golden Era*'s masthead with that of the *St. Paul Pioneer and Democrat* and the way in which in both images, the Native American is figured as voyeur, either to the "dawning" of Western civilization in the frontier as is the case with the *St. Paul Pioneer and Democrat*, or to his own passing existence and significance (see Figure 6).

41. *Overland Monthly* (October 1868): 303.

42. Ibid., 303, 305.

43. Ibid., 305.

44. Much has been written about the history of the Chinese in America. Some of the key texts that discuss the nineteenth century include: Andrew Gyory, *Closing the Gate: Race, Politics, and the Chinese Exclusion Act* (Chapel Hill: University of North Carolina Press, 1998); Robert G. Lee, *Orientals: Asian Americans in Popular Culture* (Philadelphia: Temple University Press, 1999); Charles McClain, *In Search of Equality: The Chinese Struggle against Discrimination in Nineteenth-Century America* (Berkeley: University of California Press, 1994); Gary Y. Okihiro, *The Columbia Guide to Asian American History* (New York: Columbia University Press, 2001); Alexander Saxton, *The Indispensable Enemy: Labor and the Anti-Chinese Movement in California* (Berkeley: University of California Press, 1971); B. L. Sung, *The Story of the Chinese in America* (New York: Collier, 1967); Ronald Takaki, *Strangers from a Different Shore: A History of Asian Americans* (New York: Penguin, 1990); and Liping Zhu, *A Chinaman's Chance: The Chinese on the Rocky Mountain Mining Frontier* (Niwot, CO: University of Colorado Press, 1997).

45. Takaki, 104–8.

46. Takaki, 105. For more on the development of the "Ah Sin" character and Twain and Harte's failed play *Ah Sin,* in which the character received greater notoriety, see Hall, 90–91.

47. Takaki, 105–6.

48. Besides sharing an ambiguously sympathetic tone, this "John" forms an attachment with a little white girl who attempts to Christianize the little "pagan" just as the little girl in "Wan Lee, the Pagan" does. "Wan Lee, the Pagan" was first published in *Scribner's Monthly* in September 1874.

49. *Golden Era* (5 April 1863): 4.

50. Ibid.

51. *Golden Era* (16 January 1869): 8.

52. *Golden Era* (28 November 1868): 4.

53. Ibid.

54. Ibid.

55. *Golden Era* (6 March 1869): 5.

56. Ibid.

57. Ibid.

58. *Golden Era* (27 March 1869): 4; Almaguer, *Racial Fault Lines,* 13. Elsewhere in the *Era,* an article criticizing the actions of strikers raises the question of the role of the Chinese in strikes, as well as their entrance into the work on the railroad. These strikes "throw wide the door and offer great inducements to Chinamen and other Asiatics to come here, and make it necessary for employers of all kinds to make use of them, if they would not have their capital idle and unproductive. It was thus that the Central Pacific Railroad was built by Chinamen instead of whitemen, whom the company would much preferred to have employed" (*Golden Era* [26 June 1869]: 4).

59. *Golden Era* (27 March 1869): 4.

60. Ibid.

61. The style and tone of the articles focusing on the Chinese in the self-consciously intellectual *Overland Monthly* is quite different from that which appears in the *Golden Era.* The first thing to notice is the sheer number of pieces published about the Chinese in the *Overland Monthly.* Volume One alone (which begins July 1868 and finishes in December of that same year) contains seven articles devoted

to various aspects of Chinese culture and society, more than were dedicated to any other single topic save California itself. Given the nature of the journal, it's not surprising that most of these pieces convey an encyclopedic, informative air, indicating that their goal is to present their readers with a more accurate depiction of Chinese life and culture than they will find elsewhere. Most of the essays were written by Reverend A. W. Loomis, a man who in 1860 was consulted by the powerful political group, the Chinese Six Companies, in the hiring of a lobbyist to represent Chinese interests in the Californian legislature (McClain 23–24). But even these texts are contradictory in their approach to the Chinese, including in Loomis's "How Our Chinamen Are Employed," praise for the industriousness of the Chinese as a means to better develop the country for whites (*Overland Monthly* [March 1869]: 231). Loomis's chief concern is to persuade white readers that they are intended for more advanced labor and that the Chinese will make it possible for them to do that work. As if to push this theme home, the article following "How Our Chinamen Are Employed" is called "Trade with the Cannibals," an essay that details the efforts of one man to initiate trade in the Fiji Islands, then notorious for its supposed practice of cannibalism.

62. *Golden Era* (6 March 1869): 5.
63. Ibid.
64. Ibid.
65. *Overland Monthly* (June 1869): 577.
66. Ibid.
67. Ibid.
68. *Overland Monthly* (July 1869): 83.
69. *Golden Era* (14 August 1869): 4.
70. *Golden Era* (14 August 1869): 4.
71. *Overland Monthly* (October 1868): 360.
72. Ibid.
73. *Overland Monthly* (October 1868): 362.
74. Ibid.
75. Ibid., 364.
76. Ibid., 367.
77. *Overland Monthly* (October 1870): 352. All other citations to this text will be cited parenthetically.

7. The Woman Question, Coast to Coast

1. For convenience's sake, all references to the text of "Miggles" will be from Bret Harte, *The Luck of Roaring Camp and Other Stories, Including Earlier Papers, Spanish and American Legends, Tales of the Argonauts, etc.* (Boston: Houghton, Mifflin, 1900).

2. According to the official state web site, the California grizzly *(Ursus californicus)* was made the state animal in 1953. Its history, however, is another tale of the passage of the primitive: "Before dying out in California, this largest and most powerful of carnivores thrived in the great valleys and low mountains of the state, probably in greater numbers than anywhere else in the United States. As humans began to populate California, the grizzly stood its ground, refusing to retreat in the face of

advancing civilization. It killed livestock and interfered with settlers. Less than 75 years after the discovery of gold, every grizzly bear in California had been tracked down and killed" (www.library.ca.gov/history/cahinsig. html, p. 1 of 9).

3. Tomás Almaguer, *Racial Fault Lines: The Historical Origins of White Supremacy in California* (Berkeley: University of California Press, 1994), 26.

4. *Golden Era* (12 September 1869): 4.

5. *Golden Era* (19 September 1869): 4.

6. *Golden Era* (13 March 1869): 5.

7. *Golden Era* (3 April 1869): 5.

8. *Golden Era* (28 October 1860): 4.

9. *Golden Era* (4 November 1860): 4.

10. *Golden Era* (22 February 1863): 4.

11. *Golden Era* (26 April 1863): 4.

12. *Golden Era* (14 August 1869): 5.

13. Ibid.

14. Ibid.

15. Ibid.

16. Ibid.

17. *Golden Era* (24 April 1869): 5.

18. Ibid.

19. Ibid.

20. Ibid.

21. *Golden Era* (9 January 1869): 5.

22. *Golden Era* (13 February 1869): 4.

23. Almaguer, *Racial Fault Lines*, 176.

24. Almaguer, *Racial Fault Lines*, 178.

25. Ibid.

26. The demise of Miriam's marriage to E. G. Squier overlapped uncomfortably with the ascent of her relationship to Frank Leslie. The story includes a trip taken by the Squiers and Leslie to Europe that landed Squier in jail, leaving Miriam and Leslie free to tour the continent, quite conveniently, by themselves. She and Squier eventually divorced in May of 1873. A month after her next marriage commenced in July of 1874 to Frank Leslie, Squier was committed to an insane asylum. As Stern argues, Squier may well have had his revenge, possibly contributing to or even authoring the press release that followed the publication of *California: A Pleasure Trip* and which covered the more unconventional, even sordid details of Miriam's life. For more, see Stern's *Purple Passage: The Life of Mrs. Frank Leslie,* (Norman: University of Oklahoma Press, 1970), particularly 46–71.

27. Stern, *Purple Passage*, 182.

28. Ibid., 72.

29. Madeleine B. Stern, "Introduction" in *California: A Pleasure Trip from Gotham to the Golden Gate, April, May, June 1877.* Mrs. [Miriam] Frank Leslie, 1877. (Nieuwkoop, the Netherlands: B. De Graaf, 1972), xi.

30. *Frank Leslie's Chimney Corner* (8 July 1865): 91.

31. Mrs. [Miriam] Frank Leslie, *California: A Pleasure Trip from Gotham to the Golden Gate, April, May, June 1877.* (Nieuwkoop, the Netherlands: B. De Graaf, 1972), 5. All future references to this text will be cited parenthetically.

32. Miriam is endlessly fascinated with the Chinese in the book and, in fact, the most common subjects for the text's engraved illustrations are Western landscapes and scenes featuring the Chinese. As Miriam says, "the fascination of climbing Sacramento or Washington Streets and finding one's self in that swarm of Chinese is one that never wears out for us, and were it not for wearying the reader, we could go through unnumbered pages describing the quaint, queer, outlandish sights and people, whom nobody comprehends, and who, while we arrogantly try to civilize and Christianize them by our own standard, complacently seat themselves upon the heights of their own civilization, their own religion, and consider us as outside barbarians whom it is not worth their while to convince of error and ignorance" (217).

Despite this self-awareness, though, Miriam's language still typically relies on a racializing discourse. She notes, for instance, that even though the "'Heathen Chinee'" may have an "ill" odor in "Caucasian nostrils, we must say that their cleanly, smooth, and cared-for appearance was very agreeable in contrast with the wild, unkempt and filthy red man" (108).

33. Qtd. in Richard S. Van Wagoner, *Mormon Polygamy: A History* (Salt Lake City: Signature Books, 1989), 106.

34. Ibid., 105.

35. Miriam's response to this impoverished frontier home reveals the sense of alienness that pervades the text and often encapsulates Miriam as the group travels along. Time and again, Miriam comments on the civilized or uncivilized nature of the environment in which she finds herself, and can bring no higher compliment than the one she pays to a woman in Elkhart, Indiana whose "manners and appearance," she says, could have "graced any Fifth-Avenue drawing room" (26). For Miriam Leslie, a sense of national fraternity—or sorority—is not so reliably contingent on race, as it is class.

36. See Stern, *Purple Passage,* for a brief description of the reviews Miriam received for *California: A Pleasure Trip,* 90–91.

37. For more on the article, the follow-up pamphlet published in Virginia City, and her speculations regarding Squier's help in authoring the pieces, see Stern, *Purple Passage,* 90–97.

38. Qtd. in Stern, *Purple Passage,* 182.

39. Toni Morrison, *Playing in the Dark: Whiteness and the Literary Imagination* (New York: Vintage, 1993), 8.

Conclusion

1. Toni Morrison, *Playing in the Dark: Whiteness and the Literary Imagination* (New York: Vintage, 1993), 8.

2. Ibid. It's good to remember here that one of Morrison's major contentions in this study is that, for a range of reasons, literary criticism has placed itself in an adversarial relationship to literature, dismissing "the difficult, arduous work writers do to make an art that becomes and remains part of and significant within a human landscape" (9). She is chiefly concerned that critics have overlooked the Africanist presence in American literature due to an odd combination of politics and social propriety. Hers was one of the first calls to consider the role of whiteness in American

228 Notes to Conclusion

literature, something with which scholars have contended for a while now. My interest in Morrison's question about what makes "intellectual domination possible," then, does not necessarily share her own nuanced point about it.

3. The scholarship thus far completed on so-called "real readers" of this period is very scant and spotty. "Real readers" are not the projection of the scholar's imagination such as I have imagined here, but the actual flesh-and-blood consumers of texts who left traces of their reading for literary historians to study, traces that include diaries, library charge records, marginalia, and other markers of readers past. As Susan K. Harris has noted, nineteenth-century readers often recorded *what* they were reading, but few thought or had the time to record their reflections on that reading (*Nineteenth-Century American Women's Novels: Interpretive Strategies* [New York: Cambridge University Press, 1990], 12–30). When such rare and valuable records have been found, they often belong to an elite body of readers. Barbara Sicherman's case study of Victorian women's reading, for example, focuses on the Hamiltons of Fort Wayne, Indiana; two of the seven women discussed in the piece eventually attain international renown ("Sense and Sensibility: A Case Study of Women's Reading in Late-Victorian America" in *Reading in America: Literature and Social History*, Cathy N. Davidson, ed. [Baltimore: The Johns Hopkins University Press, 1989]). Ronald J. Zboray and Mary Saracino Zboray are in the process of changing these trends and their work is and will continue to be of enormous importance to scholars of nineteenth-century readership and publishing. In their two latest studies, *Literary Dollars and Social Sense: A People's History of Mass Market Publishing* (New York: Routledge, 2004) and *Everyday Ideas: Socio-Literary Experience among Antebellum New Englanders* (Knoxville: University of Tennessee Press, 2005), they note that, counter to prevailing beliefs, readers of popular periodicals like *Frank Leslie's Illustrated Newspaper* came from a range of class backgrounds and labor interests, as did readers of the more supposedly "genteel" *Harper's Monthly*. But as they themselves have reported in other, earlier work, studies of nineteenth-century readership have typically focused on "the more privileged, who, being generally well-educated and financially secure, not only had backgrounds that encouraged appreciation of diverse literature, but who could afford to own a wide variety of books and to subscribe to sundry periodicals" ("Books, Reading, and the World of Goods in Antebellum New England," *American Quarterly* 48.4 [1996]: 590). The readers with whom I am primarily concerned, however, would not necessarily have belonged to this elite faction of Americans, but would have been the working- and middle-class readers who comprised the trunk and limbs of the American body politic, readers whom the work of Zboray and Saracino Zboray are just now starting to bring to light. The lack of existing scholarship on these readers makes the correspondence columns contained in the weeklies and miscellanies all the more vital as some kind of representation—"real" or virtual—of the periodicals' consumers.

4. *Saturday Night* (31 July 1869): 8.

5. *The New York Mercury* ran from 1838 to 1870; a weekly miscellany, it was published on Saturday and contained light features, fiction, and general interest items.

6. *New York Mercury* (16 March 1861): 8.

7. For more on Miriam Leslie's "Ladies' Conversazione" column in *Frank Leslie's Illustrated Newspaper*, see Linda Frost, "Where Women May Speak for Themselves": Miriam Frank Leslie's "Ladies' Conversazione," in *Blue Pencils and Hidden Hands:*

Women Editing Periodicals, 1830–1910 (Boston: Northeastern University Press, 2004): 60–79.

8. Ronald and Mary Saracino Zboray, "Books, Reading, and the World of Goods," 588.

9. Ronald Zboray, "The Letter and the Fiction Reading Public in Antebellum America," *Journal of American Culture* 10.1 (1987): 30, 31.

10. *New York Mercury* (19 February 1859): 8.

11. *New York Mercury* (18 May 1861): 8.

12. *New York Mercury* (26 March 1859): 8.

13. *New York Mercury* (12 March 1859): 8.

14. *New York Mercury* (7 May 1859): 8.

15. *New York Mercury* (20 April 1861): 7.

16. *New York Mercury* (18 May 1861): 8.

17. *New York Mercury* (7 May 1859): 8.

18. *New York Mercury* (12 March 1859): 8.

19. Ibid.

20. *Frank Leslie's Chimney Corner* (2 September 1865): 219.

21. *New York Mercury* (16 April 1859): 8; *Frank Leslie's Chimney Corner* (3 June 1865): 10.

22. *New York Mercury* (18 June 1859): 8.